OPPOSING VIEWPOINTS® SERIES

Animal Experimentation

Other Books of Related Interest:

Opposing Viewpoints Series

Cloning

Ethics

Current Controversies Series

Medical Ethics

At Issue Series

Animal Experimentation

Do Animals Have Rights?

Prescription Drugs

"Congress shall make no law . . . abridging the freedom of speech, or of the press."

First Amendment to the U.S. Constitution

The basic foundation of our democracy is the First Amendment guarantee of freedom of expression. The Opposing Viewpoints Series is dedicated to the concept of this basic freedom and the idea that it is more important to practice it than to enshrine it.

OPPOSING VIEWPOINTS® SERIES

Animal Experimentation

David M. Haugen, Book Editor

GREENHAVEN PRESS

An imprint of Thomson Gale, a part of The Thomson Corporation

THOMSON

GALE

Detroit • New York • San Francisco • New Haven, Conn. • Waterville, Maine • London

Christine Nasso, *Publisher*
Elizabeth Des Chenes, *Managing Editor*

© 2007 Thomson Gale, a part of The Thomson Corporation.

Thomson and Star logo are trademarks and Gale and Greenhaven Press are registered trademarks used herein under license.

For more information, contact:
Greenhaven Press
27500 Drake Rd.
Farmington Hills, MI 48331-3535
Or you can visit our Internet site at http://www.gale.com

LIBRARY OF CONGRESS CATALOGING-IN-PUBLICATION DATA

Animal experimentation / David M. Haugen, book editor.
        p. cm. -- (Opposing viewpoints)
    Includes bibliographical references and index.
    ISBN-13: 978-0-7377-3346-4 (hardcover : alk. paper)
    ISBN-10: 0-7377-3346-2 (hardcover : alk. paper)
    ISBN-13: 978-0-7377-3347-1 (pbk. : alk. paper)
    ISBN-10: 0-7377-3347-0 (pbk. : alk. paper)
    1. Animal experimentation--Moral and ethical aspects. 2. Animal experimenta-tion--United States. I. Haugen, David M., 1969–
        HV4915.A635 2006
        179'.4--dc22
                                                    2006031196

Printed in the United States of America
10 9 8 7 6 5 4 3 2 1

Contents

Chapter 3: Does Animal Experimentation Aid Medical Progress?

Chapter 4: Are New Forms of Animal Experimentation Worth Pursuing?

Why Consider Opposing Viewpoints?

> *"The only way in which a human being can make some approach to knowing the whole of a subject is by hearing what can be said about it by persons of every variety of opinion and studying all modes in which it can be looked at by every character of mind. No wise man ever acquired his wisdom in any mode but this."*
>
> *John Stuart Mill*

In our media-intensive culture it is not difficult to find differing opinions. Thousands of newspapers and magazines and dozens of radio and television talk shows resound with differing points of view. The difficulty lies in deciding which opinion to agree with and which "experts" seem the most credible. The more inundated we become with differing opinions and claims, the more essential it is to hone critical reading and thinking skills to evaluate these ideas. Opposing Viewpoints books address this problem directly by presenting stimulating debates that can be used to enhance and teach these skills. The varied opinions contained in each book examine many different aspects of a single issue. While examining these conveniently edited opposing views, readers can develop critical thinking skills such as the ability to compare and contrast authors' credibility, facts, argumentation styles, use of persuasive techniques, and other stylistic tools. In short, the Opposing Viewpoints Series is an ideal way to attain the higher-level thinking and reading skills so essential in a culture of diverse and contradictory opinions.

In addition to providing a tool for critical thinking, Opposing Viewpoints books challenge readers to question their own strongly held opinions and assumptions. Most people form their opinions on the basis of upbringing, peer pressure, and personal, cultural, or professional bias. By reading carefully balanced opposing views, readers must directly confront new ideas as well as the opinions of those with whom they disagree. This is not to simplistically argue that everyone who reads opposing views will—or should—change his or her opinion. Instead, the series enhances readers' understanding of their own views by encouraging confrontation with opposing ideas. Careful examination of others' views can lead to the readers' understanding of the logical inconsistencies in their own opinions, perspective on why they hold an opinion, and the consideration of the possibility that their opinion requires further evaluation.

Evaluating Other Opinions

To ensure that this type of examination occurs, Opposing Viewpoints books present all types of opinions. Prominent spokespeople on different sides of each issue as well as well-known professionals from many disciplines challenge the reader. An additional goal of the series is to provide a forum for other, less known, or even unpopular viewpoints. The opinion of an ordinary person who has had to make the decision to cut off life support from a terminally ill relative, for example, may be just as valuable and provide just as much insight as a medical ethicist's professional opinion. The editors have two additional purposes in including these less known views. One, the editors encourage readers to respect others' opinions—even when not enhanced by professional credibility. It is only by reading or listening to and objectively evaluating others' ideas that one can determine whether they are worthy of consideration. Two, the inclusion of such viewpoints encourages the important critical thinking skill of objectively evaluating an author's credentials and bias. This evaluation will illuminate an author's reasons for taking a particular stance on an issue and will aid in readers' evaluation of the author's ideas.

It is our hope that these books will give readers a deeper understanding of the issues debated and an appreciation of the complexity of even seemingly simple issues when good and honest people disagree. This awareness is particularly important in a democratic society such as ours in which people enter into public debate to determine the common good. Those with whom one disagrees should not be regarded as enemies but rather as people whose views deserve careful examination and may shed light on one's own.

Thomas Jefferson once said that "difference of opinion leads to inquiry, and inquiry to truth." Jefferson, a broadly educated man, argued that "if a nation expects to be ignorant and free . . . it expects what never was and never will be." As individuals and as a nation, it is imperative that we consider the opinions of others and examine them with skill and discernment. The Opposing Viewpoints Series is intended to help readers achieve this goal.

David L. Bender and Bruno Leone,
Founders

Introduction

> "No one can make an informed decision without free and open discussion. But how can you be informed if the people who have the information are threatened or even attacked whenever they speak out?"
>
> —Professor Steve Bloom,
> Hospital Doctor

> "Action is everything. Words and tears mean nothing to the animals trapped in their cages inside [Huntingdon Life Sciences] waiting to die. They deserve nothing less than our utmost commitment to take action every day to close down the lab that holds them captive and slowly kills them."
>
> —Stop Huntingdon Animal Cruelty
> Web site

Since the mid-1970s the Hall family of Staffordshire, England, had raised guinea pigs to supplement the earnings from their chief livelihood, sheep herding. The guinea pigs were sold to research laboratories that used them in various animal experiments. The added income helped the Halls' Darley Oaks Farm remain profitable throughout the 1980s and 1990s. But around 1999 the Halls' fortunes changed. Darley Oaks became the target of animal rights protesters who objected to the raising of guinea pigs for research. Over the next six years the Halls, their workers, and their business partners were subjected to taunts and scare tactics. As the British newsmagazine the *Economist* described in an August 2005 article,

[The Halls] have been abandoned by frightened suppliers and employees and lost their entire dairy herd, which was slaughtered when their tormentors made it impossible for the milk to be collected. The nadir came last year, when activists stole the body of Gladys Hammond, mother-in-law of one of the Hall brothers, from its grave in the churchyard at Yoxall in Staffordshire.

In hopes of regaining Gladys Hammond's remains and ending the terror campaign, the Hall family announced it would cease the breeding of guinea pigs for science.

The majority of animal rights protests have been vocal but peaceful, a trend that most animal rights spokespeople are quick to point out. In the past several years, however, the notoriety of a few campaigns involving intimidation and violence has captured the attention of the media, the scientific community, and the public in both England and the United States. Fear of the type of scare tactics experienced at Darley Oaks has influenced Cambridge University's decision to forgo plans to build a primate research facility, and Oxford University has been fighting in the courts to keep animal protesters from terrorizing contractors working on a new animal laboratory. Both English institutions have been the targets of organized rallies, and animal activist Web sites have published the names and addresses of university faculty, which Oxford authorities claim is an "incitement to harass" staff.

The most notable and sustained protest in recent years— one that has provided the impetus for the Oxford and Cambridge campaigns—has been the continuing demonstrations against Huntingdon Life Sciences, Europe's largest laboratory for conducting toxicity tests on animals. Huntingdon performs about seventy-five thousand toxicity tests each year. The animals used in such tests are primarily rodents, but a few hundred dogs and primates are also part of Huntingdon's testing procedures. Animal rights groups began targeting Huntingdon Life Sciences (then Huntingdon Research Centre) in the late 1980s after an activist infiltrated the labs and exposed the rough treatment of animals, poor caging facilities, and the grim reality of toxicity testing. The story broke in 1989 and garnered much public sympathy but no official sanctions for the lab. Subsequent infiltrations in the late 1990s supplied some filmed abuse of dogs that was aired on British television. In response, two animal activists formed Stop Huntingdon Animal Cruelty (SHAC), a British organization—with international support—aimed at shutting down Huntingdon Life Sciences.

Since its founding SHAC has come under fire for exceeding the bounds of peaceful protest. Death threats, vandalism, and false bomb threats have been linked to SHAC's campaign against Huntingdon employees. According to the Victims of Animal Rights Extremism Web site, one computer scientist at Huntingdon wrote of his experience:

> I recently woke up to find two of my cars trashed and the graffiti "puppy killers" sprayed on the side of one of them. They had punctured two tyres. One car was effectively written off. There were slogans sprayed on my house. . . . That in itself was bad enough but over the weekend my name, address and telephone number went up on the SHAC website, which was effectively inviting local activists to come and have a go.

> Besides targeting employees, SHAC has also been accused of intimidating suppliers and contractors working with Huntingdon Life Sciences. These efforts have been so successful that prominent financial backers have pulled their interests out of the corporation.

The unparalleled efforts of SHAC and other animal rights organizations operating in the United Kingdom have brought about some reaction from authorities. In April 2005 the British Parliament passed the Serious Organised Crime and Police Act, which, in part, makes it illegal to harass people at their homes or to cause interference in business concerns as part of a demonstration. One result of the British law was to quell some of the terror tactics at home while simultaneously igniting them overseas. Protests of Huntingdon Life Sciences lab facilities in New Jersey began to swell in the new millennium after SHAC's unusual brand of dissent showed results in Britain. Kevin Kjonaas, the twenty-eight-year-old president of SHAC USA, the U.S. counterpart of Stop Huntingdon Animal Cruelty, organized protests outside employees' homes and allowed the posting of employees' phone numbers and addresses, as well as the names of their children, on the SHAC USA Web site.

Like Britain, the United States has laws meant to curb intimidation campaigns. Originally passed in 1992 and strengthened after the September 11, 2001, terrorist attacks, the Animal Enterprise Protection Act protects animal testing institutions and their employees. In May 2004, Kjonaas and six other SHAC members were indicted under the act—primarily for what the government calls an Internet fear campaign. As reported in a January 2006 issue of *Mother Jones*, "John Lewis, the FBI's deputy assistant director for counterterrorism, told Congress . . . that SHAC and other animal rights groups represent America's No. 1 domestic terror threat."

The trial of Kjonaas and his colleagues in the United States as well as the conflict that still rages in England reveal the extremes reached in the debate over animal experimentation. Defenders of animal research claim that animals provide the best nonhuman testing models for determining the risks of new drugs and medical treatments. Using animals in experiments will also increase the understanding of human and animal physiology and psychology, advocates say. Such arguments are embraced by a large percentage of the scientific community. In a 2004 issue of *Hospital Doctor*, Professor Tipu Aziz of University of Oxford and Imperial College London encouraged scientists to speak out against intimidation by animal activists. He told his peers, "Anyone who has been to medical school and treated patients will understand the vital contribution made by animal research."

Detractors, however, tell a different story. Many believe animal research has never influenced the great medical discoveries of the past and is not likely to do so in the future. They argue that animals do not provide proper models for human physiology, and therefore any drug testing or other experiments cannot provide results that would translate to humans. Animal activists, such as those involved with the fight against Huntingdon Life Sciences, also contend that it is unethical to treat animals as a means to human ends. These activists assert that the pain and suffering experienced by test animals should not be tolerated by any empathetic and reasonable person. University lecturer Sharon Howe wrote in a March 2006 editorial to the *Independent* (a UK newspaper), "How can painfully and artificially inducing human diseases in other species with a different genetic make-up to our own possibly advance the cause of modern medicine?"

The impassioned arguments of animal activists coupled with evidence of inhumane treatment of animals at some research institutions have already brought about legislation in many countries that subjects animal experimentation to rigorous government oversight and inspection. In addition, the scientific community subscribes to a belief that reducing the need for animal experiments by replacing these tests with other types of experiments (computer modeling, for example) is a worthy goal. Taken together, these factors have consistently and drastically cut the number of animal experiments performed throughout the world since the 1970s. However, to animal rights advocates, reduction is not enough, and this belief has led to the extremist actions making headlines in recent years.

Although the lawyer for Kevin Kjonaas and his six colleagues was reported in the *New York Times* as stating, "Advocating obnoxiously is not a crime," the courts have already decided otherwise. In March 2006 six of the seven convicted members of SHAC USA were found guilty by a federal jury and face maximum sentences ranging from three to five years' imprisonment and up to $250,000 in fines. The guilty verdict, however, has not stopped the protests, and the debate over the supposed terrorist actions of some animal rights groups continues. This controversy is one of many deliberated in the chapter Do Animals Have Rights? in *Animal Experimentation: Opposing Viewpoints*. Other chapters in this anthology ask the following questions: Is Animal Experimentation Justifiable? Does Animal Experimentation Aid Medical Progress? Are New Forms of Animal Experimentation Worth Pursuing? These chapters lay out the fundamental questions that surround animal experimentation, a contentious issue that has prompted reasoned debate as well as intimidation and criminal behavior.

OPPOSING
VIEWPOINTS®
SERIES

CHAPTER 1

Do Animals Have Rights?

Chapter Preface

In a July 2000 essay, Tibor Machan, a professor of business ethics, points out that animals are sometimes driven by instinct to kill their own offspring. Fish, he notes, occasionally eat their young, and lions often slaughter chosen cubs. Although Machan acknowledges that the reasons for this are not clear, he states that the conduct is a matter of "genetic disposition." Why then, he asks, are humans subject to criminal prosecution if they engaged in similar behavior?

Machan's question strikes at the heart of the controversy over animal rights. Those, like Machan, who believe there is a fundamental difference between animals and humans contend that the concept of "rights" cannot apply to creatures that are driven primarily by instinct. On the other hand, humans, Machan says, "have the capacity to make choices, they possess free will and have the responsibility to act ethically and respect the rights of other human beings. . . . Human beings, in short, are free and morally responsible. And it is this fact that gives rise to their having basic rights that others ought to respect and they may protect with force and law."

Critics of Machan's argument, however, insist that animals need not be granted rights by humans. To them, people and animals possess natural rights to share the planet and live freely. Some animal rights advocates also claim that human morality approves of the concept of animal rights. They contend that moral principles are based on the capacity to suffer because it is the only ethically relevant standard that is common to all people. These critics charge that because people would be acting immorally if they caused suffering to others, then they are acting immorally if they cause suffering to animals. For this reason, people should refrain from using animals to their own ends—especially in scientific experiments in which animals are made to suffer to advance human knowledge. Or more broadly, as the international animal rights group Animal Liberation argues: "Animals may not be killed, exploited, cruelly treated, intimidated, or imprisoned for no good reason. Animals should be able to live in peace, according to their own needs and preferences."

Some of the authors in the following chapter debate whether animals possess rights and whether these rights or the inherent worth of animals should deter people from using them in scientific experimentation. Other authors represented in this chapter extend this argument to question whether there are limits on how far champions of animal rights should go in carrying out what they see as a moral duty to protect animal interests.

"There is no 'superior' species. To think otherwise is to be no less prejudiced than racists or sexists."

Animals Have Rights

Tom Regan

Tom Regan is an emeritus professor of philosophy at North Carolina State University and the author of The Case for Animal Rights. *In the following viewpoint, Regan explains why animals should be afforded the same rights claimed by humans. He argues that it is just and ethical to concede rights to animals because to treat animals with less respect than humans is speciesism—a form of prejudice. People should protect and defend animals, Regan states, because animals cannot speak up for themselves. If humans wish to live up to their ethical natures, he insists, then they should act with compassion; they should recognize that animals have inherent worth and are not commodities to be used.*

As you read, consider the following questions:

1. In Regan's view, what is the highest principle of ethics? How does he apply this principle to the case for animal rights?

Tom Regan, "The Philosophy of Animal Rights," The Culture & Animals Foundation, 1997. www.cultureandanimals.org. Reproduced by permission.

2. What four things do all ethical philosophies emphasize, according to Regan?

3. In the author's view, how is animal exploitation connected to environmental degradation?

It is not rational to discriminate arbitrarily. And discrimination against nonhuman animals is arbitrary. It is wrong to treat weaker human beings, especially who are lacking in normal human intelligence, as "tools" or "renewable resources" or "models" or "commodities." It cannot be right, therefore, to treat other animals as if they were "tools," "models" and the like, if their psychology is as rich as (or richer than) these humans. To think otherwise is irrational.

The Philosophy of Animal Rights Is Scientific

The philosophy of animal rights is respectful of our best science in general and evolutionary biology in particular. The latter teaches that, in Darwin's words, humans differ from many other animals "in degree, not in kind." Questions of line drawing to one side, it is obvious that the animals used in laboratories, raised for food, and hunted for pleasure or trapped for profit, for example, are our psychological kin. This is no fantasy, this is fact, proven by our best science.

The Philosophy of Animal Rights Is Unprejudiced

Racists are people who think that the members of their race are superior to the members of other races simply because the former belong to their (the "superior") race. Sexists believe that the members of their sex are superior to the members of the opposite sex simply because the former belong to their (the "superior") sex. Both racism and sexism are paradigms of unsupportable bigotry. There is no "superior" or "inferior" sex or race. Racial and sexual differences are biological, not moral, differences.

So Close to Human

To people used to dividing the world up into "humans" and "animals" it comes as a shock to realise that the genetic differences between humans and chimpanzees are smaller than those between chimpanzees and gorillas. . . . Why, then, do we continue to insist that even the most basic rights, like those to life, liberty and protection from torture, are for humans only?

Peter Singer, "Some Are More Equal,"
Guardian (UK), May 19, 2003.

The same is true of speciesism—the view that members of the species *Homo sapiens* are superior to members of every other species simply because human beings belong to one's own (the "superior") species. For there is no "superior" species. To think otherwise is to be no less prejudiced than racists or sexists.

The Philosophy of Animal Rights Is Just

Justice is the highest principle of ethics. We are not to commit or permit injustice so that good may come, not to violate the rights of the few so that the many might benefit. Slavery allowed this. Child labor allowed this. Most examples of social injustice allow this. But not the philosophy of animal rights, whose highest principle is that of justice: No one has a right to benefit as a result of violating another's rights, whether that "other" is a human being or some other animal.

The Philosophy of Animal Rights Is Compassionate

A full human life demands feelings of empathy and sympathy—in a word, compassion—for the victims of injustice—whether the victims are humans or other animals. The philosophy of animal rights calls for, and its acceptance fosters the growth of, the virtue of compassion. This philosophy is, in [Abraham] Lincoln's words, "the way of a whole human being."

The Philosophy of Animal Rights Is Unselfish

The philosophy of animal rights demands a commitment to serve those who are weak and vulnerable—those who, whether they are humans or other animals, lack the ability to speak for or defend themselves, and who are in need of protection against human greed and callousness. This philosophy requires this commitment, not because it is in our self-interest to give it, but because it is right to do so. This philosophy therefore calls for, and its acceptance fosters the growth of, unselfish service.

The Philosophy of Animal Rights Is Individually Fulfilling

All the great traditions in ethics, both secular and religious, emphasize the importance of four things: knowledge, justice, compassion, and autonomy. The philosophy of animal rights is no exception. This philosophy teaches that our choices should be based on knowledge, should be expressive of compassion and justice, and should be freely made. It is not easy to achieve these virtues, or to control the human inclinations toward greed and indifference. But a whole human life is impossible without them. The philosophy of animal rights both calls for, and its acceptance fosters the growth of, individual self-fulfillment.

The Philosophy of Animal Rights Is Socially Progressive

The greatest impediment to the flourishing of human society is the exploitation of other animals at human hands. This is true in the case of unhealthy diets, of the habitual reliance on the "whole animal model" in science, and of the many other forms animal exploitation takes. And it is no less true of education and advertising, for example, which help deaden the human psyche to the demands of reason, impartiality, compassion, and justice. In all these ways (and more), nations remain profoundly backward because they fail to serve the true interests of their citizens.

The Philosophy of Animal Rights Is Environmentally Wise

The major cause of environmental degradation, including the greenhouse effect, water pollution, and the loss both of arable land and top soil, for example, can be traced to the exploitation of animals. This same pattern exists throughout the broad range of environmental problems, from acid rain and ocean dumping of toxic wastes, to air pollution and the destruction of natural habitat. In all these cases, to act to protect the affected animals (who are, after all, the first to suffer and die from these environmental ills), is to act to protect the earth.

The Philosophy of Animal Rights Is Peace-Loving

The fundamental demand of the philosophy of animal rights is to treat humans and other animals with respect. To do this requires that we not harm anyone just so that we ourselves or others might benefit. This philosophy therefore is totally opposed to military aggression. It is a philosophy of peace. But it is a philosophy that extends the demand for peace beyond the boundaries of our species. For there is a war being waged, every day, against countless millions of nonhuman animals. To stand truly for peace is to stand firmly against speciesism. It is wishful thinking to believe that there can be "peace in the world" if we fail to bring peace to our dealings with other animals.

We and They Are Equal

We are not saying that humans and other animals are equal in every way. For example, we are not saying that dogs and cats can do calculus, or that pigs and cows enjoy poetry. What we are saying is that, like humans, many other animals are psychological beings, with an experiential welfare of their own. In this sense, we and they are the same. In this sense, therefore, despite our many differences, we and they are equal.

"The nature of animals makes them worthy of human compassion, kindness and care, but never of any human rights."

Animals Do Not Have Rights

Ilana Mercer

In the following viewpoint, Ilana Mercer claims that people have a distorted view of animal nature. Instead of recognizing that animals have no conscience and act out of instinct, many people tend to treat animals as rational creatures with near-human attributes. According to Mercer, this has prompted activists to suggest that animals are deserving of the same rights possessed by humans. Such a view is unfounded, Mercer says, because rights only exist among moral beings with the capacity to reason. Animals, therefore, can be worthy of human compassion but could never possess human rights. Ilana Mercer is an analyst for the Internet's Free Market News Network and the author of Broad Sides: One Woman's Clash with a Corrupt Culture.

As you read, consider the following questions:

1. In Mercer's examples, how has the media altered people's perceptions of animals?

2. How does Mercer counter the argument that some primates deserve rights because they are genetically similar to humans?

3. According to the author, from what two attributes are human rights derived?

A vague anxiety underlies the media's preoccupation with the recent attacks on people by predators—Roy Horn of the "Siegfried and Roy" act was mauled by a tiger, and grizzly-bear advocate Timothy Treadwell and his companion were gobbled up in Alaska while traveling across bear country (without weapons).

As more wild animals brazenly make themselves at home in manicured suburbs, people, including media top dogs, worry. And for good reason. They are taught from cradle to crypt that humans have encroached on the animals' territory. On television, "Animal Planet" *experts* tell them (mostly incorrectly) how rare, essential to the "ecosystem," and misunderstood these creatures are.

Equally unassailable is the premise that you don't shoot alligators, bears, coyotes and cougars—not even when they threaten hearth and home. Should a "situation" arise, to avoid criminal charges, one is expected to practically Mirandize the animal [read it its criminal rights] before eliminating it.

[Television commentator] Bill O'Reilly conducted a species-sensitive interview with a couple of animal trainers following Horn's mauling. The urban legend now making the rounds has it that, after being reluctantly dragged by the animal to a more secluded picnic spot, Horn, a jet of blood squirting from his neck, told paramedics not to kill the tiger.

Well, perhaps. But Roy need not have worried his poor—and by then also poorly attached—head. The O'Reilly interview was marked by the same forlorn fatalism. The typical PETA-friendly (People for the Ethical Treatment of Animals) discussion, replete with anthropomorphism (the practice of attributing human characteristics to an animal) followed. Everyone agreed solemnly that the animal didn't intend to commit a crime.

Animals Act Without Conscience

Forgive me if this is too (excuse the expression) catty a point to make, but isn't that the case with creatures that have no capacity for conscious thought? Unlike human beings, animals are incapable of forming malicious intent—they simply act reflexively, in a stimulus-response manner.

Because animals kill with no forethought or conscience, we don't hold them responsible for their actions in the legal sense, as we would a human being. We agree they were only acting on their animal instincts—they don't function on a higher plane.

Yet a public long fed a diet of Disneyfied cartoon animals has also swallowed a lot of pabulum about the "humanness" of animals. We've reached the point that even quasi-scientific National Geographic may give Christian names to its boa constrictor film stars. As the animal slithers on its random way, the creepy narrator will also imbue the creature with elaborate inner concerns. In the event that this curdled schmaltz fails to sicken viewers, it should, at the very least, have the credibility of a "Winnie the Pooh" overdub.

Not Moral Beings

Animal-rights advocates—some of whom even walk upright and have active frontal lobes—argue, for instance, that because the great apes share a considerable portion of our genetic material, they are just like human beings, and ought to be given human rights.

As of yet, though, Alexei A. Abrikosov, Vitaly L. Ginzburg and Anthony J. Leggett are not the names of lower primates—they are the names of the 2003 Nobel Prize winners in phys-

Animals Have a Fixed Value

Animals never have any potential to do anything greater than their ancestors and direct contemporaries. Animals are not individual because while they may have distinct characteristics they lack the capacity to develop themselves and transform their existence. Animals are also not social because while they may live within groups, they lack the capacity to transform that group's behavior and they cannot take collective decisions within the group. In this sense, the value of animals is fixed such that it is always comparable to any other animal currently living, dead or projected into the future.

Stuart Derbyshire, speech given at the
Edinburgh (Scotland) Book Festival, August 19, 2002.

ics. No matter how many genes these men share with monkeys and no matter how sentient chimps are, the latter will never contribute anything to "the theory of superconductors and superfluids," or author a document like the "Declaration of Independence," much less tell good from bad.

Given that human beings are so vastly different in mental and moral stature from apes, the lesson from any genetic similarities the species share is this and no more: A few genes are responsible for very many incalculable differences!

Unlike human beings, animals by their nature are not moral agents. They possess no free will, no capacity to tell right from wrong, and cannot reflect on their actions. While they often act quite wonderfully, their motions are merely a matter of conditioning.

Since man is a rational agent, with the gift of consciousness and a capacity to scrutinize his deeds and chart his actions, we hold him culpable for his transgressions. A human being's exceptional ability to discern right from wrong makes him punishable for any criminal depravity.

Animals Have No Claim to Rights

Man's nature is the source of the responsibility he bears for his actions. It is also the source of his rights. Human or individual rights, such as the rights to life, liberty and property, are derived from man's innate moral agency and capacity for reason.

Unfortunately, the new-generation, campy "conservatives," who look to Bo Derek as the Republican brain trust on animal rights, desperately need an explanation of what a right is.

A right is a legal claim against another. As author and lecturer Robert Bidinotto points out in his manifesto against environmentalism and animal rights, rights establish boundaries among those who possess them. Since animals can't recognize such boundaries, they should certainly not be granted legal powers against human beings.

Moreover, the rights human beings possess exist within the context of a moral community. Animals don't belong to a moral community—they answer the call of the wild. When a simian devours her young ones, none of her sisters in the colony hoot a la [animal activist and scientist] Jane Goodall for justice. Not one of the many tigers lounging around on Siegfried and Roy's Little Bavaria estate is catcalling for the majestic head of their errant teammate.

The nature of animals makes them worthy of human compassion, kindness and care, but never of any human rights.

The perverse, pagan, public theatre elicited by animal attacks ought to give way to some life-loving, logical lessons. It is in the nature of things for predators to kill. Wild animals have big pointy teeth for a reason, wrote John Robson of the *Ottawa Citizen*.

A civilized society places human life above all else and endorses its vigorous defense—it doesn't show resignation when beast attacks man.

In the future, if a working wild animal repeats this perfectly predictable performance, a stage hand should be poised to lodge a bullet in the critter's skull. The same goes for bears in the backyard.

| *"If animals can feel pain as humans can, and desire to live as humans do, how can we deny them similar respect?"*

Animals Are Equal to Humans

Matt Ball and Jack Norris

In the following selection, Matt Ball and Jack Norris insist that arguments against granting rights to animals are flawed. The authors claim that the only ethical criterion that should determine whether creatures should have rights is their capacity to suffer. If animals can suffer, the authors assert, then they have a subjective desire to survive, and therefore they deserve the right to pursue life. Humans cannot overlook this fact if they wish to maintain a consistent and equitable standard of morality, Ball and Norris conclude. Matt Ball is the cofounder and executive director of Vegan Outreach, an animal rights organization. Jack Norris is the president of Vegan Outreach.

As you read, consider the following questions:

1. According to Ball and Norris, why is it unsound to deny animals rights on the basis of lower intelligence and lack of technological advancement?

Matt Ball and Jack Norris, "Beyond Might Makes Right," Vegan Outreach, n.d. www.veganoutreach.org. Reproduced by permission.

2. How does the concept of "subjective experience" factor into the authors' argument about why animals should have rights?

3. As cited in the article, how have Carl Sagan and Ann Druyan illustrated that animals may be moral beings?

In most of the world, human beings are granted basic rights. These fundamental rights are usually (at a minimum): the entitlement of individuals to have basic control of their lives and bodies, without infringing on the rights of others. In other words: the right not to be killed, caged, or experimented on against their will at the hands of moral agents (persons able to understand and act from a moral code). It is assumed that the reader believes humans to have these rights.

A Difference of Degree

Many say that humans deserve rights while other animals do not because humans have a greater level of certain characteristics: humans are more intelligent, creative, aware, technologically advanced, dominant able to use language, able to enter into contracts, able to make moral choices, etc. Thus, humans deserve rights because they have a greater degree of these characteristics.

This argument has two problems:

- Rights are not relevant to a group (e.g., "humans"), but only to individuals. Individuals, not groups, are exploited and are capable of suffering and dying; individuals, not groups, are denied rights when there is a morally relevant reason (e.g., after committing a crime).

- Not all humans possess these characteristics to a greater degree than all other non-humans. There are non-humans who are more intelligent, creative, aware, dominant, technologically advanced (in reference to tool making), and able to use language, than some humans (such as infants or severely handicapped humans). Furthermore, many animals perform actions that, in humans, would be labeled moral behavior; oftentimes some animals act more ethically than many humans. If rights were granted at a certain threshold of intelligence, creativity, moral behavior, etc., some animals would have rights and some humans would not.

Value to Others

Some say that even though infants do not possess high levels of some characteristics, they should be granted rights because they are valued by other humans (their parents, for instance). By this argument, infants themselves do not possess any inherent rights, but receive them only if valued by an adult human.

At the same time, being valued by an adult human does not grant rights to pigs, parakeets, pet rocks, or Porsches. This is inconsistent: either one is granted rights by being valued by an adult human—and thus everything valued by an adult human has rights—or there must be different criteria for granting rights. . . .

Biological Rights

Another argument is that humans have rights because they belong to the species Homo sapiens. In other words, a chimpanzee may very well be as intelligent (or creative, etc.) as some humans, but chimpanzees do not have rights because they are not members of the biologically-defined rights-bearing species, Homo sapiens.

In the past, there have been a number of biological definitions of what constitutes a species. Today, it is defined genetically. The questions then become:

- Why should rights be deserved solely on the basis of a certain arrangement of genes?

- Among the genes that determine one's eye color, etc. which gene is it that confers rights?

- If rights should be based on genes, why should the line be drawn at the species level? Why shouldn't the line be drawn at race, order, phylum, or kingdom?

A thoughtful person might find having their rights (or lack thereof) determined by a molecular sequence to be a bit absurd. It is no better than basing rights on the pigmentation of one's skin (which is also determined by the individual's genetic code). . . .

The Golden Rule

In the past, humans may have respected each other's rights in order to survive without constant violence. Many people still function on this level. Yet over time, more civilized people have evolved a moral system that grants rights not just based on self-protection but on the Golden Rule—treat your neighbor as you would like to be treated. We know that we want to stay alive, do not wish to suffer, etc., and we assume others like us have the same desires. Being capable of looking beyond our own individual interests we apply the Golden Rule even to people who could not harm us.

How much like us do beings have to be before we include them under the Golden Rule? At one time, women were not enough like the men who held power to be granted many rights. Neither were minorities in the United States and other societies. Even though the circle has expanded to include these individuals in the United States, today other animals are still not considered sufficiently like us for the majority of people to treat these animals as our neighbors under the Golden Rule.

The Soul

Some would say having a God-given soul is what gives one rights. There is no way to prove that humans have souls, just

"Well, if—as everyone insists—we've a superior social organisation, communications system, ecological sense and an ability to adjust, how is it we're becoming extinct?"

Ed Fisher. © Punch Rothco. Reproduced by permission.

as there is no way to prove that all other animals lack souls. Those who insist that only humans have souls (and thus rights) are faced with a theological dilemma: it would require a cruel God to create beings with the capacity to feel pain and the desire to live, if these animals' purpose was to suffer at the hands of humans.

Animals Kill Each Other

Some defend humans killing animals on the grounds that animals kill each other in nature. These people would be hard pressed to show that our modern systems of animal agriculture or experimentation are "natural."

While it is true that some animals kill other animals in nature, moral philosophy is based on principles, not excused by the actions of others. As [animal activist and scholar] Peter Singer writes: "You cannot evade responsibility by imitating beings who are incapable of making [an ethical] choice." Some humans assault, rape, or kill other humans, yet we do not condone these actions. . . .

Suffering Is the Criterion

Searching for some characteristic to justify granting rights to all humans while denying rights to all other animals is futile. A moral system based on any of the characteristics discussed so far would either include many non-human animals or exclude some humans.

To have a consistent set of ethics a characteristic must be found that not only allows for the inclusion of all humans, but is also morally relevant. The only characteristic that simply and consistently meets these requirements is the capacity for suffering.

As Jeremy Bentham, head of the Department of Jurisprudence at Oxford University during the 19th century, said in reference to his belief that animals should be granted moral consideration, "The question is not, Can they reason? nor, 'Can they talk?' But rather, 'Can they suffer?'"

If a thing cannot suffer, then it does not matter to that being what happens to it. For example, computers have forms of intelligence (in many ways greater than that of any human), but these machines do not care whether they are turned off or even destroyed.

On the other hand, if a being is able to have subjective experiences of pleasure and pain, then it does matter—to that individual—what happens to it. Irrespective of intelligence, language, etc., a conscious, sentient being has interests in its existence—at the very least to avoid pain and to stay alive. Any complete ethic cannot ignore these concerns.

For the Love of Animals

There are many who claim that they love animals and don't want them to suffer. Few oppose "humane" treatment of animals. But fewer still are willing to give up their prejudice of human superiority. Thus, the distance between the acceptable treatment and the actual, institutionalized treatment of these animals is greater than ever: slaughterhouses are hidden away from populated areas, and vivisectors' labs are closed and locked.

Many scientists claim they use animals only when it is "absolutely necessary to save human lives." Ignoring the question of whether or not their contention of necessity is accurate and what is the ethical use of limited resources for medical care and research, these people are betrayed by their actions: how many vegetarian vivisectors are there? They can hardly argue that it is necessary for them to kill animals for food.

In general, the animal welfarist position, which has been endorsed (but sparsely adopted) by the meat industry and pro-vivisection groups, is at odds with a truly respectful relationship based on the recognition of the rights of other animals. Welfarists concede that animals have interests, but these animals remain human property. Thus, the fundamental interests of the animals remain secondary to any interests of the owners. Laws based on the welfarist position, such as the federal Animal Welfare Act, have proven to be almost useless in every practical sense as any use/abuse of an animal is allowed if deemed "necessary".

Trying to legislate a humane balance between the interests of animals and the interests of humans sounds good in principle and appeals to most. However, given that the current system still allows such atrocities as canned hunts, castration without anesthesia, factory farms, pain experiments, etc., animal abuse will continue until the current system recognizes that many animals are conscious, sentient beings whose rights are independent of the interests of humans. . . .

Even though rights can only be granted consistently and justly on the basis of the capacity to suffer and not on the ability to make moral choices, there is ample evidence that many animals can and do make moral choices, often to the shame of "superior" humans. As Drs. Carl Sagan and Ann Druyan relate in *Shadows of Forgotten Ancestors*:

> In the annals of primate ethics, there are some accounts that have the ring of parable. In a laboratory setting, macaques were fed if they were willing to pull a chain and electrically shock an unrelated macaque whose agony was in plain view through a one-way mirror. Otherwise, they starved. After learning the ropes, the monkeys frequently refused to pull the chain: in one experiment only 13% would do so—87% preferred to go hungry. One macaque went without food for nearly two weeks rather than hurt its fellow. Macaques who had themselves been shocked in previous experiments were even less willing to pull the chain. The relative social status or gender of the macaques had little bearing on their reluctance to hurt others.

If asked to choose between the human experimenters offering the macaques this Faustian bargain and the macaques themselves—suffering from real hunger rather than causing pain to others—our own moral sympathies do not lie with the scientists. But their experiments permit us to glimpse in non-humans a saintly willingness to make sacrifices in order to save others—even those who are not close kin. By conventional human standards, these macaques—who have never gone to Sunday school, never heard of the Ten Commandments, never squirmed through a single junior high school civics lesson—seem exemplary in their moral grounding and their courageous resistance to evil. Among these macaques, at least in this case, heroism is the norm. If the circumstances were reversed, and captive humans were offered the same deal by macaque scientists, would we do as well? (Especially when there is an authority figure urging us to administer the electric shocks, we humans are disturbingly willing to cause pain—and for a reward much more paltry than food is for a starving macaque.) In human history there are a precious few whose memory we revere because they knowingly sacrificed themselves for others. For each of them, there are multitudes who did nothing.

If animals can feel pain as humans can, and desire to live as humans do, how can we deny them similar respect? As moral beings, how can we justify our continued exploitation of them?

We must stand up against the idea that might makes right. We must question the status quo which allows the unquestioned infliction of so much suffering. We must act from our own ethics, rather than blindly follow authority figures who tell us it's okay and even necessary to harm animals.

Discussing the macaque monkeys who chose to starve rather than inflict pain on another, Drs. Sagan and Druyan conclude, "Might we have a more optimistic view of the human future if we were sure our ethics were up to their standards?"

| *"Humans are the measure of all things: morality starts with us."*

Animals Are Not Equal to Humans

Josie Appleton

Josie Appleton is an assistant editor for Spiked, *an Internet newsmagazine. In the following selection, Appleton argues against the notion that animals and humans are morally or otherwise equal. Appleton states that enlightened human thought has consistently disproved such equality, maintaining instead that humans are superior due to their rational and ethical capacities. Humans, Appleton points out, possess a consciousness—not merely an instinct—that allows for self-reflection and the ability to develop civilizations. Because animals can never acquire such traits, they could never be the equal to humans.*

As you read, consider the following questions:

1. According to Appleton, why does German philosopher Immanuel Kant argue that it is ethical for humans to use animals for their own interests?

2. In Appleton's view, what has been Christianity's stance on the relationship between animals and humans?

3. Referring to evolution, how does the author illustrate that the distinction between animals and humans is one of "kind" and not "degree"?

[In his 1977 book. *Animal Liberation*] Animal rights activist Peter Singer defines speciesism as 'a prejudice or attitude of bias towards the interests of members of one's own species and against those of members of other species'. Advocates argue that fighting speciesism is an extension of struggles for human equality: just as we once dehumanised others on the basis of their race or sex, so apparently we now think animals are below us. The argument goes that speciesism, racism and sexism are all examples of 'exclusionary attitudes'. In *The Political Animal: The Conquest of Speciesism*, Richard Ryder notes that Aristotle thought that animals 'exist for the sake of men' while also looking down on slaves and women. No coincidence, says Ryder. According to Ryder, either you are a caring person who recognises the value of other beings, or you are selfish and care only for yourself. He cites 'evidence of a link between caring for humans and caring for animals': one study found that opponents of animal rights tended to be male, anti-abortion, have 'prejudice against homosexuals' and 'exhibited racial prejudice'; another study of US students concluded that 'those students who favour animal experimentation tend to be male, masculine in outlook, conservative and less empathetic'. . . .

The term speciesism hasn't yet entered the popular vocabulary, perhaps partly because it is such a mouthful. But the assumption behind the term—that it is wrong to prioritise humans over animals—has become mainstream. . . . Of course, in practice most of us are speciesist: we eat animals but not humans; we buy pets and keep them locked up in cages; we support animal experimentation in order to save human lives. But increasingly these distinctions lack moral justification. It's time we developed a more human-centred morality, to provide our practical judgements with intellectual support.

Changing Notions of Human and Animal Equality

Animal rights activists get the relationship between human and animal equality completely skewed. In actual fact, the idea of the brotherhood of mankind was founded on the basis of uniquely human features. In the Enlightenment, when the notion of human equality was hammered out, it was argued that we should treat one another as equals because we were all rational, self-conscious beings. The German philosopher Immanuel Kant argued that we have to respect other human beings because they are *self-willing*: they are conscious of their existence, so you cannot merely treat them as a means to your end. By contrast, says Kant, 'Animals are not self-conscious and are there merely as a means to an end. That end is man'. It is because animals are not ends for themselves that humans can treat them as a means to our ends.

The flowering of human consciousness went hand-in-hand with a growing distinction from animals. It is when humans lived in cramped and degraded circumstances that they have felt the most commonality with the beasts. In ancient Egypt, cats and dogs were mummified because they were believed to have an afterlife, and Egyptian Gods had animal heads. Premodern societies often had animal totems, and they saw animals and humans as intertwined through reincarnation. Animals were attributed with agency: some societies tried animals in court, and prayed to fish to return to the rivers. The sense of fellowship with animals corresponded to societies subject to the whims of nature. These circumstances didn't foster brotherly love. . . .

With Ancient Greece, when humanity began to develop a fuller sense of itself and its abilities, animals began to be cast out of the picture. Greek Gods are all human—though they sometimes disguise themselves as animals, as in the myth of Leda and the swan. Human-animal hybrids remained in the form of satyrs and mermaids, but crucially these had human heads and arms and so retained the locus of personality. Theorists of ethics and the good life, such as Aristotle, generally argued that animals lacked reason and so could not be granted justice.

A Clearer Distinction Between Human and Animal

Christianity developed a broader notion of human equality, and a clearer distinction between humans and animals. We are all made in the image of God, says the Bible, even women and slaves, and we are all deserving of equal respect. Christianity respected no holy animals, a point made in the Bible where Jesus casts the swine into the sea. But Christianity understood humanity's distinctness from nature as a *gift* from God. 'I have given you all things', says God: 'Every moving thing that liveth shall be meat for you.'

The Enlightenment philosophers increasingly located the source of human distinction in mankind itself, writing excited essays about the innate 'dignity of man' and humanity's capacity for self-development. While fish worshipping corresponded to a feeble control over nature, so this notion of human uniqueness corresponded to a society that was developing science, technology and industry. Our 'dominion' over nature came to be seen not as a gift from God but as the product of our own hands.

Those who argue that human beings and animals are equal, devalue humanity. As animal rights academic Paola Cavalieri notes [in *The Animal Question: Why Nonhuman Animals Deserve Human Rights*, 2001], new notions of animal rights are the result of changing definitions of humans, with a shift from 'high-sounding claims about our rationality and moral capacity' to 'work on a much more accessible level'. The ability to feel pain is the definition of moral worth suggested by Peter Singer (who calls it sentience) and Richard Ryder (who calls it painience). Human beings' superior mental abilities are apparently of no moral consequence: Singer talks about humans' 'self-awareness, and the ability to plan for the future and have meaningful relationships with others', but argues [in *Animal Liberation*] that they are 'not relevant to the question of inflicting pain—since pain is pain'. Here commonality with other human beings (and animals) is based on our central nervous systems. We are all part of a 'community of pain', says Ryder. Singer suggests that a human life is worth (a bit) more than an animal's, because we have a slightly higher level of sentience. We should therefore treat sentient animals as we would a mentally handicapped human being.

Others take a behavioural psychological approach. Primate studies have found that they form relationships among members of the group; that they have some kind of memory of events; that they can use twigs and rocks as tools and have different 'tool cultures' for different groups; that they can communicate with one another and can learn basic signs to communicate with humans. Here the question of moral value is decided in a laboratory or in field tests, weighed on the basis of cognitive and awareness skills. Humans come out better than chimps, but it is a quantitative rather than qualitative difference. . . .

Finally, others take DNA as their measure of moral value. Studies have shown that we share some 98.4 per cent of our DNA with chimpanzees, and an even greater proportion of our genes. When recent research showed that humans shared a closer evolutionary relationship with chimps than previously thought, calls started for chimps to be removed from the *pan* genus and welcomed into *homo*. Many drew the assumption that shared DNA made chimpanzees into moral agents. 'Could a chimp ever be charged with murder?', asked the UK *Daily Mail*. . . .

How Humans Are Different

Human beings are not just a variation on chimps. What is at question is not *awareness* of our world, but *consciousness*. Humans are the only beings that are an object for themselves: that not only exist but know that they exist; that don't just act, but reflect on their activity. 'Man makes himself', is the title of a book on human history by archaeologist V. Gordon Childe. He notes that biological evolution selects characteristics that will be useful for a particular environment—a tough hide for protection, fast running to escape predators, or sharp claws with which to kill. Human beings have virtually no useful biological adaptations: we are slow, naked and thin-skinned. Instead we consciously fashion our own adaptations, from clothes to cars to weapons. Rather than being a product of evolutionary improvement, we improve ourselves.

This is not a question of degree: it is a question of kind. Over time evolution has produced increasingly complex species, which have a greater control over and awareness of their environment—from bacteria to plants to reptiles to primates. Evolution is the equivalent of a plane speeding up on a runway, and then with the emergence of humans it takes off and operates according to completely different laws. Whatever chimps' and gorillas' genetic similarity to humans, they are primarily creatures of evolution. A chimp community from two million years ago would be completely indistinguishable to one today. . . .

Who knows what the key ingredient was that allowed human beings to take off. Some scientists suggest that it was a refinement in the vocal tract, allowing a greater range of sounds for speech. Certainly consciousness is intrinsically social: we only become aware of ourselves as individuals by seeing ourselves in the eyes of others; we only have inner thoughts through the common symbols of language. . . .

In the development of humans, there was a weakening of biological adaptation and an increasing reliance on culture. We became upright, leaving our hands free; our hands lost their adaptations for swinging (chimps) or bounding (gorillas) and became primarily for manipulation of tools; our mouths

The Moral Difference

Human beings are fundamentally different from their animal kin in the wild. They have the capacity to make choices, they possess free will and have the responsibility to act ethically and respect the rights of other human beings. Why? So these others can carry out their morality responsibilities on their own initiative. Human beings, in short, are free and morally responsible.

Tibor R. Machan, "The Myth of Animals Rights,"
lewrockwell.com, July 25, 2000.

lost their adaptations for tearing food (such as tough tongues and lips, heavy jaws, large teeth) and became sensitive and versatile for speech. The hand and the mouth are the key human organs. Aristotle called the hand the 'organ of organs' because of its versatility. Thomas Aquinas looked down on the 'horns and claws' and 'toughness of hide and quantity of hair or feathers' in animals: 'Such things do not suit the nature of man. ... Instead of these, he has reason and hands whereby he can make himself arms and clothes, and other necessities of life, of infinite variety'. Reason, Aquinas said, was 'capable of conceiving of an infinite number of things' so it was fitting that the hand had the 'power of devising for itself an infinite number of instruments'.

Some suggest that we have been in denial about the moral implications of Darwinism for the past 150 years. Richard Ryder argues: 'Thanks to Darwin, many of the huge and self-proclaimed differences between humans and animals were revealed to be no more than arrogant delusions. Surely, if we are all related through evolution we should also be related morally'. In fact, the opposite is true. First, knowledge of Darwinism shows just how much we have managed to break free of the process of natural selection that holds every other living creature in its yoke. Second, in finding that we evolved rather than were created by God, perhaps we truly became our own gods. After all, what kind of species manages to find out the secret of its own origins?

Crossing the Species Barrier

In purely practical terms, modern society is more distinguished from animals than ever before: we live more than ever in conditions of our own creation, immune from natural pressures of hunger and cold. Yet there is a curious dissonance between practical reality and consciousness. Whereas in the past human beings' practical mastery went hand-in-hand with an expanding consciousness, now the two have come apart. While practical mastery continues apace, it lacks the moral foundations to justify it. As a result, we are effectively living in two worlds: one composed of the things we do, and one of the things we can justify. Behind this lies doubt about the point to human existence. E.O. Wilson's 1978 book *On Human Nature* argued: 'We have no particular place to go. The species lacks any goal external to its own biological nature'. Wilson perceptively noted how such 'evolutionary ethics' were a fill-in for 'the seemingly fatal deterioration of the myths of traditional religion and its secular equivalents'. It was a loss of faith in our ability to make our own history that encouraged the view that we are just a bundle of nerves and DNA.

Some humans are now trying to cross the species barrier, seeking again a kinship with animals. Indeed such is the real content of many of the primate experiments with chimps and gorillas. Jane Goodall in Gombe National Park was less observing chimps from outside than trying to become one with them, empathising with their courtships and fights and injuries. . . .

This blurring of the boundaries between animals and humans means a loss of moral sense, and a disgust at humanity.

... We are in a paradoxical situation today, of using our capacity for consciousness and creativity to devalue that consciousness and creativity. Scientists use their ability to analyse DNA to prove that we are little more than chimps. Philosophers use their reasoning powers and the accumulated knowledge of human history to try to prove that humans have no special ethical value. ...

There are severe consequences of holding human life so cheap. For a start, it is demoralising, drumming home the notion that our lives are futile. There are practical implications too. Animal research has produced key medical breakthroughs, from insulin to heart transplants to vaccines. Many of us would now be dead were it not for these discoveries. Now that animal rights concerns hold back research, this will mean needless human deaths in the future. Meanwhile, in wildlife sanctuaries in the developing world the welfare of chimps or tigers is placed above that of local villagers. The biologist Jonathan Marks sums up the crude calculations he heard from a colleague: 'A British professor thinks there are too many Asians and not enough orangutans.'

It is only a human-centred morality that can provide for fertile and equal relationships among human beings. We should relate to each other and respect one another as conscious, rational beings, rather than as DNA databases or collections of nerve endings. Attempts to find equality between humans and animals are founded in a loss of moral compass, and a disgust at humanity. As such, they are antithetical to historic attempts to fight for human equality. Moreover, it is our sense of humans as a common family that means that we can treat those who lack full agency and rationality—such as disabled people and children—with love and respect. These humans live in a network of relationships, and are loved and valued by those around them.

None of this means that we should be nasty to or disinterested in animals. Wanton torture is wrong, though less because of the pain it causes to the animal than because it reflects badly upon the torturer. The same level of animal pain, existing for a clear purpose in a slaughterhouse or a science lab, would be entirely justified. A proper relationship to animals consists in using them in a controlled, conscious manner—for the varied ends of the butcher, the nature photographer, the poet, the scientist, or the pet-owner. These relationships with animals are founded on our different aims and values, and as such are moral. A human-centred approach could mean spending hours in the wild studying animals, or painting and admiring them—but seeing them through a human eye rather than trying to escape our humanity.

What is at question is the position from which we see the world. Taking a bear-centred perspective makes no more sense than a DNA-centred perspective. Humans are the measure of all things: morality starts with us.

> *"It should be no surprise that many in the animal-rights movement use violence to pursue their man-destroying goals."*

Animals Rights Activists Are Terrorists

Alex Epstein

In the following viewpoint, Alex Epstein claims that animal rights activists who resort to violence to thwart animal experimentation are terrorists. Epstein argues that animal experimentation is vital to medicine, and those who would put the interests of animals before the interests of people are dangerous to both science and society. According to Epstein, right-thinking people should make sure that animal rights terrorists are jailed for their crimes and that the antihuman philosophy of animal rights should be condemned. Alex Epstein is a writer for the Ayn Rand Institute, a California-based educational organization advocating rational self-interest, individual rights, and free-market capitalism.

As you read, consider the following questions:

1. What acts of terrorism does Epstein say animal rights activists have used to intimidate those who conduct animal experimentation?
2. According to Epstein, in what way is animal experimentation vital?
3. What is the purpose of rights, as Epstein defines them?

The "animal rights" movement is celebrating its latest victory: an earlier, more painful death for future victims of Alzheimer's, Parkinson's, and Huntington's disease.

Thanks to intimidation by animal rights terrorists, Cambridge University ... [in England] dropped plans to build a laboratory that would have conducted cutting-edge brain research on primates. According to *The Times* of London, animal-rights groups "had threatened to target the centre with violent protests ... and Cambridge decided that it could not afford the costs or danger to staff that this would involve."

The university had good reason to be afraid. At a nearby animal-testing company, Huntingdon Life Sciences, "protestors" have for several years attempted to shut down the company by threatening employees and associates, damaging their homes, firebombing their cars, even beating them severely.

Many commentators and medical professionals in Britain have condemned the animal-rights terrorists and their violent tactics. Unfortunately, most have cast the terrorists as "extremists" who take "too far" the allegedly benevolent cause of animal rights. This is a deadly mistake. The terrorists' inhuman tactics are an embodiment of the movement's inhuman cause.

Why Experimentation Is Vital

While most animal-rights activists do not inflict beatings on animal testers, they *do* share the terrorists' goal of ending animal research—including the vital research the Cambridge lab would have conducted.

There is no question that animal research is absolutely necessary for the development of life-saving drugs, medical procedures, and biotech treatments. According to Nobel Laureate Joseph Murray, M.D.: "Animal experimentation has been essential to the development of all cardiac surgery, transplantation surgery, joint replacements, and all vaccinations." Explains former American Medical Association president Daniel Johnson, M.D.: "Animal research—followed by human clinical study—is absolutely necessary to find the causes and cures for so many deadly threats, from AIDS to cancer."

Millions of humans would suffer and die unnecessarily if animal testing were prohibited. Animal rights activists know this, but are unmoved. Chris DeRose, founder of the group Last Chance for Animals, writes: "If the death of one rat cured all diseases, it wouldn't make any difference to me."

An Anti-Human Position

The goal of the animal-rights movement is not to stop sadistic animal torturers; it is *to sacrifice and subjugate man to animals*. This goal is inherent in the very notion of "animal rights." According to People for the Ethical Treatment of Animals, the basic principle of "animal rights" is: "animals are not ours to eat, wear, experiment on, or use for entertainment" —they "deserve consideration of their own best interests regardless of whether they are useful to humans." This is in exact contradiction to the requirements of human survival and progress, which demand that we kill animals when they endanger us, eat them when we need food, run tests on them to fight disease. The death and destruction that would result from any serious attempt to respect "animal rights" would be catastrophic—for humans—a prospect the movement's most consistent members embrace. "We need a drastic decrease in human population if we ever hope to create a just and equitable world for animals," proclaims Freeman Wicklund of Compassionate Action for Animals.

Extreme Tactics by Animal Rights Group

According to [a 2002 Southern Poverty Law Center report], ARL [animal-rights/liberation] terrorists such as ALF [Animal Liberation Front] and SHAC [Stop Huntingdon Animal Cruelty] regularly employ "death threats, fire bombings, and violent assaults" against those they accuse of abusing animals. Some of the cruelest attacks have been mounted by SHAC against executives for Huntingdon Life Sciences, a British drug-testing facility that uses animals to test drugs for safety before they are tested on people. Indeed, the threats and violence became so extreme that Huntingdon fled Britain out of the fear that some of their own were going to be killed. They had good cause. The company's managing director was badly beaten by three masked assailants swinging baseball bats, while another executive was temporarily blinded with a caustic substance sprayed into his eyes.

Wesley J. Smith, "Terrorists, Too: Exposing Animal Rights Terrorism," National Review *online, October 2, 2002. www.nationalreview.com.*

To ascribe rights to animals is to contradict the purpose and justification of rights—to protect the interests of *humans*. Rights are moral principles necessary for men to survive as human beings—to coexist peacefully, to produce and trade, to provide for their own lives, and to pursue their own happiness, all by the guidance of their rational minds. To attribute rights to nonrational, amoral creatures who can neither grasp nor live by them is to turn rights from a tool of human preservation to a tool of human extermination.

It should be no surprise that many in the animal-rights movement use violence to pursue their man-destroying goals. While these terrorists should be condemned and imprisoned, that is not enough. We must wage a principled, intellectual war against the very notion of "animal rights"; we must condemn it as logically false and morally repugnant.

> "These [animal] activists . . . are part of a relatively new, isolated social movement, and therefore more vulnerable to attacks on civil liberties."

Animals Rights Activists Are Not Terrorists

Will Potter

In the following viewpoint Will Potter, a freelance journalist, claims that animal rights activists are unfairly being labeled as terrorists by the U.S. government. According to Potter, federal authorities are making such claims because the government's War on Terror has failed to nab any real and dangerous terrorists. Thus, in Potter's view, the government is rounding up relatively harmless activists in order to convince the public that the War on Terror is achieving results.

As you read, consider the following questions:

1. As mentioned in the viewpoint, with what crime were the Stop Huntingdon Animal Cruelty (SHAC) activists charged?

2. Why does Potter describe the arrested activists as "canaries in the mine?"

3. In Potter's view, what should all political activists do in response to the arrests of the SHAC members?

The [George W.] Bush administration sent a calculated message to grassroots political activists [in May 2004]: The War on Terrorism has come home.

FBI agents rounded up seven American political activists from across the country Wednesday morning, and the U.S. Attorney's Office in New Jersey held a press conference trumpeting that "terrorists" have been indicted.

That's right: "Terrorists." The activists have been charged with violating the Animal Enterprise Terrorism Act of 1992, which at the time garnered little public attention except from the corporations who lobbied for it. Their crime, according to the indictment, is "conspiring" to shut down Huntingdon Life Sciences [HLS], a company that tests products on animals and has been exposed multiple times for violating animal welfare laws. [Huntingdon is a British company with branches in the United States and other countries.]

The terrorism charges could mean a maximum of three years in prison and a $250,000 fine. The activists also face additional charges of interstate stalking and three counts of conspiracy to engage in interstate stalking: Each count could mean up to five years in prison and a $250,000 fine.

A Sham War on Terrorism

Since September 11, the T-word has been tossed around by law enforcement and politicians with more and more ease. Grassroots environmental and animal activists, and even national organizations like Greenpeace, have been called "eco-terrorists" by the corporations and politicians they oppose. The arrests on Wednesday, though, mark the official opening of a new domestic front in the War on Terrorism.

Bush's War on Terrorism is no longer limited to Al Qaeda or [its leader] Osama Bin Laden. It's not limited to Afghanistan or Iraq (or Syria, or Iran, or whichever country is next). And it's not limited to the animal rights movement, or even the campaign against Huntingdon Life Sciences. The rounding up of activists on Wednesday should set off alarms heard by every social movement in the United States: This "war" is about protecting corporate and political interests under the guise of fighting terrorism.

To use a non-animal rights analogy, these activists are the canaries in the mine. They are part of a relatively new, isolated social movement, and therefore more vulnerable to attacks on civil liberties. But what happens to them now will happen to other movements soon enough.

The activists arrested are part of a group called Stop Huntingdon Animal Cruelty [SHAC], an international organization aimed solely at closing the controversial lab. The group uses home demonstrations, phone and email blockades, and plenty of smart-ass, aggressive rhetoric to pressure companies to cut ties with the lab. It has worked. The lab has been brought near bankruptcy, after international corporations like Marsh Inc. have pulled out their investments.

To most, this is effective—albeit controversial—organizing. According to the indictment, though, it's "terrorism" because the activists aim to cause "physical disruption to the functioning of HLS, an animal enterprise, and intentionally damage and cause the loss of property used by HLS."

That's like saying the Montgomery bus boycott, a catalyst of the civil rights movement, was terrorism because it aimed to "intentionally damage and cause the loss of property" of the bus company.

Everyone Could Be a Terrorist

It seems the biggest act of "terrorism" by the group is a website. Members of the group are outspoken supporters of illegal direct action like civil disobedience, rescuing animals from

Falsely Labeled as Terrorists

On May 26, 2005 at 6 a.m. . . . these seven activists were arrested at gunpoint by FBI, ATF [Bureau of Alcohol, Tobacco, and Firearms], Secret Service and Homeland Security agents. This after over 100 FBI agents and 11 US attorneys spent time tapping phone lines and email accounts, raiding homes and threatening friends and family with grand jury subpoenas. And all of these resources were spent, or rather wasted on these people that did the sinister act of running a website and writing letters to companies that test on animals. Beware!

Megan McGowan,
"Animal Rights Activists Shouldn't Be Labeled As Terrorists!"
Collegiate Times, *October 20, 2005.*

labs, and vandalism. Whenever actions—legal or not—take place against the lab, the group puts it on the website. The activists are not accused of taking part in any of these crimes.

Such news postings are so threatening, apparently, that the indictment doesn't even name the corporations that have been targeted. They are only identified by single letters, like "S. Inc." or "M. Corp."

"Because of the nature of the campaign against these companies, we didn't want to subject them further to the tactics of SHAC," said Michael Drewniak, spokesperson for the U.S. Attorney's Office in New Jersey, in an interview.

Some of the wealthiest corporations on the planet, and the U.S. Attorney's Office must protect them from a bunch of protesters. This is what the War on Terrorism has become: The Bush administration can't find real terrorists abroad, yet it spends law enforcement time and resources protecting corporations from political activists.

The lawsuit is so outlandish that some activists, who asked that they not be identified, said they don't think it is intended to win. Instead, they see it as an important political move in the War on Terror. In a hearing before the U.S. Senate Judiciary Committee just last week, a U.S. Attorney said the Animal Enterprise Terrorism Act needed to go further to successfully be used against Stop Huntingdon Animal Cruelty. If this lawsuit fails, the Justice Department can say, "We told you so."

So, these activists face a double-edged sword. If they lose, they go to prison, and are labeled "terrorists" for the rest of their lives. If they win, it could be fodder for an even harsher political crackdown.

Their only chance is for activists of all social movements—regardless of their political views—to support them, and oppose the assault on basic civil liberties. Otherwise, in Bush's America, we could all be terrorists.

"Silence does not protect scientists against intimidation."

Animal Researchers Should Not Be Bullied by Animal Rights Terrorists

Fiona Fox

Fiona Fox is the director of the Science Media Centre, a London-based organization that promotes the work of scientists in the British press. In the following viewpoint Fox worries that the intimidation tactics of animal rights extremists are successfully silencing scientists working in the field of animal research. Fox argues that remaining quiet or giving in to extremists' demands will ultimately hurt the research community and perhaps thwart vital work in medical and pharmaceutical science. Only by uniting against the fear, Fox claims, will scientists be able to win the fight against continued harassment.

As you read, consider the following questions:

1. How many animal researchers are members of Fox's Science Media Centre?

Fiona Fox, "Come Out and Fight: The Surest Way to Let the Animal Rights Extremists Win, Warns Fiona Fox, Is for Scientists to Hide Away and Refuse to Argue Their Case," *New Scientist*, vol. 187, no. 2518, September 24, 2005, p. 22. Copyright © 2005 Reed Elsevier Business Publishing, Ltd. Reproduced by permission.

2. According to Fox, what was the response of Britain's Research Defence Society to the forced closure of the Darley Oaks Farm, where guinea pigs were raised for animal testing?

3. According to Fox, in what two ways does silence on the part of the scientific community hamper the fight against animal extremists?

In 2001, the New York stock exchange reopened just days after the attacks of 11 September in a symbolic act of defiance against terrorism. How times change. Earlier this month, the same organisation apparently caved in to intimidation from a small group of animal rights extremists over the flotation of Life Sciences Research, the parent company of the UK-based animal research company Huntingdon Life Sciences.

This loss of nerve came hot on the heels of the closure of a UK-based business that bred guinea pigs at Darley Oaks Farm in Staffordshire, which was forced to shut down by a sustained campaign of intimidation. You might be forgiven for thinking that the extremists are winning.

Whether or not they are winning depends, for me, on whether they are managing to silence the scientific community. And that certainly seems to be happening. I work for the Science Media Centre, an independent press office based in London that was set up in 2002 to encourage scientists to speak out on the controversial stories of the day. On issues ranging from genetically modified crops to designer babies and nanotechnology, the centre has been hugely successful in signing up scientists willing to enter the media fray.

But not so for animal research. Getting scientists to speak on this topic has been a dispiriting affair. The number registered on our database is limited to about 20 brave souls. Most scientists and their institutions in the UK, it appears, are allowing themselves to be silenced on the issue of animal testing by the violent activities of a handful of animal rights extremists.

Terrorists Oppose Democratic, Free Discussion

Professor Steve Bloom, head of metabolic medicine at Imperial College London, is among the many UK researchers who have been targeted by extremists. He has had phone calls threatening violence against his children. Prof Bloom is angry that the actions of a few can undermine open public discussion. And he believes extremists are actually impeding improvements to the [animal welfare] law. 'The terrorists are against democracy. They inhibit free discussion. People are afraid to speak out because they know they might become the next target. 'No one can make an informed decision without free and open discussion. But how can you be informed if the people who have the information are threatened or even attacked whenever they speak out?'

Janis Smy, "Can Doctors Safely Talk about Testing?"
Hospital Doctor, *October 7, 2004.*

The extremists' actions have led many universities, healthcare charities and drug companies to maintain a "no comment" policy on animal testing. One press officer in a university planning to build a new animal facility says that his proposal to invite the local media in at an early stage was met with horror by colleagues, whose instinct was to keep the project quiet. Another leading university that does animal research recently offered the Science Media Centre a venue for press conferences—but only on condition that the topics steered clear of animal testing. And several press officers from other institutions say it is their policy to remove references to animal research from press releases about medical breakthroughs.

Fortunately, there are signs that such attitudes are changing. Simon Festing, director of the UK's Research Defense Society [RDS], which represents medical researchers in the debate on animal testing, points out that 10 years ago almost no scientists ever spoke out on animal research. But on the day the news broke about the closure of Darley Oaks Farm, the RDS released a declaration of support for animal research signed by more than 700 scientists.

More voices are desperately needed. Hundreds of institutions and tens of thousands of scientists conduct animal research that they consider to be crucial to curing human disease, yet refuse to say so publicly. While individually the reasons for their reticence are often compelling and hard to challenge, collectively this must surely amount to one of the most catastrophic collapses of nerve in our society today. The failure is all the more regrettable when you consider that support for animal testing from the public, government and media has never been greater.

What's more, silence does not protect scientists against intimidation. The long-standing campaigns against Darley Oaks Farm, Huntingdon Life Sciences and more recently the University of Oxford's planned new animal facility show that all too clearly. Extremists targeted these organisations despite the silence of the people who work there.

Keeping silent can even make matters worse, attracting accusations of secrecy and allowing activists' unfounded allegations of malpractice to go unanswered. And there is no evidence that speaking out in the media is the spark for intimidation and attacks. My own straw poll of scientists on our database revealed that most of those who spoke out had not been targeted. And many of those who had spoken out, such as Colin Blakemore, a neurosurgeon at the Radcliffe Infirmary in Oxford, started doing so only after becoming targets.

The way forward is clear. If all those scientists who support animal testing started to say so publicly they would drown out the small number of extremists and make it harder for them to pick out individuals from the crowd. My hunch is that extremists, who clearly prefer midnight attacks to open debate, steer clear of those robust enough to take to the airwaves.

Despite the animal rights activists' apparent successes, the battle over animal research is far from over. While government and the police must continue do their bit, and do it better, this alone is unlikely to stop the attacks. The real test will be whether those who perpetrate physical attacks against those who use animals in experiments will succeed in driving animal research abroad. Only if the scientific community is willing to stand up and be counted will the extremists be defeated.

Periodical Bibliography

The following articles have been selected to supplement the diverse views presented in this chapter.

Gary Block   "The Moral Reasoning of Believers in Animal Rights," *Society & Animals*, July 2003.

Jeffrey Brainard   "Undercover Among the Cages," *Chronicle of Higher Education*, March 3, 2006.

Heidi Brown   "Beware of People," *Forbes*, July 26, 2004.

Kerry Capell   "Animal-Rights Activism Turns Rabid," *Business Week*, August 23, 2004.

Gary Francione   "One Right for All," *New Scientist*, October 8, 2005.

Brad Knickerbocker   "Crackdown on Animal-Rights Activists," *Christian Science Monitor*, March 7, 2006.

David Kocieniewski   "Accused of Aiding Animals by Making Prey of People," *New York Times*, March 1, 2006.

Zeeya Merali   "Animal Activists Flee UK Clampdown," *New Scientist*, May 13, 2006.

Iain Murray and Ivan Osorio   "PETA: Cruel and Unusual," *Human Events*, January 16, 2006.

R. Scott Nolan   "Activists Seek Personhood for Animals," *Journal of the American Veterinary Medical Association*, September 15, 2003.

Scott Smallwood   "Speaking for the Animals, or the Terrorists," *Chronicle of Higher Education*, August 5, 2005.

OPPOSING
VIEWPOINTS®
SERIES

CHAPTER 2

Is Animal Experimentation Justifiable?

Chapter Preface

Many American high school teenagers attend at least one biology class in which the dissection of a frog, fetal pig, or other small animal is part of the curriculum. Most schools and teacher organizations support the practice of vivisection in the classroom because it gives students a unique opportunity to see the complex inner workings of a living organism. The National Association of Biology Teachers (NABT), for example, states that "no alternative can substitute for the actual experience of dissection or other use of animals." The NABT also "urges teachers to be aware of the limitations of alternatives."

Opponents of dissection in the classroom believe that studying the internal anatomy of dead animals is not essential for learning. The majority of students, these critics assert, will not be pursuing a career in which intensive biological examination is necessary, and those who might choose to become medical practitioners can acquire this knowledge using other tools such as computer models. The New England Anti-Vivisection Society (NEAVS) further contends that compelling hesitant students to participate in dissection can reduce the value of the exercise. "When forced to use animals in ways the student objects to," NEAVS states, "the student is traumatized and invariably learns *less*."

Because more students are voicing their objection to dissection labs on religious grounds or conscientious concerns, many schools across the nation have begun offering alternatives. Computer simulation, multimedia coursework, and other educational tools have been used as substitute learning aids for those who dissent. These options have allowed students to feel more comfortable about their decision to refrain from dissecting animals. The authors in the following chapter discuss the justification for experimenting on animals beyond the classroom setting. These critics and scholars—like their school-age counterparts—have varying opinions on the ethical merits of using animals to advance scientific knowledge.

"Observing that all species strive to stay alive and then handicapping ourselves deliberately by not trying to understand the biological world would be just plain stupid."

Animal Experimentation Is Ethical

Adrian R. Morrison

Dr. Adrian R. Morrison works in the Laboratory for Study of the Brain in Sleep at the University of Pennsylvania's School of Veterinary Medicine. As an animal researcher, Morrison believes that animal experimentation is both ethical and necessary to medical progress. In the following viewpoint Morrison defends the ethics of his work by explaining that the human race's overriding duty is to keep itself alive. Humans, like all species, are struggling to survive, he maintains, and medical advancement through animal experimentation serves this purpose. He insists, though, that people have an obligation to look after the needs of animals in their care but that this concern does not contradict the use of animals in purposeful experimentation.

Adrian R. Morrison, "Ethical Principles Guiding the Use of Animals in Research," *The American Biology Teacher*, vol. 65, no. 2, February 2003, pp. 105–08. Reproduced by permission of the National Association of Biology Teachers.

As you read, consider the following questions:

1. According to Morrison, how are humans—of all species—uniquely "burdened?"

2. How does Morrison deflate Peter Singer's notion of "speciesism?"

3. How does Morrison counter the argument that animals have rights?

As a biologist ... I recognize that all species are in a struggle for existence. As the most intelligent species on the planet, we would be extremely foolish to deny this fact and not act on behalf of our own families, friends and, ultimately, our own species by not engaging in biomedical research by all means available. Actually, we would be denying a biological imperative: the drive to survive. Clearly, in this instance one must have the long-range view that biomedical research enhances the opportunity for survival. Of course, our brains endow us with the ability to go beyond 'tooth and claw.' Only we can advance our own interests through the medium of science. Should we go through life arrogantly refusing to use our brains in such research because some philosopher has said that to use animals is wrong? Remember, research has also benefited animals by improvements in veterinary care.

Indeed, it would appear that ignorance of, or ignoring, biology has led a small group of philosophers down a foolish path. A conservation writer [Richard Conniff] has quite directly said that they and their followers have "elevated ignorance of the natural world almost to the level of a philosophical principle."

The following famous statement from the animal rights literature, at the very least, ignores the biological imperative of which I spoke earlier: "If that (abandoning animal research) means that there are some things we cannot learn, then so be it. . . . We have, then, no basic rights against nature not to be harmed by those natural diseases we are heir to" (Tom Regan, *The Case for Animal Rights*).

Of course, one can create any world one wants with words. A critical question, though, is would one be willing to live in that world? Should one force it on others for the sake of animals? Neither the philosophers nor their followers have taken a principled, public stand announcing that their world will do without the fruits of modern medicine based on animal research. . . .

With these beliefs made explicit, let me now turn to what I call my 'first principles.' I am quite certain the vast majority of scientists would readily subscribe to all five of them.

First Principles

1. Our first obligation is to our fellow humans. I have already addressed this idea from a biological point of view. Observing that all species strive to stay alive and then handicapping ourselves deliberately by not trying to understand the biological world would be just plain stupid. Indeed, I think it is my most powerful argument, one that no philosopher can defeat. But can one also support this choice philosophically? I believe so.

We are a species unique in our cognitive abilities: to use just a few examples, we create beautiful sculptures, write on philosophical issues, and devise just laws. These laws, as well as tradition handed down from long ago, bind us together in a moral community. Yet, we are autonomous beings living in that community. Only we, of all species on Earth, can be held accountable for our deeds, judged guilty in a court of law. We are burdened in a way that no other species is, even to the extent of caring for other species. These responsibilities make us special in my view and warrant special consideration and compassion. I think it follows that we owe it to our fellow man to alleviate the pain and misery of disease through biomedical research.

Furthermore, our capacity to suffer extends far beyond that of any animal. Immediate pain is one thing and something we must always consider when using animals in research. But I think now of mental suffering: the sense of loss of a child to disease or the despair of a teenager condemned to a restricted life due to a spinal cord severed in a head-on collision while playing football. We can empathize directly with these fellow humans. Being more certain of their suffering than that of any animal, we would be remiss in not putting our fellow humans first by doing research that might eventually help someone. To lack such empathy—and various animal-rightists have evidenced such a lack in their public statements—is inhuman and inhumane.

2. *All human beings are persons.* The average person says: of course! But not Peter Singer, author of *Animal Liberation*, called the 'bible' of the animal rights movement. He reasons that parents with a deformed or mentally defective infant, one with Down syndrome, to use one of his examples, would be justified in rejecting (euthanizing) this 'non-person,' for a baby only becomes a person (protected by law) at one month of age. This act would bring them more happiness if they then had a normal infant. Singer comes from the utilitarian wing of the branch of philosophy called ethics. The utilitarian perspective, at least as carried forth by Singer, allows one to seek the greater good or happiness offered by the normal replacement. This approach would be 'convenient' but dangerous, not to mention that many with Down syndrome or other 'defects' can develop into a reasonably productive and apparently happy person.

Singer is very explicit in his views. He states: "Likewise, we cannot justifiably give more protection to the life of a human being than we give to a non-human animal, if the human being clearly ranks lower on any possible scale of relevant characteristics than the animal." Animals with cognitive abilities can be persons in Singer's view. He believes that we should

Moore. © 1998 Universal Press Syndicate. Reproduced by permission.

abandon belief in the sanctity of human life and no longer exclude animals from our moral community. . . .

Singer emphasizes the concept of 'speciesism,' which means that treating members of other species without considering their interests just because they are animals is akin to racism. This concept drives his thinking. Singer says that we should not treat members of other species differently than we treat members of our own just because the former are not humans. Although he states that he wishes to elevate animals, I think he drags humanity down to the level of animals with an emphasis on the capacity of all creatures to suffer pain. But the human species is so much more than that. We are a social, highly cognitive species with the capacity to participate in the suffering of people thousands of miles away. This enables rescue operations aided by people from far away after an earthquake or flood. Again, this makes us special in my view. Certainly, we should not treat members of another species with wanton cruelty just because they are not human—in this sense we are considering their interests, but our special duty to fellow humans warrants the use of other species in biomedical research.

3. Animals are not little persons. This principle strikes at the heart of the dilemma faced by a scientist who is very fond of animals, enjoys their company, and yet uses them in research. Although we know they are not little persons, we create our pets as such. I have a young cat, Buster, who captured my heart during his kittenhood. If I stopped walking while he was near me, he would lie on my feet so I would pet him before moving on. He would often stand on my chest while I lie in bed and look closely at me while purring very close to my face. What he was thinking, I will never know. . . .

Yet, for most of my career I used members of his species in my research on sleep mechanisms because, due to their size and habits, cats are well suited for neurophysiological studies on sleep and other phenomena. How could I do this? Indeed, I asked myself several times a year whether I really wanted to continue. The answer was always 'yes.' It came down to faith in the process of science and knowledge of medical history, a belief that my work would provide a bit of knowledge ultimately useful for solving a human problem. Otherwise, it could not be justified. Now, our work involves rats, and I am relieved. To one who keeps a rat for a pet, however, this would not be a satisfactory solution, again emphasizing the point that we decide what the animal is to be in relation to us.

4. We have a great obligation to the animals under our control. No words express this principle better than a passage from a book popular when I was a boy. For some reason the following conversation burned itself into my mind. In *My Friend Flicka* by Mary O'Hara, rancher Rob McLaughlin is speaking with one of his sons about a wild mare that had broken loose from their corral with the noose of a lariat around her neck:

> "What if it did choke her?" asked Howard. "You always say she's no use to you." "There's a responsibility we have toward animals," said his father. "We use them. We shut them up, keep their natural food and water from them that means we have to feed and water them. Take their freedom away, rope them, harness them, that means we have to supply a different sort of safety for them. Once I've put a rope on a horse, or taken away its ability to take care of itself, then I've got to take care of it. Do you see that? That noose around her neck is a danger to her, and I put it there, so I have to get it off."

The point is that although laws administered by the Public Health Service and the Department of Agriculture govern the use of animals in the laboratory, animal welfare in the laboratory must begin with the scientist. It is the scientist's competence and knowledge of the literature that determine whether the animal's participation is for a noble cause. The process is not perfect, I admit, but these standards represent an important ideal. . . .

Our obligations we commonly call 'rights': for example, the right to proper food and water when under our care and the right to be treated humanely. Some philosophers emphasize these moral rights. Indeed, they are embodied in law. But these 'rights' are far from saying animals are our moral equals, something the majority of students recognize intuitively, I am sure. They do not approach [animal rights philosopher Tom] Regan's extreme view quoted earlier. For Regan, who comes from the rights branch of ethics, argues that animals have 'inherent value,' which proscribes our harming them. He argues that they are conscious and goal-oriented; therefore they are 'subjects of a life,' the quality that gives them the inherent value upon which we cannot trample. His stance would leave us helpless in the face of nature. . . .

5. Good science requires good animal care, but bureaucracy does not necessarily equate with increased welfare. With governmental regulation comes a certain amount of bureaucracy. One must accept this because many regulations have improved laboratory animal welfare. Thus, scientists must submit a research proposal for review and approval by a committee of scientists, veterinarians and non-scientists before the research may be undertaken. I think the process is a good one, for it ensures that the plan is methodologically sound and that the welfare of the animal subjects is optimized. Required daily oversight of an institution's animals by veterinarians is also good for both the animals and the quality of the experiments.

But animal-rightist pressure has pushed us, or rather, the United States government, beyond these reasonable demands. Thus, under the illusion created by animal rights pressure claiming that scientists are bent on using animals even though there [are] other equally adequate instruments, the U.S. Congress passed legislation stating that a scientist must show that a thorough review of the literature has revealed no alternatives. We do this, even while knowing that our searches will come up empty; for after 40 years in research on a particular subject, who better than that scientist knows the answer? When another way presents itself, the scientist will take it for ethical as well as scientific reasons. . . .

Philosophy Must Apply to the Real World

Scientists are not aloof, cold-blooded individuals working under some set regimen . . . ; ethical considerations accompany their efforts in the laboratory. I accept, though, that one may disagree with my line of thinking, even rejecting the use of animals in research. In doing the latter, however, one must present his or her fellow human beings with a rational substitute, one that will work in the real world. To date, no one has succeeded. The philosophical leaders of the movement, Regan and Singer, have created unnatural worlds with words and then demolished each other's worlds with more words with philosophical jousting, still agreeing on the need to end all animal use—a political end. Their worlds may have relevance in the corridors of a philosophy department, but they have little meaning in rooms of two institutions close to me, The Hospital of the University of Pennsylvania and Children's Hospital of Philadelphia.

| "If we would not want done to ourselves what we do to laboratory animals, we should not do it to them."

Animal Experimentation Is Unethical

David Thomas

In the following viewpoint David Thomas asserts that because science does not condone experimenting on nonconsenting humans, it cannot ethically condone experimenting on animals, which never can give consent. Furthermore, if the medical community refrains from the former because of the pain such experiments would inflict, then it must logically refrain from the latter. Animals feel pain, Thomas insists, and to experiment upon them against their will is as cruel and unethical as it would be to conduct experiments upon people without consent. David Thomas is a lawyer and chairman of the Royal Society for the Prevention of Cruelty to Animals.

As you read, consider the following questions:

1. What historical examples does Thomas give of experiments involving nonconsenting humans?

David Thomas, "Laboratory Animals and the Art of Empathy," *Journal of Medical Ethics*, vol. 31, April 2005, pp. 197–202. Copyright © 2005 British Medical Association. Reproduced by permission.

2. In what way is the Helsinki Declaration important to Thomas's argument about the ethics of human and animal experimentation?

3. In the author's view, what is the difference between the deontological philosophical approach to human experimentation and the utilitarian philosophical approach to animal experimentation?

It is not clear whether Shylock would have been opposed to animal experiments. But he should have been, if he was being consistent in his ethics. He understood that, when determining how we should treat others, we should put ourselves in their shoes and ask how we would feel in the same circumstances. In other words, we should empathise. Just as Jews suffer in the same way as Christians if they are poisoned, so do animals. Like Christians and Jews, animals bleed if pricked.

In this article I will argue that consistency is the hallmark of a coherent ethical philosophy and that the obvious comparator with animal experiments is non-consensual experiments on people. We regard the latter as unethical, so we should the former. As a society we have no difficulty in empathising with the victims of human experiments. Horror at the thought of being experimented upon is no doubt why we regard the practice as abhorrent. It should not take a big leap of imagination to empathise with the victims of animal experiments as well. In short: if we would not want done to ourselves what we do to laboratory animals, we should not do it to them.

Animals Suffer

Crucially for the debate about the morality of animal experiments, non-human animals suffer just as human ones do. [Seventeenth-century philosopher René] Descartes may have described animals as "these mechanical robots [who] could give such a realistic *illusion* of agony" (my emphasis) but no serious scientist today doubts that the manifestation of agony is real, not illusory. Indeed, the whole pro-vivisection case is based on the premise that animals are sufficiently similar to us physiologically, and for some experiments behaviourally too, for valid conclusions to be extrapolated from experimenting on them.

Of course, the nature and degree of suffering will not always be identical. Some species of animal will suffer less than people in eq:vialent situations, and people probably experience greater distress at witnessing someone close to them suffer than many animals would, adding to the totality of suffering in the human context.

Equally, however, lab animals will sometimes suffer more than people would, sometimes physically, sometimes psychologically. Unlike Terry Waite, who composed several novels in his head as a coping mechanism during his five years of captivity, animals are (as far as we know) not fortified by a sense of mission or injustice and do not know that their suffering will eventually come to an end.

The law has sometimes been slow to recognise that animals suffer. However, the European Union now accepts that animals are sentient beings and therefore qualitatively different from other traded "products". The European Patent Convention and th European Patent Directive each acknowledge that the genetic engineering of animals raises moral issues precisely because the engineered animals are liable to suffer; in principle, a patent could be refused on these grounds. And, in the UK, a licence to conduct an experiment on animals is only required if it is liable to cause "pain, suffering, distress or lasting harm". Nearly three million laboratory animals fell within this definition in 2003.

Suffering, indeed, lies at the heart of all morality. We have moral codes precisely because our behaviour may adversely affect others. It is not surprising, therefore, that animal experimentation has become one of the ethical issues of our time.

In a recent survey carried out by MORI [Market & Opinion Research International] for the [British] Coalition for Medical Progress (CMP), over two thirds of respondents said they were either very or fairly concerned about the issue. The Animal Procedures Committee (APC), the government's advisory body, has recently entered the ethical debate in its report on the cost: benefit test which lies at the heart of the Animals (Scientific Procedures) Act 1986. "Cost", of course, refers principally to animal suffering. The APC's contribution is intelligent but flawed in one crucial respect, as I will explain.

The Battle For Hearts and Minds

The CMP is a newly formed coalition of mulitnational pharmaceutical and contract testing companies (such as GlaxoSmithKline (GSK) and Huntingdon Life Sciences (HLS)), provivisection pressure groups such as the Research Defence Society (RDS), bodies funding animal research like the Medical Research Council, and a trade union, Amicus (which has members at HLS). The fact that yet another lobby group has been set up shows how crucial the battle for hearts and minds on this issue has become. It is fair to point out that many CMP members have a large financial interest in animal experiments.

It is beyond dispute that the present government, ever ready to promote British business, has recently entered the propaganda fray firmly on the side of animal researchers. It contributed an astonishing £85 000 towards the cost of the MORI survey. In 2002 the Prime Minister publicly supported Cambridge University's controversial planning application to extend its primate facility. Rather embarassingly for him, his intervention came on the very day that BBC's *Newsnight* carried the British Union for Abolition of Vivisection's exposé of the suffering endured by primates at the university's existing facility.

The Ethical Issue In a Nutshell

So the battle lines are drawn, sometimes literally. Although there are, increasingly, arguments around the scientific efficacy of vivisection, at root it is an ethical issue: is it justifiable to inflict suffering on animals when it is not for their benefit but rather for the benefit of those doing the inflicting (or those they purport to represent)? As with all ethical dilemmas, the proposition is capable of neither proof nor disproof. If a person's political opinions are merely the rationalisation of his or her instinctive response, so it is with matters of ethics. We react to a given situation at an emotional level and then find the reasons to justify our position. The assumptions we make in addressing an issue will often determine the outcome, and those assumptions will often be the product of our cultural conditioning. Vivisection is no different from other issues in this respect.

The 18th century Scottish philosopher David Hume put it like this:

> The approbation of moral qualities most certainly is not deriv'd from reason, or any comparison of ideas; but proceeds entirely from a moral taste, and from certain sentiments of pleasure or disgust, which rise upon contemplation and view of particular qualities or characters.

Adam Smith's view was that the general rules of morality are founded upon experience of what, in particular instances, our moral faculties and sense of propriety approve or disapprove. None of this means, of course, that rational thought has no place when considering ethical issues. As a minimum, we should, firstly, ensure that we have sufficient facts to make a reasonable judgement; and, secondly, strive for consistency across ethically comparable issues. The debate about animal experiments suffers from a deficiency in both these prerequisites, as I will try to explain.

I will focus on those animal experiments which can truely be said to be designed to address particular human diseases.

They are, in fact, a minority of those carried out but it is here that the rival ethical positions are most sharply engaged.

A Secret System

Animal experiments in this country are shrouded in secrecy. Under section 24 of the Animals (Scientific Procedures) Act 1986, the Home Secretary could be sent to prison for up to two years were he to desclose information given to him in confidence by a researcher. The RDS advises researchers to mark everything they send the Home Office "in confidence" to try to prevent disclosure. A few years ago, Smith Kline French (as it then was) took a judicial review all the way to the House of Lords in an attempt to stop the medicines regulator even *referring* to test the data (which SKF had supplied) when considering applications from other companies. Fortunately the attempt failed, but this is the secrecy mentality. Occasionally companies openly admit that they prefer their rivals to conduct "blind alley" research, irrespective of the cost to lab animals.

The Home Office claims that it makes its own judgement about what is confidential, but usually seems to find a reason to join in the conspiracy of silence.

The outcome of some research is published, of course, but only if the researcher finds it advantageous to do so. He or she is unlikely to highlight the animal suffering involved. Negative results are rarely published. As result, duplication is rife, as international institutions and the industry itself now acknowledge. Where results are published, an article in the *BMJ* has recently highlighted the flaws in the system. The authors concluded: "Systematic bias favours products which are made by the company funding the research. Explanations include the selection of an inappropriate comparator to the product being investigated and publication bias."

The public is therefore denied the information on which to make sound ethical judgements about animal experiments.

It has to rely on the media, which traditionally prefers easy sensationalism to painstaking investigation and stories about animal rights militancy to serious argument. Animal protection groups feel they have to conduct undercover investigations to educate the public.

The Ethical Judgement At The Heart of The Legislation

Crucially, the culture of secrecy means that the legislation cannot work properly. The cost: benefit test is a moral judgement. Before he grants a licence for animal experiments, the Home Secretary is enjoined to weigh the likely "adverse effects" on an animal against the likely benefits of an experiment. That is, of course, a value laden judgement. How much suffering (if any) is acceptable? Does it depend on the species? What about the fact that the animal may die in the experiment, or be killed when it is no longer required? Should commercial benefit suffice? Should society just do without certain products, such that we do not need to worry about their safety? What about fundamental research, from which the benefits are by definition speculative?

There is no arithmetical formula to be applied to these ethical questions. In a mature democracy, how they are answered should reflect informed public opinion. But, this is not possible if the public does not really know what is going on and has no opportunity of influencing regulatory decisions, at however general a level. According to the Home Office, most of its inspectors—who in practice run the system—have previously held licences to experiment on animals, and therefore inevitably bring a pro-vivisection ethical perspective to their task.

Many believe that the government should publish detailed information about animal experiments—what they involve for the animals, their purpose, and their results—unless the researchers can, in an individual case, make out a strong objection. That would reflect the presumption of openness contained in the Freedom of Information Act 2000 (FOI Act), which has just come fully into effect. Information can be made public in anonymised form, in order to protect researchers from any risk of attack; information which is truly commercially sensitive can be omitted for as long as it retains such sensitivity.

Only in this way can there be the informed debate essential for formulation of ethical principles. It remains to be seen how much difference the FOI Act will make.

So, the first prerequisite to a reasoned ethical judgement—the availability of sufficient information—is missing with animal experiments. What about consistency across comparable issues?

Most people would accept that an ethical philosophy should be internally consistent, insofar as possible, and that similar cases should be treated alike. Otherwise, the philosophy is likely to be opportunistic and self serving. To paraphrase John Donne: no ethical issue is an island.

In reaching our view about animal experiments, we should therefore search for a valid comparator and test our view about the former against our view of the latter. The obvious—and I believe correct—comparator is non-consensual experiments on people. In both cases, suffering and perhaps death is knowingly caused to the victim, the intended beneficiary is someone else and the victim does not consent.

The APC rightly raises the question of consistency in its discourse on the ethics of vivisection. However, it chooses the wrong comparator. It suggests that the "appropriate point of comparison should perhaps be with an 'improved' food animal industry". Certainly, there is an ethical overlap between the way we treat food animals and the way we treat lab animals. However, the much more pertinent comparator is non-consensual experiments on people and it is surprising that the APC missed it.

Recent Examples of Non-consensual Experiments on People

Recent history has witnessed many examples of non-consensual experiments on people. For example:

- the barbaric experiments carried out by Nazi and Japanese scientists during the second world war;

- the long running syphilis experiments on black people in Alabama over four decades up to the 1970s;

- the radiological experiments conducted at the Burden Neurological Institute in Bristol [England] during the 1950s and 1960s by British scientists for the US Office for Naval Research. According to *The Ecologist*, holes were drilled at random through the skulls and into the brains of the institute's patients. Steel electrodes, which had been coated with a radioactive chemical, were then sent deep into the brain via these holes, and electric shocks pumped through them. Some of the patients later had tumours deliberately induced in their brains.

Sometimes, the human victim gives no consent at all; on other occasions, he or she may give consent but not on an informed basis. In November 2001, BBC Radio 4's *File on Four* carried a damning report on the practice of some pharmaceutical companies, particularly in Eastern Europe and Africa, of abusing the principle of informed consent in clinical trials, including with children and mentally vulnerable people. Animals of course, cannot give any form of consent—informed or otherwise. I will return to the question of consent because it is central to the debate.

Why Experiments on People and on Animals Are Comparable

Some people will argue that, despite the superficial similarities, non-consensual experiments on people and experiments on animals are not ethically comparable. I have described these arguments below.

People have greater value than animals. It is said that, on the one hand, all people have equal intrinsic value and that, on the other, all people have greater value than all (non-human) animals. So, it is concluded, experimenting on people is unethical whereas experimenting on animals is ethical. There are two points here. Firstly, judging relative value is a subjective, wholly unscientific exercise, not least because the criteria one chooses will almost inevitably determine the outcome. There is no set of obviously correct objective criteria ready to be plucked off the shelf. It rather depends who you ask. Just as for each human being our own existence is inevitably the most important, however altruistic we may try to be, to the laboratory rat its existence matters more than anyone else's.

Secondly, and more importantly, why should the fact (if this is what it is) that A has more value than B mean that A is at liberty to cause pain to B for A's benefit? This is the crucial gap in logic which pro-vivisectionists rarely address. Let us accept for the sake of argument that it was provable that the human species was more important than other species—whether because people generally (though not always) have greater capacity for rational thought, may have greater self awareness, are better able to empathise, or have more sophisticated culture. It is not explained why those attributes mean that we can cause pain to those we relegate further down the hierarchy of value. And, if cruel exploitation of *other* species is justified on a relative value basis, then, logically, so must cruel exploitation *within* our species. Some people, indisputably, have greater capacity for rational thought, have greater self awareness, are better able to empathise, or have a deeper cultural appreciation than other people. However, most people do not conclude that the more endowed are for that reason entitled to cause pain to the less endowed for their own benefit.

The racist, the religious fundamentalist, and the misogynist do, of course, discriminate in their treatment of others according to the hierarchies of value they espouse. The majority of people may profoundly disagree with these hierarchies, but we cannot prove *empirically* that they are misconceived. Once one has breached the moral dam by allowing relative value to be the justification for cruel behaviour in one situation (vivisection), there is no rational basis on which one can tell someone that he does not have the right to be cruel to another person he genuinely (if misguidedly) believes to be of lesser value.

The important point is that the Nazis experimented on Jews *because* they regarded them as being of less value; those carrying out syphilis experiments on black men in Alabama no doubt privately justified them on the basis that they were "only" blacks. The US Bill of Rights deemed slaves to be worth only half a person, with the predictable exploitative results. In Honduras, Guatemala, and Brazil they kill street children by the thousand, because, after all, they are "only" street children, of no more value than last night's rubbish.

In truth, relative value is a very dangerous criterion for making ethical judgements.

People are more intelligent than animals. Supporters of vivisection also point out that people are more intelligent than animals. This, it is claimed, is a morally distinguishing feature. It is, of course, true that people are generally more intelligent than animals (at least according to our own perception of intelligence). However, intelligence is a morally neutral attribute, not least because no moral choice is exercised in acquiring it. We do not give greater rights to the Nobel prize winning scientist than to the unemployed labourer. As Jeremy Bentham put it over 200 years ago in his well known epithet (his italics):

> The question is not, Can [animals] *reason?* Nor, Can they *talk?*, but, Can they *suffer?*

In any event, as Bentham noted, some animals are clearly more intelligent than some people. For example, many animals are more intelligent than people with severe learning disabilities or advanced senile dementia. If intelligence were the determining factor, it would be at least as justifiable to experiment on those people as on those animals.

Only people can exercise responsibility. A linked argument is that, in the mantra of New Labour, rights and responsibilities are the flip sides of the same coin. No one is entitled to enjoy rights unless also willing to exercise responsibility. As people can and do exercise responsibility, they should, it is argued, therefore enjoy the right of not being experimented upon; animals, on the other hand, often do not exercise responsibility (in the way we understand that concept) and are therefore entitled to no concomitant right.

In fact, there is no logical reason why one's right to protection from physical harm should be conditional on what one can give back. No sensible person would deny babies, the mentally handicapped, or the comatose protection from harm because they cannot exercise responsibility.

In truth, there is no ethically relevant criterion which differentiates experimenting non-consensually on people from experimenting on animals. Ultimately, all that the proponent of vivisection has to fall back on is the fact that humans belong to one species and other animals belong to other species: "we are human and they are only animals". This is a truism but one only has to state it to see that it has no intrinsic moral relevance. There may be a natural inclination, even a genetic disposition, to "protect one's own", but as Richard Dawkins acknowledged in *The Selfish Gene*, speciesism (the word first coined by Richard Ryder) has "no proper basis in evolutionary biology". Why, then, do we allow it to determine our ethics?

Consent by People

As I have indicated, the question of consent lies at the heart of the debate about experiments on people and experiments on animals. Experiments on people are sometimes permitted by law and supported by accepted norms. Indeed, the *Declaration of Helsinki: Ethical principles for medical research involving human subjects* (the Helsinki Declaration), as amended in October 2000, says that "[m]edical progress is based on research which ultimately must rest in part on experimentation involving human subjects". However, consent is crucial; without it, the experiment may not be carried out. There are three types of situation where consent is relevant in the case of experimental treatment on people:

- *Healthy volunteers.* Healthy individuals—typically students needing money—take part in trials for new drugs for which they have no therapeutic need. Companies such as GSK advertise for volunteers in publications such as the Big Issue. The Helsinki Declaration emphasises the importance of informed consent: "each potential subject must be adequately informed of the aims, methods, sources of funding, any possible conflicts of interest, institutional affiliations of the researcher, the anticipated benefits and potential risks of the study and the discomfort it may entail". Consent can be withdrawn at any time "without reprisal". Similarly, the Nuremberg Code, which arose out of the post-war Nuremberg Trials, says that "[t]he voluntary consent of the human subject is absolutely essential". Again, the basic principle is that consent can be withdrawn.

- *Patients who have capacity.* Patients sometimes consent to treatment which, although experimental, may benefit them. People suffering from AIDS provide the obvious example. The Helsinki Declaration describes this as "medical research combined with medical care". Additional safeguards are put in place. The benefits and risks of the procedure in question must be tested against the best current prophylactic, diagnostic, and therapeutic methods and the patient must be given access to the best treatment identified by the study at its conclusion. Again, informed consent is key. The patient must be told which aspects of his care are related to the research.

- *Patients who do not have capacity.* The Helsinki Declaration provides that "[s]pecial attention is . . . required for those who cannot give . . . consent for themselves". Presumably, experimentation is only permitted where the person without capacity stands to benefit directly from the process. In the UK, the law gives a high level of protection to patients without capacity, even for non-experimental treatment. For example, under section 58 of the Mental Health Act 1983 a registered medical practitioner, before embarking on a course of psychiatric treatment for a patient who is incapable of understanding its nature, purpose, and likely effect, must consult two other people who have been professionally concerned with the patient. It must be convincingly shown that the treatment is in the patient's best interests. In some circumstances the consent of the High Court must be obtained before treatment is given to patients lacking capacity. What happens is that, where the safeguards are met, the law in effect presumes that the patient would have given consent had he or she been able to—because the treatment is in his or her best interests.

In each of these cases, consent is either volunteered or presumed; and in each case the subject's interests are paramount.

Animals and Consent

Animals, of course, cannot give consent. In a therapeutic setting, they rely on their owners to give consent on their behalf. The fact that treatment may be experimental is no bar, provided again that the particular animal may benefit. As with patients lacking capacity, the consent of the animal is, in effect, presumed if the treatment is in its best interests.

Animal experiments, by contrast, never benefit the particular animals experimented upon and are not designed to. This is why the correct comparison is with *non-consensual* experiments on people. A devil's advocate might nevertheless argue that, as with people without capacity, a lab animal's consent might sometimes be *presumed*. He might paint an optimistic scenario in which a mouse is adequately fed and watered and is housed in a laboratory in a way that is environmentally enriching and comfortable. He might also ask us to imagine that the procedures to which the particular mouse is subjected are only mild, such as the occasional taking of a blood sample, and not the more invasive procedures to which many lab mice are subjected (such as the creation of cancerous tumours and ascitic monoclonal antibody production).

Of course, the mouse would prefer not to be subjected to any procedure. But a rational mouse in its position, so the argument could run, might conclude that its life in the laboratory is nevertheless better than life outside, where it would have to search for food and live in constant danger from predators. It might judge that the loss of freedom and the occasional mild discomfort (under our scenario) are worth the security gained. Even if it is likely to be killed prematurely, it might reason that, but for its proposed use in an experiment, it would not have been born in the first place. Better to have a life cut short than no life, it might ponder in an insightful moment.

In reality, even our hypothetical mouse might well prefer to take its chances in the wild. It is a reasonable assumption that primates and domesticated species such as dogs and cats would be most unlikely, under any circumstances, to swap freedom in the wild or a comfortable home for life in the laboratory. Clearly, one could not look to researchers (or government inspectors immersed in the culture of lab animal research) to make an impartial judgement that an animal would have given its consent had it been able to. In addition, the suffering experienced by lab animals is usually greater than mild discomfort, often far greater, even ignoring the distress caused by confinement in unnatural conditions.

However, the important point for the purpose of philosophical discourse is that it is *theoretically possible* to conceive of cases where, *looked at from an animal's perspective*, the cost of being involved in an experiment might be outweighed by other considerations, in the same way as a poor student [contemplating volunteering for medical trials] might make that judgement. Crucially, however, prevailing morality treats the two situations very differently. The law is simply not interested in whether an animal might be presumed to consent to an experiment. Its interests are overridden, ultimately rendered at naught. By contrast, the interests of the human experimental subject are always paramount. Intriguingly, the Helsinki Declaration and the Nuremberg Code embody the fundamental difference in approach. The Helsinki Declaration requires that experiments on people must, where appropriate, be based on information derived from animal experiments; and the Nuremberg Code says that the experiment "should be ... based on the results of animal experiments".

In other words, the codes stress the importance of consent with experiments on people but brush it aside when it comes to experiments on animals. There is a complete absence of consistency. Lord Winston recently fell into the same trap. He complained that doctors trying out new IVF techniques were effectively experimenting, without informed consent, on patients and babies. His solution? More experiments, necessarily without any consent, on apes and other primates.

Benefit to Other Animals

It is often pointed out, in defence of animal experiments, that animals also benefit from them (from the development of veterinary drugs and so forth). So they may, although in fact most experiments on animals for the benefit of animals are in the context of the farming and pet food industries—in other words, for (human) commercial benefit. In any event, here again the glaring inconsistency in approach manifests itself. The proposition is that it is justifiable to experiment on, say, a dog (against its will) so that dogs as a species may benefit. But if that is right, it must, by parity of reasoning, also be justifiable to experiment on a person (against his will) so that people generally will benefit. However, very few pro-vivisectionists subscribe to this view, at least openly.

Experiments on animals and non-consensual experiments on people are obvious comparators because both involve physical and psychological suffering for an unwilling, sentient victim. In each case consent is neither sought nor presumed and the victim is not the intended beneficiary.

However, society treats the two cases very differently. This is because ethical sleight of hand is deployed. Different ethical principles are applied to the two types of experiment.

With non-consensual experiments on people, a *deontological* approach is taken. The prevailing view is that such experiments are *inherently* wrong, whatever the potential benefits to others. Even where consent is given, the interests of the experimental subject are emphasised. The Helsinki Declaration states as one of its key principles: "In medical research on human subjects, considerations related to the well-being of the human subject should take precedence over the interests of science and society". Science engages in a self-denying ordi-

The Nonconsenting Human Guinea Pig

One notable case in human experimentation involved an Irish servant girl, Mary Rafferty, who entered the Good Samaritan Hospital in Cincinnati in 1874, with an ulcerated tumor on the side of her head, caused by a bad burn. Her physicians diagnosed the ulcer on her scalp as cancerous and apparently attempted to treat her condition surgically. When they believed that her situation could not be remedied, they proceeded to experiment on her. One of Mary's physicians was interested in experiments that Dr. David Ferrier had undertaken with dogs using electric shock to determine the localization of epilepsy. The experiments with Mary are described as follows:

> When the needle entered the brain substance, she complained of acute pain in the neck. In order to develop more decided reaction, the strength of the current was increased by drawing out the wooden cylinder one inch. When communication was made with the needles, her countenance exhibited great distress, and she began to cry. Very soon, the left hand was extended as if in the act of taking hold of some object in front of her; the arm presently was agitated with clonic [alternately contracting and relaxing] spasm; her eyes became fixed with pupils widely dilated; her lips were blue, and she frothed at the mouth; her breathing became stertorous [horase and gasping]; she lost consciousness and was violently convulsed on the left side. The convulsion lasted five minutes, and was succeeded by a coma. . . .

This particular example illustrates a persistent pattern in issues of human experimentation: despite her death a few days later and her unnecessary suffering through the experimentation, her death certificate stated that she had died from cancer.

"The Absurdity of Vivisection," ca. 2000.
http://www.vivisection-absurd.org.uk/.

nance: the interest of the individual trumps that of humanity as a whole, *even though* this probably slows the search for a cure for AIDS.

With animals, by contrast, the approach is a kind of *utilitarianism*. The law allows scientists to cause pain to animals if *others* might benefit. The Royal Society [for the Prevention of Cruelty to Animals] has recently argued that it is the alleged benefits of animal experiments which justify them. What it apparently failed to notice is that, if all that was needed for moral justification was a successful outcome, experiments on people would also be justified—indeed, much more so because people are indisputably a much better scientific model than animals for inquiries into human disease.

Some people, of course, do adopt a utilitarian approach to non-consensual experiments on people. The *BMJ*'s correspondent at the Nuremberg trial of Nazi scientists, Kenneth Mellanby, was prepared to justify those experiments which produced benefits. For example, he praised the notorious paper on typhus vaccines which an SS medical officer, Erwin Ding, published in 1943 as an "important and unique piece of medical research" which might lead to 20 000 people being saved for every victim of the research. We have, fortunately, advanced as a society from the Machiavellian ends and means guide to a moral life—except when it comes to animals.

In making the sort of moral judgement discussed in this article, the best guide, as Shylock realised, is to empathise. The *New Oxford Dictionary of English* defines empathy as "the ability to understand and share the feelings of others". The *Oxford English Dictionary* definition is a little more sophisticated: 'the power of projecting one's personality into (and so fully comprehending) the object of contemplation'. As a moral principle empathy finds best expression in St Matthew's Golden Rule: "Do unto others as you would have them do unto you". If I do not want pain inflicted on me, I should not inflict it on others. The reason we should include animals in our circle of compassion, as Albert Schweitzer put it, is because they, too, can suffer.

The ancient Greek poet Bion summarised it in this way: "Boys stone a frog in sport, but the frog dies in earnest". In other words, we should look at things from the perspective of the victim—human or animal—not that of the would-be exploiter. By this yardstick, animal experiments must be immoral, just as non-consensual experiments on people are. In each case, the degree of immorality is in direct proportion to the degree of suffering caused—experiments causing severe suffering are more immoral than those causing only mild, transient suffering.

Consistency demands that, if we condemn one form of highly invasive physical exploitation, we must condemn all forms. In matters of ethics, the identity of the victim—black or white, Aryan or Jew, man or woman, human or non-human animal—should be irrelevant.

"Monkey models are vital to evaluate promising new drugs for efficacy."

Using Primates in Medical Experimentation Is Justifiable

Scientific Steering Committee of the European Commission

The European Commission works to advance the interests of its twenty-five member nations. The commission's Scientific Steering Committee advises on matters of health and consumer protection within those nations. In the following viewpoint the committee argues that nonhuman primates are valuable to medical research because they most closely resemble humans in terms of genetic structure. Most significantly, chimpanzees, macaques, and rhesus monkeys are useful as test subjects for new vaccines and therapies designed to counter human diseases. Without the use of nonhuman primates in drug trials, the committee maintains, diseases such as hepatitis, malaria, multiple sclerosis, and AIDS may never be eradicated.

As you read, consider the following questions:

1. What is the significance of Council Decision 1999/575/ EC, according to the committee?

Scientific Steering Committee of the European Commission, "The Need for Non-Human Primates in Biomedical Research," *Statement of the Scientific Steering Committee of the European Commission*, April 4–5, 2002, pp. 1–4. Copyright © 2002 European Communities. Reproduced by permission.

2. What does the committee believe are the two compelling reasons to use nonhuman primates in biomedical research?

3. What animals were used in clinical trials to prove the effectiveness of the Hepatitis C vaccine?

For finding new ways of improving the living standards of humans and animals the scientists use a lot of different approaches. Some of them do not involve live animals, including *in vitro* [outside a living body] techniques, modelling and epidemiological studies. However experiments on live animals are powerful ways of better understanding the complex biological mechanisms. The community is very aware of the consequences of those experiments on the living conditions of the animals involved in experiments. As a consequence a whole set of regulations have been published to avoid unnecessary suffering during the experiments and to provide optimum living conditions during their whole lives (in particular D86/609/EEC, Council Decision 1999/575/EC).

In the Council Decision 1999/575/EC, it is stated that " . . . , accepting nevertheless that man in his quest for knowledge, health and safety has a need to use animals where there is a reasonable expectation that the result will be to extend knowledge or to be the overall benefit of man or animal, just as he uses them for food, clothing and as beasts of burden". The question remains however to weight the costs on the experimental animals and the benefits for the future of humans or animals.

That type of questions is particularly sensitive when primates are involved in experiments. The reasons for this are said to be related to their high cognitive abilities and complex social life which are more easily disrupted than those of other animals by living conditions in laboratories and more specifically during the experiments.

Why Primates Are Needed

The Scientific Steering Committee (SSC) believes that there are scientific reasons why primates will be particularly useful in future European research programs. It should allow the scientific European community to contribute better to the future of human health. It should also insure that the experiments are done under good laboratory practice. By contrast, the SSC however does not feel competent to decide whether or not to use primates in research but that it should be better commissioned by the European Group of Ethics of Sciences and New Technologies of the European Commission. If it is accepted that the use of primates in research is ethical, those animals should be housed and treated in a way that fulfils their species-specific requirements and avoids any unnecessary suffering. . . .

The Scientific Steering Committee considers that non-human primates are required in biomedical research for the following reasons:

1. To ensure safety. Many new vaccines or biologicals must be assessed for specificity and safety in a "near-human" immune system before they enter the clinic.

2. To determine the efficacy of non-human primate models for infections for which no other suitable animal models exist. These so-called "proof of principle" studies are critical in catalysing interest and development capital for development and clinical trials.

It is important to note that to develop specific vaccines, non-human primate models are often required because of safety risks and the chance of unexpected autoimmune or hyper immune reactions and even enhanced infection and or disease (e.g. Respiratory Syncitial Virus). This problem becomes clear when one examines the very specific interactions that parasites and viruses have with their hosts. For instance they are often able to evade the immune system by mimicking immune molecules or altering the regulation of these immune molecules. In most cases their interactions with their host are so species specific that they can only be studied *in vivo* [within living bodies] in hosts very closely related to man.

The following 5 examples, which are far from being exhaustive, illustrate the above:

1. *AIDS*: The epidemic is still rapidly spreading and, with more than 40 million infected, a vaccine is desperately needed. The etiologic agent HIV-1 is an example of a virus with a very complex interaction with the immune system and a very limited host range. It only readily infects humans and to a lesser extent chimpanzees. Macaques are an important surrogate model which when infected with SIVsm [simian immunodeficiency virus, Sooty Mangabey strain] develop an AIDS-like disease which is almost indistinguishable from AIDS in humans. . . .

2. *Malaria*: This is a major cause of human morbidity and mortality in developing countries that is having more impact on developed countries each year. In sub-Saharan Africa up to 2 million children under 5 years of age die from malaria annually. The relationship between the parasite and the host is quite specific, such that human malaria parasites will not infect rodents. They do however infect some non-human primate species, and other malaria parasites of non-human primates are very closely related to the human parasites. Therefore, using both old world and new world monkey models, the relationship between the parasite and the host can be investigated to identify therapeutic and prophylactic possibilities. Although considerable research can be done *in vitro*, the parasite has obligatory intra-hepatic developmental phases that are not amenable to *in vitro* cultivation. To date primates have been used as pre-clinical screens for a variety of new vaccine candidates. . . . Dif-

ferent malaria vaccines will require different immune responses ... and well-characterised models with similar immune responses to humans (such as macaques) are essential in vaccine development. New malaria drugs will have to work effectively *in vivo*, and many drugs that are effective *in vitro* fail *in vivo*. Monkey models are vital to evaluate promising new drugs for efficacy. More recently genetically modified parasites of primates have been developed and the modifications are allowing vital insight into the critical areas of interaction between the parasite and the host.

3. *Tuberculosis*: One third of the world's population is estimated to be infected with TB. It is a major killer in its own right, and combination with HIV is proving even more of a problem. The current vaccine, BCG, is highly variable in efficacy (in some trials it is ineffective) and existing drugs require long-term treatment and suffer from problems of increasing resistance. Highly virulent new strains such as the Beijing strain are now spreading within Europe, with potentially serious results. Mouse and guinea pig models are used to screen potential new vaccines and drugs, however their patterns of disease and their immune responses are often markedly different from those seen in humans. Recently a careful analysis of two macaque models ... has shown the value of these two models and their similarity to the human situation. These models are now being used to screen and select among new candidate vaccines before embarking on the complex, protracted and expensive clinical phase.

4. *Hepatitis*: Hepatitis C is the major cause of chronic liver disease leading to hepatocellular carcinoma in humans. More than 200 million people are infected with this virus throughout the world and most of them are unknowing carriers. Hepatitis C cannot be cultured [*in*

vitro] and the only other species other than man that can be infected is the chimpanzee. Early HCV vaccine studies in chimpanzees have begun to show progress but non-human primate research is essential to bring a truly effective vaccine to the clinic. Thanks to studies in chimpanzees which are still alive and healthy today, millions of doses of a very successful Hepatitis B vaccine have been given World-wide. However, Hepatitis B is still transmitted and many new infections occur daily. New less expensive HBV vaccines are required for developing countries to halt and eliminate this chronic human pathogen.

5. *Immune-based diseases*: Non-human primate models of immune-based clinical disorders, such as rheumatoid arthritis, multiple sclerosis, type I diabetes, allergy/asthma and transplant rejection, are needed for the development and evaluation of new immunomodulatory/immunosuppressive therapies. This is in particular the case with biological reagents that by their species specificity work insufficiently in rodent models and of which the potential toxicity in humans is insufficiently clear to test them directly in patients.

There is an increasing need of non-human primates as models for CNS [central nervous system] biology and disease. Multiple sclerosis is one such disease for which there is no cure. MS is an invalidating neurological disease with an underlying autoimmune etiology affecting one in 1,000 young adults. . . . The close genetic, immunological and virological relation with humans makes non-human primates an excellent model of this disease.

Why Alternatives Fail

Thus the problems faced in developing vaccines or therapeutics against these modern day plagues can be summarised as follows;

Recent Medical Advances Achieved Through Primate Research

1980s

- Processing of visual information by the brain.
- Treatment of congenital cataracts and "lazy eye" in children.
- First animal model for research on Parkinson's Disease, enabling doctors to more accurately research human Parkinson's Disease.
- Heart and lung transplant to treat cardiopulmonary hypertension.
- First Hepatitis B vaccine.
- Rhesus monkey model for AIDS used to establish the effectiveness of early administration of AZT in cases of diagnosed infection.

1990s

- Lead toxicity studies help U.S. fight childhood lead exposure.
- First controlled study to reveal that even moderate levels of alcohol are dangerous in pregnancy.
- Parent to child lung transplants for cystic fibrosis.
- Monkey model developed for curing diabetes.
- Naturally regenerative mechanism discovered in the mature primate brain, spurring new research toward curing Alzheimer's [Disease and] other degenerative brain disorders.
- Rhesus and cynomolgus monkey kidneys developed for use in diagnosing influenza.
- Development of anthrax vaccine.

2000s

- Monkey model developed to study the effects of malaria in pregnant women and their offspring.
- Dietary restriction without malnutrition provides major health benefits and may extend maximum lifespan.
- Rhesus monkeys are now prime model for development of HIV treatments and potential vaccines. There are 14 licensed anti-viral drugs for treatment of human immunodeficiency virus (HIV) infection alone.

California Biomedical Research Association,
"Fact Sheet: Primates in Biomedical Research." ca-biomed.org.

Host-viral/parasite relationship:

1. For instance some agents such as HCV and malaria intra-hepatic stages cannot be cultured *in vitro* or, they are so species specific that they only infect humans or other closely related primates.

2. An infectious agent may only cause disease due to its specific interaction with the affected host. A good example is HIV-1 which causes disease in almost all humans, but very rarely in chimpanzees.

Specificity of new generation drugs/biologicals:

1. New generation therapeutics are often so specific that sometimes a change in a single amino acid can result in the difference between a beneficial or deleterious effect. These positive or negative effects cannot be predicted by computer models nor by testing in rodents. Often these important side effects can only be detected in specific primate models.

2. Outbredness and the need to consider genetic resistance & susceptibility:

3. Inbred species of mice and even transgenics cannot predict accurately for how long a drug, biological, or vaccine will work or possibly cause adverse effects in an outbred population. An outbred population with specific characteristics, which resemble the human population, is often the most relevant model. Unfortunately, the numbers of captive bred animals needed to maintain this "outbred quality" are high. Smaller colonies of non-human primates will result in a smaller genetic pool in which the predictable value will be lost, or may even result in selective inbreeding, defeating one of the most important needs of primates for research. Thus large, diverse, well-characterised, captive-breeding colonies are needed in Europe to maintain this outbred character.

> *"Can there be any compelling ethical defence of using creatures so like ourselves in ways that we would find unbearable?"*

Using Primates in Medical Experimentation Is Unjustifiable

John Gray

John Gray argues in the following viewpoint that it is unethical to use nonhuman primates in medical experiments. According to Gray, scientists use apes in experiments because they are close to humans in their mental capacity and genetic composition. Gray suggests, however, it is precisely these near-human characteristics that should persuade primate researchers to abandon their work. In Gray's opinion, experimenting on apes is tantamount to experimenting on humans. John Gray is a professor of European Thought at the London School of Economics and the author of Straw Dogs: Thoughts on Humans and Other Animals.

As you read, consider the following questions:

1. To Gray, why is the issue of "consent" immaterial to the arguments for or against primate experimentation?

John Gray, "The Best Hope for Animal Liberation Is That Humans Kill Each Other in Wars," *New Statesman*, vol. 133, no. 4674, February 9, 2004, pp. 29–31. Copyright © 2004 New Statesman, Ltd. Reproduced by permission.

2. How does Gray deflate secular humanist views that place humans in a superior position to the animal kingdom?

3. According to the author, what is the "chief difference" between animals and humans that allows humans to believe they have dominion over other species?

In [Franz] Kafka's story "A Report to an Academy", an ape called Red Peter delivers a lecture to a learned society in which he gives an account of the life he led before he acquired human ways. Captured on the Gold Coast (now Ghana), Red Peter was transported in a cage to Hamburg [Germany]. In that city, he reports, he faced two alternatives—the zoological gardens or the variety stage. Life in the zoological gardens meant only another cage, so he chose the stage. It was not easy to get into the variety hall, but once there Red Peter was an enormous success. Soon he learnt to talk like a human, and it was not long before he achieved what he termed "the cultural level of an average European". His stage performances enabled him to enjoy a distinctly human way of life. As he described it in his report to the academy: "When I come home late at night from banquets, from scientific receptions, from social gatherings, there sits waiting for me a half-trained little chimpanzee, and I take comfort from her as apes do."

Kafka's story is cited in J.M. Coetzee's *The Lives of Animals*, a profound fictional meditation on the contradictions that beset our attitudes to other animal species. The story of Red Peter is a fantastical version of the fate that befell many apes, and—as one of Coetzee's characters notes—there were real-life prototypes of Red Peter. In 1912, the Prussian Academy established a research centre on the island of Tenerife to study the mental powers of apes; and in 1917, the director of the centre, Wolfgang Köhler, published some of the results of this in his celebrated study *The Mentality of Apes*. Like Red Peter, Köhler's apes underwent a period of training designed to induce them to adopt human ways. Among the pedagogic methods used was slow starvation, with the apes being repeatedly shown and denied food until they developed something resembling human faculties.

It is not clear how researchers today would assess the results of this experiment, but Köhler—one of the founders of cognitive psychology—seems to have seen it as a success, noting with satisfaction how the captive chimpanzees ran in a circle round their compound, some draped in old strips of cloth and others carrying pieces of rubbish, "for all the world like a military band".

So Like Ourselves

Köhler's experiments were cruel and demeaning to the animals on which they were inflicted, but they are chiefly notable for the deep confusion they exhibit in his—and our—view of our closest evolutionary kin. We have come to view apes as proto-humans, yet we subject them to treatment we would not dream of inflicting on members of our own species. If apes were not similar to us in important respects, many of the experiments to which they are subjected would be impossible or pointless. Few now deny that apes share much of our intellectual and emotional inheritance. They have many of our own capacities and vulnerabilities: they can think and plan, and they feel fear and love. Without these similarities, Köhler's experiments would have been unfeasible and could not have yielded the knowledge he was seeking. Yet these very similarities undercut the ethical basis of such experimentation.

We do not put humans into captivity and starve them in order to test their intellectual abilities because we know that such treatment would cause severe suffering. How can we justify such experimentation on apes, knowing that it can work only to the extent that their capacities—including the capacity to suffer—are much like our own? Can there be any compelling ethical defence of using creatures so like ourselves in ways that we would find unbearable? Or is the answer that the animals used in such experiments are simply unfortunate—that we have them in our power and their suffering is a regrettable but unavoidable result of our using them for our benefit?

The last of these options appears to have been taken by a recent spokesman for Cambridge University. Responding to protests against plans to establish a primate research centre there, he observed that it is an unfortunate fact that only primates have brains like our own. The implication is that it is precisely because apes have many of the capacities of humans that they are used for experimentation. It is true that experimenting on primates is a productive research technique; but if their similarities with us justify using apes in this way, it would surely be even more effective to use humans. The argument for experimenting on primates leads inexorably to the conclusion that it is permissible—in fact, preferable—to experiment on humans.

The Capacity for Suffering

Quite rightly, the idea that humans should be used in painful or dangerous medical experiments evokes intense moral horror; but this has not always been so. Powerless and marginal people—in prisons and mental hospitals, for example—have in the past often been used as guinea-pigs, and it is all too easy to imagine the forcible use of humans in scientific research practised on a far wider scale. The Nazis saw nothing wrong in subjecting members of what they considered to be inferior populations to the most horrible experiments; and there can be little doubt that had the outcome of the Second World War been different, the use of humans for scientific research would have been institutionalised across Europe. No doubt it would have been condemned by a dedicated few, but the historical experience of occupied Europe suggests that the majority of the population would have accepted the practice.

It will be objected that there is a vital difference between using animals for scientific research and using humans: humans have the capacity for consent, whereas animals do not. It is true that adult humans can express their wishes to other humans in ways that even our closest animal kin cannot; but consent is not the heart of the matter. Even if they agreed, it would be morally intolerable to use prison inmates in dangerous medical experiments. No form of consent they might give could make the injury done to them less real; it would only reflect their powerlessness. Similarly, it is not the inability of human infants to give their consent that justifies an absolute ban on experimenting on them. It is the terrible damage we would inflict on them merely to produce benefits for ourselves.

The same is true of experiments on animals. It is not the capacity for consent that is most relevant, but the capacity for suffering. I am no Utilitarian[1], but [utilitarian philosoper] Jeremy Bentham hit the spot when he wrote of animals that the crucial question is not "Can they speak?" Rather, it is "Can they suffer?"

At this point, those who support animal experimentation have a habit of wheeling out some extremely familiar arguments. Animals lack the capacity for personal autonomy, they tell us, and so cannot recognise duties to others. For the same reason, they cannot have rights. Humans have the power of choice, and this entitles them to a moral status denied to other animal species.

The Opposing View

We hear this tired refrain whenever the subject of animals is discussed, but it is significant not so much for any intellectual content it may have, but for what it shows about the lingering influence of religious belief. If you are a Christian, it makes perfect sense to think of humans as standing in a dif-

1. One who believes that the best course of action is the one that causes "the greatest happiness for the greatest number."

Results from Primate Research Cannot Be Extrapolated to Humans

Primates have been very disappointing with regard to their ability to predict dangerous side effects of medications, especially pertaining to the induction of birth defects. Aspirin produces birth defects in primates, but not in babies. Almost all currently used medications cause birth defects in some animal species. PCP, better known as angel dust, sedates chimpanzees but causes humans to have severe experiences including paranoia. Nitrobenzene is toxic to humans but not monkeys. Isoprenaline (isoproterenol) doses were worked out on animals, but proved too high for humans. People died as a result. Even when the researchers knew what to look for they were unable to reproduce this effect in monkeys. . . .

What about infectious diseases? Are we able to draw results from primates about viruses? Chimpanzees harbour Hepatitis B asymptomatically. Humans die from it. Vaccines for polio and rabies were tested safe in primates but killed humans. Even the inventor of the polio vaccine, Dr. Sabin, stated under oath that the polio vaccine was long delayed because of misleading results in primates. AIDS researchers have fared no better. The huge number of differences between the immune system of humans and nonhuman primates invalidates any experimental results. Dr. Mark Feinberg, a leading HIV/AIDS researcher stated: 'What good does it do you to test something [a vaccine] in a monkey? You find five or six years from now that it works in the monkey, and then you test it in humans and you realise that humans behave totally differently from monkeys, so you've wasted five years'. Monkeys do not die of AIDS—but humans do.

Ray Greek, "The Absurdity of Primate Experimentation,"
Absurdity of Vivisection Web site, n.d.,
http://vivisection-absurb.org.uk.

ferent category from other animals. Humans have free will and an immortal soul, and these attributes confer an incomparable importance on human life. No doubt we should refrain from cruelty to other creatures, but they have no claim to value in their own right; they are instruments for achieving human ends. Humans have dominion over animals because humans alone are made in the image of God.

Secular thinkers find it extremely difficult to come up with reasons for thinking that the human species has some kind of unique standing in the world. Darwin showed that we share a common lineage with other animals, and subsequent genetic research has shown the closeness of these evolutionary links. Insofar as humans do have morally relevant attributes that other animals lack, it is right to treat them differently. But within a purely secular perspective there can be no good reason for thinking the human species is supremely valuable.

In the context of their beliefs about animals, as in many other areas, secular humanists parrot a Christian hymn of human uniqueness. They prattle on about the supreme value of human personality as if it were a self-evident truth. Yet it is not accepted in most of the world's religions, and is strikingly absent in some—such as Buddhism—that have never thought of other species as mere instruments of human purposes. Secular humanists are adopting the anthropocentric viewpoint of Christianity—while abandoning the theistic belief-system from which it sprang, and without which it is meaningless.

Humans Are the Chief Threat to Animal Welfare

Once Christianity and humanism have been set aside, it becomes clear that the chief difference between humans and other animals is simply that humans have acquired enormous power. In evolutionary terms, the human species has been an astonishing success. In the space of a few thousand years, it has achieved a seeming mastery over its environment, which is reflected in a vast increase in human population. At the same time, humans have had a huge—and almost entirely harmful—impact on other animal species. The mass extinction of wildlife we are seeing throughout the world comes from the destruction of habitat—itself largely a result of rising human numbers. The damage done to the welfare of other animal species by human expansion is on an incomparably larger scale than anything that is done in scientific laboratories. This does not mean vivisection is unimportant—after all, no one thinks that since millions of people are slaughtered in wars it does not matter if some die as a result of murder—but it does mean that anyone who focuses on animal experimentation is missing the big picture.

The chief threat to animal welfare today comes from the unchecked expansion of homo rapiens. Wherever humans have entered a new environment the result has been a wave of extinctions. . . . The history of human relations with other species is a record of almost unbroken rapacity. Wrecking the environment seems to be in the nature of the beast. . . .

One way or another, human expansion will be curbed; and a plausible scenario is that this will occur as a by-product of war. Globalisation supports the present high levels of human population, but its logic is to intensify the struggle for scarce natural resources. Resource wars, such as the two Gulf wars, look set to dominate the coming century. Such conflicts would be damaging to animals as well as humans, but because of their disruptive effect on the global supply chain, their impact on humans is likely to be much more severe. The end result could be a less crowded world in which other species have room to breathe. Homo rapiens is a ferociously destructive creature, but its capacity for self-destruction is even greater. The human behaviour that Wolfgang Köhler was so pleased to observe being parodied by his captive apes may yet prove to be the ultimate guarantee of animal liberation.

> "[Deadlock] has arisen ... because the animal research community holds an ethical view that the animal movement rejects."

The Animal Experimentation Debate Has Reached a Moral Deadlock

Peter Singer

Peter Singer is a professor of bioethics at Princeton University and the author of the influential animal rights book, In Defense of Animals. *In the following viewpoint Singer claims that the debate over animal experimentation has reached an impasse. According to Singer, those who experiment on animals are unlikely to change their view that sacrificing animals is worthwhile to further science. On the other hand, the ethical arguments of animal rights activists are being undermined by violence from extremists within the movement. Although Singer supposes that the extremists' actions may be the result of continual failure to stop animal experimentation, the violence has further divided the opposing camps and reinforced the notion that the debate is deadlocked.*

As you read, consider the following questions:

1. According to Singer, how does the biblical view of the animal kingdom conflict with the naturalist view of Charles Darwin?

2. Why does Singer argue that nonviolent demonstration serves the animal rights movement's cause better than violent actions?

3. In the author's opinion, who bears the responsibility for ending the violence that has become part of the animal experimentation debate?

The debate over animal experimentation appears to be moving rapidly towards a state of mutual incomprehension and deadlock. The [British] home secretary is debating whether to allow the American animal rights activist Dr Jerry Vlasak into Britain after it was reported that he had said that killing five to 15 vivisectors could save millions of non-human lives. (He has subsequently denied that he was encouraging anyone to act in this way.) Animal activists have damaged trucks and other equipment used by construction companies working on Oxford University's new animal laboratory. Even this paper [the *Guardian*], in an editorial, likened British animal activists to al-Qaida terrorists.

The outcome of this process is unlikely to be positive for either side. For those who favour experiments on animals, it will mean keeping a low profile and meeting increased security costs. For the overwhelmingly non-violent animal movement, consisting of many millions of people around the world, there is a risk of serious damage from being identified with the handful of activists who are prepared to go beyond peaceful protest.

Conflicting Ethical Views

This situation has arisen, in part, because the animal research community holds an ethical view that the animal movement rejects. That view is, in essence, that animals are things for us to use, as long as we spare them unnecessary pain. The animal activists, on the other hand, reject the assumption that animals are inferior beings, and that their interests should always be subordinate to our own. They see this as "speciesism" —a prejudice against beings that are not members of our own species, and similar in many respects to racist or sexist prejudices against beings who are not members of a dominant race or sex.

Ironically, in this situation, it is the defenders of scientific research who are most likely to cling to an ethic that clearly has an unscientific basis. If we believe the account of creation given in Genesis, including its divine grant of dominion over all animals, then it makes sense to think that we are justified in using animals for our own purposes, as scientists wish to do. But if, on the other hand, we think [naturalist Charles] Darwin was right, and we are all here because of an unplanned process of evolution, there is no reason to assume that human interests should always take precedence over the interests of non-human animals. As [utilitarian philosopher] Jeremy Bentham wrote almost 200 years ago: "The question is not 'Can they reason?', nor, 'Can they talk?', but 'Can they suffer?'"

It may be possible to carry out some experiments on animals that do not cause them to suffer. And it may even be that, consistently with Bentham's principles, one can imagine situations in which, without treating the interests of animals as less weighty than those of humans, the benefits of an experiment on an animal would outweigh the costs to the animal. But the entire institution of animal research, as it exists in Britain today, is based on a different foundation: that animals count for less, and those that we are not especially fond of count for less still. Otherwise, why would Oxford University have said, in defending its proposed laboratory, that "98% of the animals involved would be rodents". Does the university believe that the interests of rats do not count?

Violence Undermines Ethics

Those who oppose treating animals as if they were mere tools for research therefore have a strong ethical argument. But when a few people use violence and intimidation to achieve the desired goal, they undermine the animal movement's ethical basis. In a democratic society, change should come about through education and persuasion, not intimidation.

Those who advocate violence may claim, with some justice, that the democratic process has been tried, and has failed. Despite decades of widespread popular support for reform, little has changed. Even the recent *Guardian* leader that began with the incendiary comparison between al-Qaida and animal rights extremists observed that more should be invested in finding alternatives—and it pointed out that a House of Lords committee stacked with scientists made the same recommendation two years ago. Yet in comparison to the funds that go into research using animals, the amount spent on developing alternatives is still very small. The extremist tactics we are now seeing may well be the result of the frustration caused by the failure of the democratic process to lead even to measures on which virtually everyone agrees.

Nevertheless, I cannot support the use of violence in the cause of animal liberation. It sets a dangerous precedent—or, one might say, it follows dangerous precedents. In the United States, "pro-life" extremists have fire-bombed abortion clinics and murdered doctors who terminate pregnancies. I consider these defenders of the sanctity of human life from conception to be misguided; but no doubt they are just as sincere in their convictions as defenders of animals. It is difficult to find democratic principles that would allow one group to use intimidation and violence, and deny the same methods to the other.

Non-violent responses to the frustrations of the democratic process do less damage to the fabric of civil society. Gandhi and Martin Luther King have shown that civil disobe-

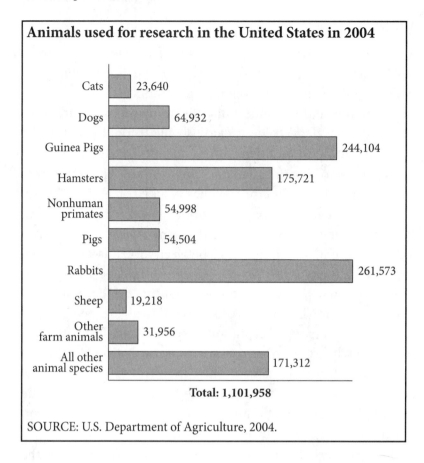

Animals used for research in the United States in 2004

Cats	23,640
Dogs	64,932
Guinea Pigs	244,104
Hamsters	175,721
Nonhuman primates	54,998
Pigs	54,504
Rabbits	261,573
Sheep	19,218
Other farm animals	31,956
All other animal species	171,312

Total: 1,101,958

SOURCE: U.S. Department of Agriculture, 2004.

dience can be an effective means of demonstrating one's sincerity and commitment to a just cause, while at the same time eschewing violence. Those who break the law openly, and are prepared to pay the price for doing so, are more likely to gain the respect and support of the public than those who strike secretly in the dark, and use fear, rather than persuasion, to change behaviour.

The Scientific Community Must Make the Next Move

Is there a way out of the present deadlock? Some opponents of experiments on animals will be satisfied with nothing less than the immediate and total abolition of all animal research.

In a society that continues to eat meat, however, that is an unrealistic goal. If people think that their enjoyment of the taste of animal flesh is sufficient reason to confine millions of animals in horrific factory farms, transport them to slaughterhouses and then kill them, why would they reject the use of relatively smaller numbers of animals in experiments designed to find cures for major diseases?

The mainstream animal movement has repeatedly condemned the use of violence against sentient beings, human or non-human. My own statements against it now stretch back nearly 20 years. But every large movement attracts extremists who are impatient at the slow pace of change. There is little more that the non-violent majority of the animal movement can do. The next step is really up to the government and the research community. If animal activists could see that serious efforts were being made to find new ways of doing research without animals, the violent fringe of the movement would become even more isolated than it now is.

> "It is possible to achieve fair agreements
> between reasonable people who accept
> that they must give some ground in or-
> der to achieve a peaceful solution."

The Moral Deadlock
Concerning Animal
Experimentation Can
Be Broken

Patrick Bateson

*Sir Patrick Bateson is a professor of ethology at the University of
Cambridge in England. He is also president of the Zoological Society of London's Animal Welfare Committee. In the following
viewpoint Bateson acknowledges that minority extremists' views
on both sides of the animal experimentation debate are unyield-
ing and unlikely to change. He believes, however, that the majority of researchers and animal rights activists may come to an
understanding about continuing some animal research if specific
rules were enacted. According to Bateson, these rules would permit animal experiments if the research was of high value and
the suffering of the animals involved was tolerable. Only by balancing the quality of the research with its benefit to humans and*

Patrick Bateson, "Using Animals in Research: There Is, Perhaps, No More Contentious
Area of Psychology Than Research with Animals," *Psychology Review*, vol. 11, no. 3,
February 2005, pp. 2–6. Copyright © Philip Allan Updates. Reproduced by permission.

its impact on the animal subjects can all parties, in Bateson's view, resolve the explicit moral dilemma.

As you read, consider the following questions:

1. How does Bateson liken his "shoe shopping" example to the moral debate surrounding animal experimentation?
2. In Bateson's view, under what conditions should animal suffering be tolerated in scientific experiments?

Public concern about animal welfare has increased greatly in recent years. Scientists who simply want to be left alone to get on with their work cannot and should not ignore such concern about the ways animals are treated in laboratories. Nor should they brush aside the animal suffering that can undoubtedly arise in research.

As this conflict intensifies, reason seems to have flown out of the window. The positions on the use of animals in scientific work have become so polarised that useful dialogue between experimenters and their critics is exceedingly difficult. Indeed, animal rights activists have inflicted major defeats on the scientific community. The decision by Cambridge University not to go ahead with a primate facility is one such case.

The Argument for Animal Rights

Although people feel uneasy about the use of animals in research for many reasons, one stream of thought in particular has fed into the strongly held view that animals must not be used in research under any circumstances. Certain morally based actions are absolutely good or bad and should not be influenced by cost-benefit calculations.

It is argued that animals have rights that are as important as those of humans. But what is an 'animal'? Does a rat have the same moral status as a chimpanzee? Does an ant have the same status as a rat? Does an amoeba have the same status as an ant? The answer given by Tom Regan, the most influential philosopher guiding animal rights activists, is that rights should be granted to animals which have beliefs, desires, perceptions, memories, a sense of the future, feelings of pleasure and pain accompanying a rich emotional life, an ability to initiate action in pursuit of desires and goals and a psychological identity over time. Even so, identifying the animals that might qualify for rights on this basis is not easy.

More fundamentally, human rights are part of an implicit contract with the social community; people accept conventions upon which the smooth functioning of society depends and these lead inevitably to the need to honour commitments. In short, rights bring with them responsibilities. These considerations suggest that giving a right to an animal is about as sensible as giving it a vote.

Although the rights position underpinning the wish to stop all research using animals is readily criticised, nobody can doubt the strength with which it is held. The end justifies the means and, for some, that involves intimidation and violence. Laboratories are wrecked, scientists' homes are attacked and their children are abused. But strength of feeling does not necessarily mean that the animal rights activists occupy the moral high ground. Strong ethical arguments are also mounted for the use of animals in scientific studies. In the past, many biologists took the view that they had a right to pursue knowledge for its own sake and this aspect of academic life, highly valued in universities, trumped all other considerations. Not many would adopt such an unvarnished view these days, but most scientists would continue to argue that great benefits flow from biological research. These benefits might be improvements in medical or veterinary practice achieved in the short to medium term or fundamental contributions to the understanding of biological processes. The provision of such benefits is seen as good and morally important.

Critics respond by questioning the motives of biologists, suggesting that the real goals are fame, career advancement and occasionally fortune, coupled with extraordinary wickedness when it comes to the treatment of animals used in research. An unwillingness to use alternatives to living animals is attributed to vanity, laziness or conservatism. I would argue that these are cheap shots. Doubtless some scientists have the base motives attributed to them. You will find some who are just as vain, lazy and conservative as some members of any other group of people. However, in a serious moral argument it is discreditable to question the sincerity and integrity of those who hold a different position from yourself. Those who dislike the use of animals in research are confronted by moral convictions that are as strongly held as their own.

A more serious moral argument is that animals which suffer in the course of scientific research do not benefit from any advances in knowledge derived from their suffering. In human and veterinary medicine, causing pain or suffering in a patient is considered unethical unless it is for the direct benefit of that patient. The great majority of us who work on animals in the course of our research are strongly bound to an ethic of caring for them. That means that we are forced into accepting that one moral principle is in direct conflict with another. The dilemmas seem inescapable. Before considering how they might be resolved, I shall discuss briefly whether scientists are correct in their belief that work on animals has led to major medical and veterinary benefits.

The Value of Animal Research

In justifying the demand that current research be stopped, activists suggest that behavioural work is scientifically trivial, of no medical importance, could be done without using animals or would be better done on humans. Most scientists would disagree and . . . a House of Lords Select Committee, after hearing both sides, concluded that the case for research on animals was strong. They also argued that more effort should be made to find replacements—a view I support.

However, in behavioural biology, necessarily involving work on intact systems, the opportunities for replacements are limited. Even computer simulations of complex systems have to be carried out alongside work on real animals in order to be effective. Studies of animal behaviour should flourish in the interests of both human and, indeed, animal welfare. An understanding of the social conditions necessary for the normal development of behaviour in animals has proved to be of direct medical benefit to humans. For instance, losing a mother early in life can lead to long-lasting mental and physical disorders in humans. Thanks to the work on animals, the developmental processes that depend on interaction with the mother are being uncovered. Effective forms of therapy for humans have been found and brought into practice.

Knowledge of the natural behaviour of animals and the way they respond to stress is improving conditions for farm animals and for those kept in zoos and laboratories. Veterinary practice is powerfully supplemented by behavioural expertise when assessing the condition of an animal or when designing quarters in which the animals should live. An animal's behaviour is one of the best guides to its state of well-being. Training veterinary surgeons to detect abnormalities of behaviour can provide them with quick, non-invasive methods for assessing distress. The knowledge acquired during training is increasingly recognised within the veterinary profession as an important contribution to animal welfare.

As far as the public is concerned, the studies of animal behaviour made famous through television programmes give pleasure and understanding to millions of people. At a practical level, this knowledge of the relationship between the behaviour of animals and their natural environment is of major value when planning the conservation of wildlife. Finally, solving how and why animals behave as they do raises some of the most challenging and exciting problems in science. It is not possible to crack these problems with tissue culture or by computer simulations. . . .

Reconciling Different Moral Positions

Even when people holding utterly different moral positions are totally inflexible and seem set for a fight to the finish, it is possible to devise practical ways of helping the majority resolve the undoubted moral conflicts. The alternative to absolutism on either side of the debate is to respect both positions and attempt to minimise suffering inflicted on animals used in research, while maximising the scientific and medical gains. I believe it is possible to achieve fair agreements between reasonable people who accept that they must give some ground in order to achieve a peaceful solution. . . .

Seemingly irreconcilable views can sometimes be brought together because a lot of one desirable outcome does not have to mean a little of another. It is possible to reconcile a strong moral commitment to understand biology and benefit from such understanding by using scientific methods with an equally strong moral desire to minimise animal suffering. Alternatives can be found to the destructive opposition between the morality of advancing our understanding of the natural world through science and the morality of eliminating the suffering that science sometimes brings with it.

Making Difficult Decisions

Most people consciously, or more often unconsciously, take many different things into account when making everyday decisions. Suppose, for instance, you want to buy a new pair of shoes. You will want good quality and you may well want shoes that are fashionable. At the same time, you are also likely to want to pay as little as possible. You will probably set an upper limit for how much you are prepared to pay and a lower limit for the quality. If you are forced to pay more, you will expect higher quality. I think the analogy is relevant to the present case: a much lower amount of animal suffering would be tolerated in scientific research if the work were not regarded as being important.

A Zoology Professor Expresses His View on Limiting Animal Experimentation

I . . . believe that some work using laboratory animals should continue because there is important work that we should try to do for medical and other reasons. But I also believe that many medical and other biological scientists are not seriously attempting to address the Three Rs [the principles of Reduction (reducing numbers of animals used), Refinement (refining experiments to cause minimal suffering), and Replacement (replacing animal experiments with viable alternatives)] in their work: because they have done a particular type of experiment for several years they see no reason to alter or abandon a 'proven' procedure.

Statements such as 'there is no alternative to using animals for this type of work' are easy to make and difficult to either challenge or sustain with sound evidence. Too many physiologists and other researchers are simply not prepared to step back and ask themselves if they really should be doing so many experiments using live animals.

Malcom Edmunds, "Animals in Research,"
Biologist, *vol. 52, no. 5, October 2005.*

When I first suggested it at a scientific meeting some 25 years ago, the shoe-shopping analogy grated on many people because they felt that no animal suffering could be justified merely in the name of good science. If the words 'medical benefit' were added to 'good science', the answer seemed clear to most of these critics. Great human suffering—and plenty of it exists in the world—is felt to be worse than the possibility of mild discomfort inflicted on an animal in the course of research. Of course, the likely benefits of biological science for human and animal welfare are not easily predicted. The best bet in general is to back science that is likely to lead to the discovery of fundamental and unifying principles. Many governmental and charitable funding bodies accept that the funding of high quality biological research is one of the best ways of contributing to the medicine of the future. Nonetheless, the delivery of real benefits to humans or animals is uncertain. It was for this reason that I included in the decision rules the probability of generating medically important results. . . .

Decision Rules for Animal Research

For the purposes of making a judgment, three separate dimensions are to be considered:

- the scientific quality of the research

- the probability of human benefit

- the likelihood of animal suffering

Animal suffering should be tolerated only when both research quality and certainty of benefit are high. Moreover, certain levels of animal suffering would generally be unacceptable, regardless of the quality of the research or its probable benefit. The decision rules used would permit research of high quality involving little or no animal suffering, even if the work had no obvious potential benefit to humans. This feature takes note of the concern of scientists who want to understand phenomena that have no immediate or obvious benefit for humans. . . .

Assessing Quality. Assessing the quality of research presents its own problems. Nevertheless, virtually all funding of future scientific research depends on making informed judgments about how particular projects will develop. Nobody denies that funding decisions are difficult and can be mistaken, but nobody who lives in the real world supposes research funding should be decided by tossing a coin. Similarly, difficult though it may seem, committees judging planned medical research are asked to assess the probability of a therapeutic outcome.

Assessing Animal Suffering. How do we assess suffering? This question is more likely to be asked by members of the scientific community than by many animal rights activists, who seem to think that the answer is obvious. The intrinsic difficulty is that suffering is a subjective state and no person can be sure that another would, in the same circumstances, suffer as they do. The usual way of dodging this ancient philosophical catch is to rely on the similarities between people. So if I suffer when I am burnt, I assume that you, too, will suffer in much the same way when you are burnt. Undoubtedly this is the implicit assumption of most vets when dealing with the issue of pain in animals. If the animal has the same neural equipment for detecting damage and processing the information in its central nervous system as humans and if it behaves in situations that humans would find painful in much the same way as a human, the intuitive rule is that the animal should be treated humanely. Identical arguments are mounted for other aspects of suffering by those concerned about animal welfare. . . .

The assessment of suffering is not straightforward, but can be greatly assisted by expert knowledge. In general, I believe that we can reach a reasonable consensus on what would constitute low, intermediate and high levels of suffering in a particular animal.

Out of the Deadlock

One advantage of a set of rules . . . is the acknowledgment that, in deciding whether a particular activity should be tolerated in a civilized society, more than one thing matters. Both the extreme animal rights activists and my more conservative scientific colleagues tend to suppose that the values they hold dear are the only ones that could possibly be important. Even when people holding such different moral positions are so in-flexible and seem set for a fight to the finish, it is possible to devise practical ways of resolving the conflict.

Periodical Bibliography

The following articles have been selected to supplement the diverse views presented in this chapter.

Colin Blakemore	"Medical Experimentation," *Chronicle of Higher Education*, December 2, 2005.
Malcolm Edmunds	"Animals in Research," *Biologist*, October 2005.
Simon Festing	"The Animal Research Debate," *Political Quarterly*, October–December 2005.
Alan M. Goldberg and Thomas Hartung	"Protecting More than Animals," *Scientific American*, January 2006.
Sharon Howe	"Animal Testing Is Both Cruel and Unnecessary," *Independent* (London, England), March 6, 2006.
Roman Kolar	"Animal Experimentation," *Science & Engineering Ethics*, January 2006.
Lancet	"Animal Research in the Post-Genome Era," March 17, 2001.
Edwin H. McConkey and Ajit Varki	"Thoughts on the Future of Great Ape Research," *Science*, September 2, 2005.
Doug Moss	"He Ain't Hairy, He's My Brother," *E: The Environmental Magazine*, March–April 2003.
Nutrition Health Review: The Consumer's Medical Journal	"Is Animal Experimentation Worthwhile?" 2003.
Gina Solomon	"The Lesser Evil," *Earth Island Journal*, Autumn 2002.
Peter Tatchell	"Why Animal Research Is Bad Science," *New Statesman*, August 9, 2004.

OPPOSING
VIEWPOINTS®
SERIES

CHAPTER 3

Does Animal Experimentation Aid Medical Progress?

Chapter Preface

More than 17 million animals are used in medical research in the United States each year. Of these, more than 95 percent are mice, rats, or other rodents. The remainder of animals range from cats and dogs to pigs and sheep to squids and apes. Each animal species is selected because researchers believe it serves as an exceptional model of some aspect of human physiology. As the North Carolina Association for Biomedical Research claims:

> Crayfish are used to study muscle functions. Armadillos are used to study leprosy. Pigs are used to study influenza and to develop new surgical techniques. Woodchucks infected with a virus similar to the human hepatitis B virus are ideal models to study new treatments for the disease. Sheep, because they share anatomic similarities with humans, are becoming popular models to study diseases and injuries of the bones, joints, and muscles. The squid, octopus and sea snail are important models for neurobiological studies.
>
> Proponents of animal experimentation attest that even the vast array of mice are invaluable to medical research. Some of these rodents are genetically modified so that they can better simulate human biological systems. This has allegedly given researchers a better understanding of Parkinson's disease, cancer, heart conditions, and muscular dystrophy.

The majority of the animals used in research are bred in captivity for this purpose. Their care and treatment is dictated by the Animal Welfare Act (AWA). This piece of legislation, passed in 1966, allows oversight committees to inspect animal research facilities to make sure that the animals in their care are housed, cleaned, and fed properly. It also stresses that pain and suffering must be minimized during procedures. Infractions of the law can result in steep fines or even the closure of the lab in question. The AWA, however, does not delineate what procedures can or cannot be done to animals during experiments.

In the following chapter, some authors debate the appropriateness of animal experimentation in medical science. Defenders of animal research insist that the aforementioned studies have yielded valuable insight into human and animal diseases. Critics, however, maintain that few if any major medical breakthroughs have come about as a result of animal research. Other authors in this chapter address the similar controversy over animals used in drug and toxicity trials.

> "Research using animals has led to some of the most important medical discoveries in history."

Animal Experimentation Is Vital to Medical Research

American Physiological Society

The American Physiological Society (APS) is a national, non-profit organization devoted to fostering education, scientific research, and dissemination of information in the physiological sciences. In the following viewpoint the APS argues that animals are vital to medical research. According to the APS, animals are living models that can help researchers study the progress and consequences of both human and animal diseases. Animal models also aid in testing drugs before trials with human subjects. Without animal experimentation, the APS maintains, it would be impossible to improve the quality of life for both people and animals.

As you read, consider the following questions:

1. The APS cites three animal biological systems that are similar to those in humans. What are they?

American Physiological Society, "Laboratory Animals' Contributions to Medicine," American Physiological Society, n.d. www.the-aps.org. Reproduced by permission.

2. According to the APS, what animals are aiding in new research on epilepsy?

3. What are three of the ways in which animal experimentation is aiding in veterinary research?

Research in physiology provides the scientific basis for much of medical practice, and is thus critical for maintaining health as well as for the diagnosis, prevention, and treatment of health problems. In order to understand and treat disease, physiologists need to understand how the body works under both normal and abnormal conditions before they can develop ways to prevent and treat disease.

Since some health problems involve processes that can only be studied in a living organism, it is necessary to perform research on animals when it is impractical or unethical to use humans. Additionally, research using animals has led to some of the most important medical discoveries in history. Animal research continues to help humans, as well as animals, live longer and healthier lives.

What Humans Have in Common with Animals

Animal research has helped scientists to understand and find ways to prevent and treat diseases historically (in diseases that are no longer widespread, like polio) and at present (for health conditions that are still prevalent), including:

- Heart disease

- Diabetes and obesity

- Neurological diseases such as Alzheimer's and Parkinson's

- Cancer

- Infectious diseases including AIDS and tuberculosis

- Inflammatory bowel diseases like Crohn's disease

In these and other instances, animals make good research subjects because they are biologically similar to humans. For example, the immune system of mice, the cardiovascular system of dogs, and the reproductive system of guinea pigs all function in much the same way as in humans. Humans also share many of their genes not only with other primates, but also with animals as far removed as mice and fruit flies.

So Why Use Animals for Research?

- Animals are used for biomedical research because it would be wrong to deliberately expose human beings to health risks in order to observe the course of a disease or use humans in invasive experiments to study normal organ function.

- Animals are susceptible to the development of many of the same health problems as humans.

- Their shorter life cycles make it easier to study them throughout their whole life span or across several generations.

- Scientists can better control variables (such as diet, age, weight, and physical activity), which would be difficult to do with human patients.

- Scientists can also change an animal's genes to study genetic diseases that cause illness in people.

Animal research is helping to elucidate the following human conditions:

Obesity and Diabetes: People with obesity and diabetes are at risk for a number of potentially serious complications that can cause premature death. For instance, researchers have used genetically engineered mice to better understand how liver damage occurs in people with Type 2 diabetes.

Epilepsy: People that are born with brain malformations sometimes have a kind of epilepsy that is not easily treat-

Humans Are Equally Vital to Medical Research

'The' use of one rodent and one non-rodent species will predict seven of ten toxic reactions in human beings. About 350 human diseases have an animal counterpart. For each drug tried in humans, about 350 animals will have been tested. Human trials need 3000–4000 participants. They enter studies for no known efficacy benefit to themselves, that being the purpose of the trial to discover. To argue that human beings do not subject themselves to research, research that can lead to harm or even death, is to grievously misunderstand medical science.

Lancet, *"Animal Research Is a Source of Human Compassion, Not Shame,"* vol. 364, no. 9437, September 4, 2004.

able with medicines. Using rats that exhibit the same kind of symptoms, scientists at Stanford University Medical Center were able to study the differences in how the brain functions in rats with epilepsy compared to healthy rats.

Parkinson's Disease (PD): Researchers studying the development of PD have used a mouse model to study genetic changes that occur in brain cells (neurons) during the earliest stages of disease, even before the substantial loss of neurons associated with the classic symptoms of PD occurs. These types of studies could lead to early detection and treatment that would ultimately minimize the severity of symptoms associated with PD.

How Animals Help Us Find Cures

Animals also play a critical role in development of new drugs and new medical procedures to treat diseases. For example, studies in animals were used to establish the safety of drugs that are widely used to treat high cholesterol, ulcers, depression and a slew of other common conditions and illnesses. In fact, almost every drug used in humans is first tested in animals.

Animal studies are done first to give medical researchers a better idea of what benefits and complications they are likely to see in humans. If the new therapy seems promising, it is tested in animals to see whether it appears to be safe and effective. Researchers use animal testing to discover what toxic side effects a drug might have, what doses are safe, and how a drug is absorbed and broken down in the body. Only after scientists have seen that the drug can be safely and effectively used in two or more species of animals do they begin testing in humans.

Scientists sometimes discover such drugs and procedures using alternative research methods that do not involve animals. While there is currently no substitute for animal testing in drug development, scientists are continually looking for other ways to test therapies for safety and efficacy.

How Animals Help Other Animals

Often times, animal research elucidates cures and treatments for ailments that afflict animals and humans alike. Many of these advances can then be used in veterinary medicine to improve the length and quality of animals' lives.

Veterinary medicine has benefited from discoveries found through animal research that alleviates animal pain and sickness and prevents disease in our pets, food animals and wildlife. Just some of the areas where animal research has helped other animals include:

- Development and testing of animal vaccines

- Detection and prevention of infectious diseases

- Food animal health and safety

- Treatments for lameness and arthritic pain

- Development of artificial joints

- Cancer therapies

- Treatment of genetic and acquired heart problems

- Animal responses to exercise

How Animal Research Is Regulated

An important part of doing animal research is making sure that laboratory animals are always treated humanely. The Animal Welfare Act is a law that regulates the use of many animals including dogs, cats and primates in scientific research and drug testing. In addition, the US Public Health Service Act requires that all research institutions receiving federal funds review and approve all research projects using vertebrate animals, and adhere to the guidelines in the "Guide for the Care and Use of Laboratory Animals."

Scientists care very much about the health and welfare of their laboratory animals. In addition to having to follow the rules put in place by their employers and the government, scientists know that unhealthy animals do not yield reliable experimental results.

Animal research is vital to advancing medicine. Physiologists will continue to learn from animals through humane research, with the goal of improving human and animal health and longevity.

> "Many ... important medical advances have been delayed because of misleading information derived from animal models."

Animal Experimentation Is Not Vital to Medical Research

Christopher Anderegg et al.

Christopher Anderegg and his colleagues who wrote the following viewpoint argue that animal research has had little consequence upon human medicine. According to the authors, using animals as models for human physiology has resulted in misleading data and unforeseen consequences in drug testing. The inherent differences between animals and humans have also delayed the proper understanding of how certain diseases progress through human bodies. Instead of investing in more animal research, the authors suggest, science should focus on more clinical research involving people. Christopher Anderegg and his colleagues are members of the Medical Research Modernization Committee, a national health advocacy group that evaluates the benefits and risks of medical research methods and technologies.

As you read, consider the following questions:

1. Why are animal models not useful in predicting psychological problems in humans, according to the Medical Research Modernization Committee report?
2. According to Anderegg and his colleagues, what—at best—can animal testing suggest to researchers? Why do the authors believe such results do not merit continuing animal experimentation?
3. Despite animal testing, what percent of drugs were taken off the market between 1975 and 1999 because of unforeseen health risks?

Proponents of animal experimentation (tests, experiments, and "educational" exercises involving harm to animals) claim that it has played a crucial role in virtually all medical advances. However, several medical historians argue that key discoveries in such areas as heart disease, cancer, immunology, anesthesia, and psychiatry were in fact achieved through clinical research, observation of patients, and human autopsy.

Human data has historically been interpreted in light of laboratory data derived from nonhuman animals. This has resulted in unfortunate medical consequences. For instance, by 1963 prospective and retrospective studies of human patients had already shown a strong correlation between cigarette smoking and lung cancer. In contrast, almost all experimental efforts to produce lung cancer in animals had failed. As a result, Clarence Little, a leading cancer animal researcher, wrote, "The failure of many investigators to induce experimental cancers, except in a handful of cases, during fifty years of trying, casts serious doubt on the validity of the cigarette-lung cancer theory." Because the human and animal data failed to agree, this researcher and others distrusted the more reliable human data. As a result, health warnings were delayed for years, while thousands of people died of lung cancer.

By the early 1940s, human clinical investigation strongly indicated that asbestos caused cancer. However, animal studies repeatedly failed to demonstrate this, and proper workplace precautions were not instituted in the U.S. until decades later. Similarly, human population studies have shown a clear risk from exposure to low-level ionizing radiation from diagnostic X-rays and nuclear wastes, but contradictory animal studies have stalled proper warnings and regulations. Likewise, while the connection between alcohol consumption and cirrhosis is indisputable in humans, repeated efforts to produce cirrhosis by excessive alcohol ingestion have failed in all nonhuman animals except baboons, and even the baboon data is inconsistent.

Many other important medical advances have been delayed because of misleading information derived from animal models. The animal model of polio, for example, resulted in a misunderstanding of the mechanism of infection. Studies on monkeys falsely indicated that polio virus was transmitted via a respiratory, rather than a digestive route. This erroneous assumption resulted in misdirected preventive measures and delayed the development of tissue culture methodologies critical to the discovery of a vaccine. While monkey cell cultures were later used for vaccine production, it was research with human cell cultures which first showed that poliovirus could be cultivated on non-neural tissue. . . .

Nevertheless, society continues to support animal experimentation, primarily because many people believe that animal experimentation has been vital for most medical advances. However, few question whether such research has been necessary or even, on balance, helpful in medical progress.

Contemporary Animal Experimentation

Cancer: In 1971 the National Cancer Act initiated a "War on Cancer" that many sponsors predicted would cure cancer by 1976. Instead, this multibillion dollar research program has proven to be a failure. . . .

Why hasn't progress against cancer been commensurate with the effort (and money) invested? One explanation is the unwarranted preoccupation with animal research. Crucial genetic, molecular, immunologic, and cellular differences between humans and other animals have prevented animal models from serving as effective means by which to seek a cancer cure. Mice are most commonly used, even though the industry's own *Lab Animal* magazine admits: "Mice are actually poor models of the majority of human cancers." Leading cancer researcher Robert Weinberg has commented: "The preclinical [animal] models of human cancer, in large part, stink. . . . Hundreds of millions of dollars are being wasted every year by drug companies using these models." According to Clinton Leaf, a cancer survivor himself: "If you want to understand where the War on Cancer has gone wrong, the mouse is a pretty good place to start."

AIDS: Despite extensive use, animal models have not contributed significantly to AIDS research. While mice, rabbits, and monkeys born with severe combined immunodeficiency can be infected with HIV, none develops the human AIDS syndrome. Of over 150 chimpanzees infected with HIV since 1984, only one allegedly developed symptoms resembling those of AIDS. Even AIDS researchers acknowledge that chimpanzees, as members of an endangered species who rarely develop an AIDS-like syndrome, are unlikely to prove useful as animal models for understanding the mechanism of infection or means of treatment. . . .

Psychology and Substance Abuse: Animal "models" of psychology, traditionally employing painful stimuli to study behavior, have been strongly criticized in part because human psychological problems reflect familial, social, and cultural factors that cannot be modeled in nonhumans. Indeed, most psychologists disapprove of psychological animal experiments that cause animal suffering.

Harry Harlow's "maternal deprivation" experiments involved separating infant monkeys from their mothers at birth and rearing them in total isolation or with "surrogate" mothers made of wire and cloth. Their terror and subsequent psychopathology, Harlow claimed, demonstrated the importance of maternal contact. However, this had been shown conclusively in human studies.

Despite its conceptual shallowness, numerous maternal deprivation studies continue, claiming relevance to human developmental psychology, psychopathology, and even immune and hormone function.

Animal models of alcohol and other drug addiction are similarly ill-conceived, failing to reflect crucial social, hereditary and spiritual factors. . . .

Genetic Diseases: Scientists have located the genetic defects of many inherited diseases, including cystic fibrosis and familial breast cancer. Trying to "model" these diseases in animals, researchers widely use animals—mostly mice—with spontaneous or laboratory-induced genetic defects. However, genetic diseases reflect interactions between the defective gene and other genes and the environment. Consequently, nearly all such models have failed to reproduce the essential features of the analogous human conditions. For example, transgenic mice carrying the same defective gene as people with cystic fibrosis do not show the pancreatic blockages or lung infections that plague humans with the disease, because mice and humans have different metabolic pathways.

Toxicity Testing: Numerous standard animal toxicity tests have been widely criticized by clinicians and toxicologists. The lethal dose 50 (LD50), which determines how much of a drug, chemical, or household product is needed to kill 50% of a group of test animals, requires 60 to 100 animals (usually rats and mice), most of whom endure great suffering. Because of difficulties extrapolating the results to humans, the test is highly unreliable. Also, since such variables as an animal's age,

Animal Models Prove Useless to the Testing of AIDS Drugs

Some of the most successful [AIDS] drugs, the protease inhibitors, were developed when the structure of an important HIV enzyme was discovered by non-animal test-tube methods. One of the first protease inhibitor drugs was indinavir (Crixivan), which progressed to clinical trials on the basis of its anti-HIV activity in test-tube studies using proteins and human cells (but not animal models of AIDS). Tests were done in rats, dogs and monkeys to see how indinavir was absorbed, metabolised and excreted by the body. Ironically, these tests revealed significant differences between the three species. For example, the amount of indinavir absorbed was 14% in monkeys, 23% in rats and 72% in dogs, and rates of metabolism varied too. Until human volunteer studies of indinavir were conducted, the equivalent values for humans were unknown. In fact livers of monkeys generate a unique metabolite of indinavir not seen at all in humans.

British Union for the Abolition of Vivisection (BUAV), Medical Research: HIV Research Fact Sheet, BUAV Web site, n.d. www.buav.org.

sex, weight, and strain can have a substantial effect on the results, laboratories often obtain widely disparate data with the same test substances. . . .

Scientific Limitations of Animal Models

Animal studies can neither confirm nor refute hypotheses about human physiology or pathology; human clinical investigation is the only way such hypotheses can be tested. At best, animal experiments can suggest new hypotheses that might be relevant to humans. However, there are countless other, often superior, ways to derive new hypotheses.

How valuable is animal experimentation? The Medical Research Modernization Committee's review of ten randomly chosen animal models of human diseases did not reveal any important contributions to human health. Although the artificially induced conditions in animals were given names analogous to the human diseases they were intended to simulate, they differed substantially from their human "counterparts" in both cause and clinical course. . . .

In contrast to human clinical investigation, animal experimentation involves manipulations of artificially induced conditions. Furthermore, the highly unnatural laboratory environment invariably stresses the animals, and stress affects the entire organism by altering pulse, blood pressure, hormone levels, immunological activities, and myriad other functions. . . .

Animal tests frequently mislead. Milrinone increased survival of rats with artificially induced heart failure, but humans taking this drug experienced a 30% increase in mortality. Fialuridine appeared safe in animal tests, but it caused liver failure in 7 of 15 humans taking the drug, five of whom died and two required liver transplantation. Animal studies failed to predict the dangerous heart valve abnormalities in humans induced by the diet drugs fenfluramine and dexfenfluramine.

Hormone replacement therapy increased women's risk of heart disease, breast cancer, and stroke, but experiments with mice, rabbits, pigs, and monkeys had predicted the opposite effect. The widely prescribed arthritis painkiller Vioxx, which was withdrawn from the global market in 2004 after causing an estimated 320,000 heart attacks, strokes, and causes of heart failure worldwide, 140,000 of them fatal, appeared safe and even beneficial to the heart in animal tests. David Graham, the Associate Director for Science and Medicine in the Office of Drug Safety at the FDA, described Vioxx as the "single greatest drug safety catastrophe in the history of this country or the history of the world." Animal tests also failed to predict the cases of partial or total blindness suffered by men taking the popular impotence drug Viagra. Despite mandatory, extensive animal testing, adverse drug reactions remain the fifth leading cause of mortality in the United States, accounting for more than 100,000 deaths per year. . . .

Scientists recognize that, even between humans, gender, ethnicity, age, and health can profoundly influence drug effects. Perhaps the most striking example of the specificity of drug effects comes from the demonstration that even human monozygotic twins display different drug responses, and that such responses become more disparate as the twins age. Obviously, extrapolating data between species is much more hazardous than within a species. Indeed, according to the FDA, a staggering 92% of all the drugs found safe and therapeutically effective in animal tests fail during human clinical trials due to their toxicity and/or inefficacy, and are therefore not approved. Furthermore, over half of the mere 8% which do gain FDA approval must be later withdrawn or relabeled due to severe, unexpected side effects. . . .

The Value of Redirecting Research

The value of animal experimentation has been grossly exaggerated by those with a vested economic interest in its preservation. Because animal experimentation focuses on artificially created pathology, involves confounding variables, and is undermined by differences in human and nonhuman anatomy, physiology, and pathology, it is an inherently unsound method to investigate human disease processes. The billions of dollars invested annually in animal research would be put to much more efficient, effective, and humane use if redirected to clinical and epidemiological research and public health programs.

"Animal experimentation has been the foundation for medical advances that have literally changed the world."

Drug Testing on Animals Is Beneficial

Jennifer A. Hurley

In the following viewpoint Jennifer Hurley asserts that animal experimentation is vital in fighting diseases such as AIDS. Jennifer Hurley writes and edits reference books for young adults.

As you read, consider the following questions:

1. How did animal research help create a polio vaccine?
2. How is animal experimentation better than in vitro research?
3. According to the author, why is animal testing vital to medical research?

When animal rights activists assert that animal experimentation does not save human lives, an obvious question comes to mind: Why would researchers choose to experiment on animals if it wasn't essential to medical progress? The answer is, of course, that they wouldn't. No scientist, researcher, or doctor enjoys experimenting on animals, espe-

Jennifer A. Hurley, "Animal Experimentation Is Always Justified," *Opposing Viewpoints Digest*, 1999. Reproduced by permission of Thomson Gale.

cially if those experiments involve suffering. However, animal-based research is the only safe and effective way to develop the therapeutic drugs and medical procedures that save countless human lives. Would antivivisectionists really begrudge people their lives because a few animals had to die?

Eliminating the Plague of Polio

Animal experimentation has been the foundation for medical advances that have literally changed the world. Insulin for diabetes; organ, corneal, and bone marrow transplants; antibiotics for pneumonia; surgery for heart diseases; and the development of nonaddictive painkillers—all of these astounding medical breakthroughs were made possible through animal testing. Perhaps most significantly, the polio vaccine, given to every child in America, owes its existence to animal-based research. In the early 1950s, thousands of Americans, many of them children and young adults, were crippled or paralyzed by polio. Among the most hideous aspects of the disease was the iron lung, a huge steel breathing device that encased polio patients from the neck down. Some patients spent their entire lives inside an iron lung, with the ceiling as their only view of the world. Until the polio vaccine was introduced in 1961, parents were so afraid of their children catching the disease that "summer public beaches, playgrounds and movie theaters were places to be avoided." All of this ended when a vaccine for polio was developed through experimentation on monkeys. Albert Sabin, one of the researchers who developed the vaccine, claimed that "there could have been no oral polio vaccine without the use of innumerable animals, a very large number of animals." Today, animals are still needed to test the safety of each new batch of polio vaccine before it is given to children.

Animal Research and AIDS

Many researchers believe that animal-based research will eventually make acquired immunodeficiency syndrome (AIDS) as rare as polio is today. All of the treatments used to fight AIDS have been tested on animals. One experimental treatment involved the transplantation of baboon bone marrow cells into an AIDS patient. Once the transplant had been conducted, the baboon was killed painlessly with a lethal injection so that all of his tissues were available for future scientific study. Animal rights activists condemned the treatment, claiming it was wrong to kill the baboon. Would it have been right to let the AIDS patient die untreated? The sacrifice of any animal is unfortunate, but if that sacrifice saves human lives, it is completely justified. Not only do animal transplants have the potential to save AIDS patients, but they also have enormous possibilities for leukemia and lymphoma patients, who frequently go without transplants because of the lack of donors. Most importantly, almost all scientists believe that animal experiments are essential to finding an AIDS vaccine; in fact, one researcher asserts that excessively restrictive animal rights laws are the biggest obstacle to AIDS research. And, according to Joseph E. Murray, the 1990 Nobel Laureate in medicine, "Whenever a cure for AIDS is found, it will be through animal research."

No Alternative to Animals

Animal rights activists sometimes contend that, since almost all disease can be effectively prevented by a healthy lifestyle, medical research is unnecessary. It would certainly be nice if this were true. Unfortunately, prevention only plays a small part in combating disease because many illnesses are either due to genetic factors or their causes remain unknown. Disease prevention can never eliminate the need for medical research, and medical research will always need animals.

The study of human cell cultures, also referred to as in vitro research, has been touted as a viable alternative to animal experimentation; after all, say animal activists, what could be a better model for humans than actual human cells? How-

The U.S. Government's Opinion on Animal Testing

Animal testing by manufacturers seeking to market new products may be used to establish product safety. In some cases, after considering available alternatives, companies may determine that animal testing is necessary to assure the safety of a product or ingredient. FDA [Food and Drug Administration] supports and adheres to the provisions of applicable laws, regulations, and policies governing animal testing, including the Animal Welfare Act and the Public Health Service Policy of Humane Care and Use of Laboratory Animals. Moreover, in all cases where animal testing is used, FDA advocates that research and testing derive the maximum amount of useful scientific information from the minimum number of animals and employ the most humane methods available within the limits of scientific capability.

We also believe that prior to use of animals, consideration should be given to the use of scientifically valid alternative methods to whole-animal testing. In 1997, FDA joined with thirteen other Federal agencies in forming the Interagency Coordinating Committee on the Validation of Alternative Methods (ICCVAM). ICCVAM and its supporting center, the National Toxicology Program Interagency Center for the Evaluation of Alternative Toxicological Methods (NICEATM), coordinate the development, validation, acceptance, and harmonization of alternative toxicological test methods throughout the U.S. Federal Government. The ICCVAM/NICEATM mission statement indicates that these organizations "focus efforts on alternatives that may improve toxicity characterization, increase savings in time and cost, and even refine, reduce, or replace animal use."

Center for Food Safety and Applied Nutrition, "Animal Testing,"
April 5, 2006. www.cfsan.fda.gov.

ever, in vitro research has limitations. A cell culture cannot tell us the effects a drug will have on an entire human body, nor can it help doctors develop new surgical procedures. Computer-based approaches to medical research also have limitations. As David Hubel, the 1981 Nobel Prize winner in medicine states, "You can't train a heart surgeon on a computer, and to study a brain, you need a brain; a man-made machine is no substitute."

In the United States, we are so accustomed to the amenities of modern medicine that we take them for granted. All of our prescription drugs, medical procedures, cosmetics, and household products have undergone animal tests to assure their safety. Because of the medical progress made possible by animal research, we live in a world in which disease no longer threatens us at every moment, and most illnesses are completely curable. According to the American Association for Laboratory Animal Science, "There is not a person in the United States who has not somehow benefited from the results of research involving animals." Without the medical breakthroughs gained through animal experimentation, many of the animal rights activists who vehemently protest vivisection would not be around to voice their opinions. Perhaps there will be a day when medicine is so advanced that the use of animals will be superfluous; however, until every American is healthy, we cannot abandon the use of animals in research.

> "It has been known among scientists and the pharmaceutical industry for decades that animal testing is scientifically unreliable."

Drug Testing on Animals Is Not Beneficial

Kathy Archibald

Kathy Archibald is the science director for Europeans for Medical Progress, a nonprofit organization that insists most animal experimentation is valueless and delays medical advances. In the following viewpoint, Archibald claims that drug testing on animals is done for legal reasons, not for scientific ones. That is, drug companies perform tests of new drugs on animals to convince the public that the drugs are safe and to protect themselves from legal liability if the drugs are later proven dangerous. Many licensed drugs do harm humans, Archibald notes, and such dangers are not always apparent in animal test subjects. Therefore, there is no scientific basis for continuing animal tests, Archibald maintains.

Kathy Archibald, "Animal Testing: Science or Fiction?" *Ecologist*, vol. 35, no. 4, May 2005, pp. 14–16. Copyright © 2005 MIT Press Journals. Reproduced by permission.

As you read, consider the following questions:

1. According to Archibald's article, what drug's release was referred to as the "single greatest drug-safety catastrophe in the history of the world" and why?

2. In the author's view, why are pharmaceutical companies "pragmatic" in selecting species to test drugs on?

3. What is "microdosing," as Archibald explains it, and how could it reduce animal testing?

Most of us know that cancer, heart disease and stroke are the leading causes of death in the West. But many people would be surprised by the next biggest killer: side effects of prescription medicines. Adverse drug reactions kill more than 10,000 people a year in the UK (and more than 100,000 in the US), costing the NHS [National Health Service of England] alone £466m[illion] per year.

The pharmaceutical establishment constantly reassures us that all drugs are tested for safety and efficacy on animals before they can be administered to humans. When challenged about the ethics of vivisection, their defence typically goes like this: 'Which do you think is more important: your child's life or a rat's?' Given this choice most people would thankfully sacrifice the rat.

Animal Testing Fails

But what if you were told that the current animal testing procedures are seriously flawed? Consider the following evidence:

- Arthritis drug Vioxx, withdrawn from the global market in September 2004, appeared to be safe and even beneficial to the heart in animals, but caused as many as 140,000 heart attacks and strokes in the US alone. The associate safety director of the US Food and Drug Administration (FDA) described it as the 'single greatest drug-safety catastrophe in the history of the world'.

- Many studies published in the scientific literature comparing drug side effects in humans and animals have found animal tests to be less predictive than tossing a coin. One review of human-animal correlation in drugs that had been withdrawn because of adverse reactions found that animal tests predicted the human side effects only six out of 114 times.

- Hundreds of drugs to treat strokes (eg, Cerestat, Maxi-Post, Zendra, Lotrafiban, gavestinel, nimodipine, clomethiazole) have been found safe and effective in animal studies and then injured or killed patients in clinical trials.

- Hormone-replacement therapy (HRT), prescribed to many millions of women because it lowered monkeys' risk of heart disease and stroke, increases women's risks of these conditions significantly. The chairman of the German Commission on the Safety of Medicines described HRT as 'the new thalidomide'. In August 2003 The Lancet estimated that HRT had caused 20,000 cases of breast cancer over the past decade in Britain, in addition to many thousands of heart attacks and strokes.

- Dr. Richard Klausner, former director of the US National Cancer Institute (NCI), lamented: 'The history of cancer research has been a history of curing cancer in the mouse. We have cured mice of cancer for decades, and it simply didn't work in humans.' The NCI also believes we have lost cures for cancer because they were ineffective in mice.

- Cigarette smoke, asbestos, arsenic, benzene, alcohol and glass fibres are all safe to ingest, according to animal studies.

- Of 22 drugs shown to have been therapeutic in spinal cord injury in animals, not one is effective in humans.

- Of 20 compounds known not to cause cancer in humans, 19 do cause cancer in rodents.

- Dr. Albert Sabin, the inventor of the polio vaccine, swore under oath that the vaccine 'was long delayed by the erroneous conception of the nature of the human disease based on misleading experimental models of [it] in monkeys'.

- Penicillin, the world's first antibiotic, was delayed for more than 10 years by misleading results from experiments in rabbits, and would have been shelved forever had it been tested on guinea pigs, which it kills. [The discoverer of penicillin] Sir Alexander Fleming himself said: 'How fortunate we didn't have these animal tests in the 1940s, for penicillin would probably never have been granted a licence, and possibly the whole field of antibiotics might never have been realised.'

- Thalidomide, the infamous cause of birth defects in more than 10,000 children in the early 1960s, induces birth defects in very few species. Dr. James Schardein, the doyen of birth defect studies, says: 'In approximately 10 strains of rats, 15 strains of mice, 11 breeds of rabbits, two breeds of dogs, three strains of hamsters, eight species of primates, and in other such varied species as cats, armadillos, guinea pigs, swine and ferrets in which thalidomide has been tested, teratogenic effects [i.e., those that cause birth defects] have been induced only occasionally.' Ironically, if thalidomide, the drug whose side effects made animal testing obligatory, were assessed exclusively on its results in such tests it would still be passed today.

Even the *Handbook of Laboratory Animal Science* admits that 'uncritical reliance on the results of animal tests can be dangerously misleading and has cost the health and lives of tens of thousands of humans'.

Animal Tests Provide Liability Protection

Animal testing became legally enshrined in response to the thalidomide tragedy. The UK Medicines Act 1968 followed the US Kefauver-Harris Act, which was implemented in 1961 in the midst of the thalidomide furor to ensure that the FDA received proof of safety and efficacy for all new drugs. The intention was good but the reliance placed on animal tests to ensure safety was tragically ill-informed.

It has been known among scientists and the pharmaceutical industry for decades that animal testing is scientifically unreliable. As long ago as September 1962 *The Lancet* commented: 'We must face the fact that the most careful tests of a new drug's effects on animals may tell us little of its effect in humans.' In 1964 Dr. J. Gallagher, the medical director of Lederle Laboratories, admitted: 'Animal studies are done for legal reasons and not for scientific reasons.'

So, pharmaceutical companies conduct animal tests simply to satisfy government regulators. Crucially, animal data also provide liability protection when drugs kill or injure people. Industry can point to the rigorous animal tests they have performed and claim that they have done their best to ensure against tragedies occurring, thus minimising any damages awarded against them.

From the perspective of satisfying the regulators, pragmatic selection of species will demonstrate whatever is required of a drug, whether it is favourable safety or efficacy. And companies are not required to submit all their animal data, but only that from any two species (one rodent and one higher mammal). Dr. Irwin Bross, former director of the world's largest cancer research institute, the Sloan-Kettering, observed: 'Whenever government agencies or polluting corporations want to cover up an environmental hazard, they can always find an animal study to "prove" their claim. They can even do a new animal study which will come out the way they want by choosing the "right" animal model system.'

Killer Drugs

Many drugs that have been pronounced safe on the basis of animal tests have gone on to injure or kill people. For example:

- Vioxx, for arthritis, caused up to 60,000 deaths between its launch in 1999 and its withdrawal in 2004;

- Baycol (Lipobay), used to treat cholesterol, caused more than 10,000 cases of serious muscle-wasting or death between 1997 and its withdrawal in 2001;

- Rezulin (troglitazone), for diabetes, killed more than 400 people between 1997 and its withdrawal in 2000;

- Propulsid (cisapride), for heartburn, killed more than 300 adults and children before being withdrawn in 2000;

- Opren, for arthritis, caused 61 deaths and 3,500 serious injuries and was withdrawn in the 1980s;

- Eraldin, a heart treatment, killed 23 people and blinded many more, and was withdrawn in the 1970s. Its devastating side effects were not reproducible in any species except man;

- Isoprenaline, for asthma, killed 3,500 young people in Britain alone and was withdrawn in the 1960s. Intensive studies with rats, guinea pigs, dogs and monkeys, at huge dosages, failed to elicit similar results.

Kathy Archibald, "Animal Testing: Science or Fiction?"
Ecologist, vol. 35, no. 4, May 2005, pp. 14–16.

Avoiding More Extensive Clinical Trials

Placing massive emphasis on animal-safety data has also allowed pharmaceutical companies to avoid the expense of conducting clinical trials as extensively as they should. Since the

1950s doctors have been saying that clinical trials should involve more people, last for a longer period of time and use representatives of a broader swathe of society than the young, white males of standard practice. Women are generally not utilised in case they might be pregnant: the manufacturer would be held liable for any unanticipated birth defects. Very often trials do not even include representatives of the patient population the drug is designed to treat. This absurd situation clearly needs to be addressed.

There is no getting away from the fact that people have to be the ultimate guinea pigs for testing new treatments. Clearly, the health and safety of research volunteers and patients should be paramount and the best safeguards should be in place to protect them.

Alternatives Are Available

New drugs go through three basic testing phases: in vitro (test-tube) and in silico (computer) modelling; animal testing; and, finally, human trials.

Before a drug is tested in humans, there should be persuasive evidence that it is safe and effective. No method, neither animal, human nor test-tube, can predict the reactions of every patient with 100 per cent accuracy. Reactions differ between sexes, ages, ethnic groups, even between family members. We are all different, but not as different from each other as we are from animals, with which the differences are so great that they render extrapolation hazardous. Non-animal methods are not completely fail-safe, but do offer more security.

There are excellent in silico and in vitro testing methods available today. Many companies specialise in virtual screening or drugs for potential toxic effects. A wide range of predictive software is available, including complete clinical trial simulations. Other companies focus on safety and efficacy assessments in human tissues. A 10-year international study proved that human cell culture tests are more accurate and yield more useful information about toxic mechanisms than traditional animal tests.

In place of animal-based pre-clinical studies, subsequent clinical trial patients and volunteers would be better protected by the adoption of preliminary microdosing studies (or 'phase 0' clinical trials). Microdose studies involve the administration of ultra-small (and safe) doses of the test drug to volunteers monitored by scanners. Human microdosing, based on the concept that the best model for man is man, helps in selecting the best drug candidates before advancing into full development, thereby reducing the chances of failure in later, more risky and more expensive phases.

During clinical trials, relevant pharmacological measurements should be made, which would give early warning of potential problems. It is true that some rare side effects will only be detected when drugs are prescribed to large numbers of people. This is why post-marketing drug surveillance is so important and should be strengthened, in order to pick up these effects as quickly as possible. Reports of adverse reactions to drugs are currently soaring in the US, where a record 422,500 adverse events were reported to the FDA in 2004. The FDA cautions that the actual number is likely to be between 10 and 100 times greater because of under-reporting.

"*[A microchip] system could not only replace conventional cell cultures but also reduce a reliance on animal experiments.*"

Microchip Technologies Could Make Drug Testing on Animals Unnecessary

David H. Freedman

In the following viewpoint David H. Freedman, a freelance journalist, states that a technological breakthrough could make animal drug testing unnecessary. As Freedman writes, scientists are merging human tissue cultures with microchips to create minute replicas of human internal systems. These miniature systems are better able to predict the effects of untried drugs on human physiology than charting the reactions of animals to such drugs. Researchers are hopeful, Freedman reports, that the new microchip testing methods will thus reduce the need for extensive, wasteful, and often inconclusive animal testing.

As you read, consider the following questions:

1. According to Freedman, why are drug companies eager to obtain the new "animal on a chip" testing devices?

David H. Freedman, "The Silicon Guinea Pig," *Technology Review*, vol. 107, June 2004, pp. 62–69. © 2004 by the Association of Alumni and Alumnae of MIT. Reproduced by permission.

2. As the author reports, why are traditional cell-culture tests not always accurate?

3. Using the naphthalene example, explain how Michael Shuler's chip model detected toxicity problems that traditional cell cultures could not.

Michael Shuler's chip could pass for any small silicon slab pried out of a computer or cell phone. Which makes it seem all the more out of place on a bench top in the Cornell University researcher's lab, surrounded by petri dishes, beakers, and other bio-clutter and mounted in a plastic tray like a dissected mouse. The chip appears to be on some sort of life support, with pinkish fluid pumping into it through tubes. Shuler methodically points out the components of the chip with a pencil: here's the liver, the lungs are over here, this is fat. He then injects an experimental drug into the imitation blood coursing through these "organs" and "tissues"—actually tiny mazes of twisting pipes and chambers lined with living cells. The compound will react with other chemicals, accumulate in some of the organs, and pass quickly through others. After several hours, Shuler and his team will be closer to answering a key question: is the compound, when given to an actual human, likely to do more harm than good?

This so-called animal on a chip was designed to help overcome an enormous obstacle to discovering new drugs: there is currently no quick, reliable way to predict if an experimental compound will have toxic side effects—if it will make people sick instead of making them well. Testing in animals is the best drug-makers can do, but it is slow, expensive, often inaccurate, and objectionable to many. To minimize the number of animal tests, drug companies routinely screen drug candidates using cell cultures—essentially clumps of living human or animal cells growing in petri dishes or test tubes. The approach is relatively cheap and easy, but it gives only a hazy prediction of what will happen to a compound on the circuitous trip through the tissues and organs of an animal.

Eagerly Anticipated Technology

Shuler is among a handful of researchers who are developing more sophisticated cell cultures that simulate the body's complex organs and tissues. MIT [Massachusetts Institute of Technology] tissue engineer Linda Griffith, for one, has built a chip that mimics some of the functions of a liver, while Shuichi Takayama, a biomedical engineer at the University of Michigan, has built one that imitates the behavior of the vasculatory system. But while such efforts have produced convincing analogues of parts of human or animal bodies, Shuler has gone a step further. Working with colleague Greg Baxter, who launched Beverly Hills, CA-based Hurel to commercialize the technology, Shuler has combined replicas of multiple animal organs on a single chip, creating a rough stand-in for an entire mammal. Other versions of Shuler's chips attempt to go even further, using human cells to more faithfully reproduce the effects of a compound in the body.

Drug companies are interested, and no wonder: they routinely make thousands, even tens of thousands, of compounds in hopes of finding one that is effective against a particular target. Chips such as Shuler and Baxter's could mean a cheap, fast, and accurate way to weed out compounds that would eventually prove toxic, saving companies years and millions of dollars on the development of worthless drugs. According to a recent study by Tufts University's Center for the Study of Drug Development, for each drug that reaches market, the drug industry spends an average of $467 million on human testing—the vast majority of the money going to drugs that fail, either because they aren't effective or because they prove toxic. If more failures could be identified before animal testing even began, companies could focus more of their time and money on the winners. "Everyone in the industry hopes to have surrogates for animals and humans when it comes to testing compounds" says Jack Reynolds, head of safety sciences for Pfizer, the world's largest pharmaceutical firm. "This is the sort of technology we'd want in our toolbox." . . .

Replicating Human Systems

When a person takes a drug, its active ingredient goes on a wild ride to get to the target cells: it might be absorbed by the gut, broken down by enzymes in the liver, hoarded for weeks by fat cells, screened out by a brain membrane, and whirled through the whole ordeal over and over again by the blood. When that happens, an otherwise harmless compound can accumulate in a particular organ until it reaches toxic levels. Or it can be transformed into a different compound altogether, which itself is toxic. Pfizer's Reynolds estimates that, of drug candidates that end up proving unsafe, approximately 40 percent acquire their toxicity after being converted to other compounds in the body.

One reason that conventional cell-culture tests often mislead researchers is that they don't present the complex brew of enzymes and other chemicals that a drug can encounter and react with in the various tissues of the body. And simple cell cultures don't reveal how much of a drug actually gets to different types of cells, in what form, and for how long. Indeed, nearly half of the drugs that seem safe in cell-culture testing prove toxic in animal tests; and even more fail when they encounter the complex tissues and organs of humans. Researchers hope, however, that cell cultures that better simulate the conditions in the body will do a far better job at spotting toxic drugs, reducing the reliance on animal and human testing. . . .

Testing in Miniature

Michael Shuler is a 57-year-old, lanky chemical engineering professor who has nurtured a side interest in biological pro-

Singer. © 2005 Andrew B. Singer, www.andysinger.com. Reproduced by permission.

cesses since junior high school. By 1989 he had become interested in toxicity testing, and he had been pondering the unreliability of conventional cell cultures when an idea occurred to him: could you make a cell culture that replicates the journey through the various organs? He recognized it as a chemical engineering problem: glass chambers lined with different types of cells and hooked up via tubes to each other and to a pump that sent fluid through them would far more realistically simulate a body, and tests employing them might predict what happens in living animals much more accurately.

After several months, Shuler and students had constructed a bench-top conglomeration of cells and plumbing providing a crude working model of a set of mammalian organs. It sort of functioned, but Shuler knew there was a big problem with its fidelity: almost all of the chemistry in the body takes place in tissues packed with minute canals and chambers, where critical reactions hinge on the ability of various chemicals to concentrate in some places and diffuse in others, depending in part on the microscopic geography. Mixing everything up in big beakers would distort that delicate balance. Plus, at this size the system wouldn't be practical or cheap enough for large-scale testing.

Meanwhile, molecular biologist Greg Baxter had just joined Cornell's Nanobiotechnology Center as a research scientist. His specialty was microfluidics—essentially, microscopic plumbing on a chip. On his second day he buttonholed Shuler at his lab, wondering if he had any projects that could benefit from ultraminiaturization. Funny you should ask, said Shuler.

It took just two meetings to hammer out the basic chip design and a year to produce the first prototype. To build one of the devices, the researchers carve minute trenches that look like faint scratches into a thumbnail-sized silicon chip; these trenches serve as fluid-carrying pipes. Producing microfluidic features on chips for testing chemical reactions and imitating biological processes is not new. But by combining their skills in chemical engineering and microfabrication, Shuler and Baxter add a significant twist: they've engineered the sizes, lengths, and layout of all the trenches in an attempt to closely duplicate the fluid flows and chemical exposures that cells experience in real organs. . . .

After a test compound has circulated through the chip for several hours, the cells in the chip are monitored, either with a microscope or via embedded sensors that can test for oxygen and other indicators. Do the cells absorb the compound? Does it sicken or kill them? As in an actual animal, each organ or tissue plays a specific role in the chip. The liver and gut break some compounds down into smaller molecules, for example, while the fat—jammed not only with cells, but also with a spongelike gel—often retains compounds, allowing them to leak out later. A "target" organ or tissue is usually included to demonstrate the ultimate effects of the compound; this might be a cancer tumor, or an especially vulnerable tissue, such as the lung's, or bone marrow.

Early Signs Are Encouraging

The chips, of course, will have to be extensively tested before drug firms will use them widely. Still, early signs are encouraging. Shuler ran one experiment with naphthalene, a compound used in mothballs and pesticides. Excessive exposure causes lung damage, but you wouldn't know it from standard cell-culture tests. That's because the culprit isn't naphthalene itself but rather two chemicals produced by the liver when it breaks naphthalene down. If you knew that and splashed those by-products directly on lung cells in culture, you'd observe such a severe response that you'd conclude even slight exposure to naphthalene is extremely dangerous. But that's wrong, too; as it turns out, fat cells yank much of the toxic compounds out of the system. Shuler's chip convincingly mimics this chain of events, yielding a realistic measure of the damage.

Such precise simulation promises to help drug companies improve their screening of drug candidates—and waste less time and money on those that will ultimately rail animal tests. According to Baxter, the chips are ready for such an application right now, and six large companies are currently talking to Hurel about adopting the technology [Johnson & Johnson has since entered into collaboration with Hurel]. Shuler aided by a team of students and collaborators at Cornell and elsewhere, is working on further shrinking and automating the technology. The goal: a sheet-of-paper-sized bank of 96 chips that plugs into a robotic lab setup that very rapidly adds test drugs and monitors the results. The system could not only replace conventional cell cultures but also reduce a reliance on animal experiments, in which researchers must use a great number of animals to test different doses of a drug, and must monitor those animals over time to pick up subtle side effects. "We're talking about running a test in one or two days that would take months with animals," says Shuler. Shuler projects a per-chip production price of about $50 complete with cells, compared to the hundreds or even thousands of dollars it takes to acquire and maintain a single lab animal.

Replacing Animals

Chips that replicate the functioning of animals will likely be the first versions of the technology to make a commercial impact. But the hope is that once those prove to accurately predict the results of animal tests, human-on-a-chip versions will provide a good indication of how toxic a drug is likely to prove in human trials.

Animal testing plays that role now, but not very well. Four out of five drugs that make it through animal testing end up failing in human clinical trials, usually because of safety concerns. Part of the problem is that mice can't tell you they have headaches, blurred vision, or stomach cramps. But the larger issue is simply that animals' organs, and the processes that take place in them, are not identical to those of humans. No one knows how many drugs that would have been safe in humans were shelved because they sickened some animals. (Penicillin, for instance, is toxic to guinea pigs but fortunately was also tested on mice.) . . .

Neither Baxter nor Shuler claims that the animal on a chip is any sort of panacea for the complex and deeply challenging drug-development process. For one thing, the chips still have to prove in large-scale tests that they really do a better job than conventional cell cultures of predicting toxicity. But if they measure up, then the pills you take ten years from now may very well arrive thanks to the sacrifices of a silicon lab rat.

Periodical Bibliography

The following articles have been selected to supplement the diverse views presented in this chapter.

Celeste Biever	"Can Computer Models Replace Animal Testing?" *New Scientist*, May 13, 2006.
Bernadine Healy	"The Tribulation of Trials," *U.S. News & World Report*, April 3, 2006.
Lancet	"Animal Research Is a Source of Human Compassion, Not Shame," September 4, 2004.
Graham Lappin	"Animal Experimentation, the Worst Form of Science?" *Biologist*, April 2004.
New York Times	"Why Test Animals to Cure Human Depression?" March 28, 2004.
Ellen Frankel Paul	"Why Animal Experimentation Matters," *Society*, September–October 2002.
Katherine Perlo	"'Would You Let Your Child Die Rather than Experiment on Nonhuman Animals?' A Comparative Questions Approach," *Society & Animals*, March 2003.
Amanda Schupak	"The Bunny Chip," *Forbes*, August 15, 2005.
Science News	"Frankenstein's Chips," *Science News*, January 8, 2005.
Richard Smith	"Animal Research: The Need for a Middle Ground," *British Medical Journal*, February 3, 2001.
Barry Yeoman	"Can We Trust Research Done with Lab Mice?" *Discover*, July 2003.

OPPOSING
VIEWPOINTS®
SERIES

CHAPTER 4

Are New Forms of Animal Experimentation Worth Pursuing?

Chapter Preface

In December 2004, Genetic Savings and Clone, a San Francisco cloning and technology firm, made the first sale of a cloned house cat to a buyer in Texas. Since then, other biotechnology operations have been banking animal DNA with the prospect of following Genetic Savings and Clone's lead. The service typically costs between $300 and $1000 for the initial cryogenic freezing of animal cells, and around $100 per year for maintenance. To have a clone made, the price jumps to $50,000, so many clients are banking their beloved pets' cells until the price for the cloning procedure drops as the technology improves.

Some animal rights activists are disheartened by this aspect of the new cloning industry because they believe it is driven by human vanity and not a love for pets. After all, clones are only physical duplicates of the original animals; they do not have the same personality or habits of their progenitors. Animal activists suggest that copying pets is unnecessary given the fact that animal shelters destroy millions of animals each year because not enough people can be found to adopt them. Other critics simply find the notion of cloning so off-putting that they condemn the science as monstrous.

Cloning has met less resistance in the agricultural market. Cattle breeders, for example, have already introduced cloned cows into their herds. The cost is far less expensive than cat cloning (because cow eggs are easier to obtain in large numbers from slaughterhouses), so the economics of cloning cattle makes sense. The U.S. Food and Drug Administration has yet to allow markets to carry beef from cloned cattle; copied cows are therefore mainly used for breeding. Bio, a Web site organization that champions the biotechnology industry, explains that "the breeding technique allows a greater number of farmers the ability to preserve and extend proven, superior genetics. Ranchers would also be able to select and propagate the best animals—beef cattle that are fast-growing, have lean but tender meat, and are disease-resistant." Other livestock—such as goats and sheep—can and have also been cloned, but the economic constraints and the lack of demand for duplicating these animals has not made cloning them attractive.

Cloned cattle and other livestock can also contribute to the field of biomedicine. Genetically modified cows, for example, have been engineered to produce human antibodies that can then be administered to people in the form of vaccines. The modified cows could then be duplicated to yield more and more of these antibody factories. In a 2005 article in the *Scientist*, Jim Robl, the president of the Connecticut-based cloning firm Hematech, maintained, "Once you've got the production system in place, you can use the same system to immunize with any number of different antigens."

Cloning is one of the scientific breakthroughs debated in the following chapter. Other forms of genetically manipulating animals are also discussed. Such cutting-edge technologies have greatly expanded the arguments for and against animal experimentation and will likely continue to shape the debate as advances are made in the near future.

"Patients with a pig organ may be inherently vulnerable to infections transmitted from the pig organ itself."

The Risks of Animal-to-Human Transplants Outweigh the Benefits

Joyce D'Silva

Joyce D'Silva is an ambassador for Compassion in World Farming, an anti–animal cruelty organization that opposes factory farming. In the following viewpoint she claims that people are too eager to extend their lives. The newest medical promise, she asserts, is to replace failing human organs with healthy pig organs. Such a fix does not come without risks, however. According to D'Silva, the pig organs may carry dangerous viruses. Furthermore, in experiments using primate recipients, the pig transplant organs have been rejected by the hosts' immune systems. To continue these experiments in hopes of prolonging life, D'Silva argues, is not worth the risks nor the suffering it brings to the animals involved.

As you read, consider the following questions:

    1. What is xenozoonosis, as D'Silva defines it?

Joyce D'Silva, "Dying to Live," *Chemistry and Industry*, December 4, 2000, p. 767.

2. According to D'Silva, what kind of genetic modifications will likely be performed on donor pigs?

3. In what way does D'Silva have a personal connection to the issue of longevity?

You would think we could live forever, one day. All our expectations of medical research, all our obsessions with health and diet, even the potential of cryopreserved corpses could lead us to believe our finite, physical bodies are capable of infinite life, one day.

Hit the right spot on my genome, tweak a bit here, eliminate there and, who knows, one day?

Media headlines fuel our hopes with promises of cures for the whole range of diseases to which we may succumb, one day.

We may dream of larger houses, cottages in the country, Caribbean holidays or faster, larger cars, but, most of all, we desire our own longevity. It's as if length of chronological time is somehow a bonus in itself, quantity being the criterion for the good life, not quality.

How attached to life we are. How bound up with our careers, our homes, our hobbies and, of course, our loved ones and ourselves.

We would risk much to preserve our own personal status quo—and that includes our own physical ability to breathe and think and function. We will risk dangerous operations, because there's a chance of success. We'll willingly try new treatments, because they may work. We'll try out alternative therapies, because they may hold some ancient secret of life (and they will, usually, at least make us feel better).

And soon, there'll be a new quick-fix coming to a hospital near you: the promise of an animal heart for your failing one, a pig kidney, a pair of lungs, a liver and who knows what other organs from an animal, one day.

The Danger of Viral Disease

Patients with a pig organ may be inherently vulnerable to infections transmitted from the pig organ itself. Research has shown human cells can be infected by porcine endogenous retroviruses. What has been found in the laboratory may be even more easily replicated in the intimacy of the body.

But viruses are masters of mobility and, in a new host, they can be devastating, viz. AIDS. One person, the xenotransplant patient, is unlikely to be the end-point of their activity; they'll be spreading to family, friends and the rest of us. This is not hype. American researchers have already coined a new term for an animal disease transmitted to a xenotransplant recipient (and beyond?)—'xenozoonosis'.

These pigs will be no ordinary pigs, although almost certainly they will share the ability to enjoy life or to suffer along with all other pigs. But these are humano-pigs, genetically engineered to reduce the likelihood of their organs being rejected. Genetic engineering is still such a hit-and-miss procedure with a minute 'success' rate, that the pigs will likely be cloned too.

A huge number of female pigs will be operated on to remove egg cells for genetic modification and cloning work. Others will be operated on for implantation of the genetically modified (GM) or cloned embryos.

We know genetic engineering has produced gross malformations in many pigs, and we know cloned farm animals are frequently abnormal and die within days or are aborted before birth. We know strict hygiene requirements mean the GM piglets will be born by specific pathogen-free methods, that is hysterectomy and fatal injection for mother and sterile rearing conditions for her orphans. During their lives, repeated blood and tissue tests may be followed up by the removal of organs in sequence, while keeping the animal alive in 'hospital' conditions.

Viral Dangers of Pig Organs

Current xenotransplantation hopes are focused on pigs. Pigs, like other animals, carry bacteria and "exogenous" viruses (viruses that happen to infect particular animals). It would be premature to presume that we already know everything about pig viruses; for instance, a new virus related to human hepatitis E was reported in pigs in 1998. Many bacteria infect both pigs and humans, and human recipients of pig heart valves have been infected by *Myocardium fortuitum* complex. Pigs also harbor many viruses that could be transmitted to humans, some of which might be far more damaging to us than to their usual hosts.

Pigs also carry endogenous retroviruses (PERV), retroviruses whose DNA has become part of the pig genome. These are worrisome because retroviruses have exceptionally high mutation rates; they would also be difficult or impossible to eradicate. Pigs are also infected by many parasites. . . .

In short, several factors . . . render calculations of risk even less reliable than usual. These factors together could generate a catastrophic scenario in which a pig microorganism mutated into an easily transmissible, lethal, human disease. Such a microorganism might turn out to be unstoppable by any known treatment, and could, conceivably, threaten human existence altogether.

Laura Purdy, "Should We Add 'Xeno' to 'Transplantation'?"
Politics and Life Science, vol. 19, no. 2, September 2000.

As the [British] government's own expert committee [Advisory Group on the Ethics of Xenotransplantation] succinctly put it: 'We regret that animal suffering is caused but we conclude that these are inevitable compromises if xenotransplantation is to take place'. This committee made such a strong acknowledgement of the inevitability of the suffering of these source animals that they said it would be 'ethically unacceptable to use primates as source animals for xenotransplantation, not least because they would be exposed to too much suffering.

Failed Experiments

As for those primates, hundreds are already being used as recipients of GM pig organs. Experiment after experiment tells us how they suffer as their bodies reject the transplant, their immune systems are rendered useless and they succumb, if not to rejection, then to infection or poisoning.

Can these 'means' justify a possible 'end' for our own species, the tempting fantasy of a year or two more of life, of togetherness?

Seen in the round, it surely cries out: 'Unfair!', 'Too risky!' and 'Not worth it!'

And yet we ache for longevity. I know. I've seen my own husband struggle to live post-stroke for three years until his death. We'd have tried anything to make his stumbling fingers virtuoso-like again on the guitar and to make his shaky legs strong so we could climb those hills again.

Animal organs or tissues weren't on offer. But if they had been, would we have opted for them? Maybe. But would we have been right? I think not.

*"If we never took risks with the un-
known we would make little progress
in medicine."*

The Benefits of
Animal-to-Human Transplants
Outweigh the Risks

A physician, interviewed by Gale Scott

The following viewpoint is a New York Times *interview with a
physician concerning the potential value of animal-to-human
organ transplants. The physician claims that xenotransplants
will soon ease the need for human organs, which are often from
older or less than ideal donors. The doctor acknowledges that science must first overcome the risks of viral infection and the high
cost of using animal organs. The speaker argues, however, that
the benefits of providing human patients with healthy animal
organs outweigh these risks. The interview was conducted by
health reporter Gale Scott.*

As you read, consider the following questions:

1. In the author's view, how do brain death and brain injury make human organs less ideal to donate?

2. What viruses does the doctor note are sometimes transferred during human-to-human transplants?

3. According to the doctor, why would patient tolerance to animal transplant organs lower the cost of such transplants?

The potential benefits of xenotransplantation, most likely using pig organs and tissues, are immense. Because of a shortage of donor organs, 50,000 of the 70,000 people in the United States who are awaiting transplants will not get them this year.

Those who need kidneys may remain on dialysis, but those needing a heart or liver stand a good chance of dying. If we had an unlimited supply of animal organs, patients could receive transplants while still in reasonable health.

We frequently have to wait until the heart and liver patients have deteriorated to the extent that they need to be in an intensive care unit.

If the transplant could be performed when first needed, patients would recover more rapidly and the associated costs would decrease.

A Better Kind of Organ

The quality of donor pig organs will certainly be better than those from human cadavers. Brain injury and brain death can stress organs, particularly the heart.

Some transplanted hearts fail to support the circulation adequately even though they looked good in the donor.

Also, the pressure on surgeons to save lives is such that they are increasingly being forced to use organs from elderly or less than ideal donors, where the organ may not be perfect.

Using specially bred and housed donor pigs gives us the potential to reduce many infections. Virtually every time we transplant a human organ, we knowingly transfer an infec-

Why Xenotransplantation Should Move Ahead

Both in the UK and USA, oversight agencies are . . . increasingly eager to continue with research concerning xenotransplantation. It is indeed conceivable that we are overestimating the magnitude of the problem. As we cannot currently predict the consequences of transplantation of a transgenic porcine organ into a human, we must also bear in mind the possibility that no transmission of dangerous, uncontrollable viruses will occur. In this case, many would find it immoral to deny such a life saving intervention if it is one day thought feasible. It would be questionable to still allow transplant teams to increasingly rely on problematic strategies to widen the donor pool, such as the use of organs from so called marginal donors. The use of organs from elderly donors and donors with a health condition is not an attractive alternative to the prospect of transplanting compatible, healthy porcine organs. Safe and effective xenotransplantation would not only resolve the current allograft shortage, it would also annul the high financial and emotional burdens associated with long waiting times for an available donor organ and allow for a precisely scheduled transplant, thereby overcoming many practical problems for the transplant team. Also, specially engineered pigs may one day provide suitable organs for infants, for whom the organ shortage is the most devastating.

A. Ravelingien et al., "Proceeding with Clinical Trials of Animal to Human Organ Transplantation: A Way Out of the Dilemma," Journal of Medical Ethics, *vol. 30, 2004.*

tious agent. That includes cytomegalovirus, Epstein-Barr virus and even the hepatitis viruses.

There will always be the risk of transferring a hitherto unknown infectious agent, although many of the measures we shall take to exclude known viruses are likely also to exclude unknown viruses, if present.

If we have excluded all known infectious agents we would be justified in proceeding with trials in patients.

Many groups are investigating whether there is a potential risk in transferring porcine endogenous viruses to humans. These viruses are present in every pig cell, yet there is no evidence that they are harmful to pigs or would be harmful to humans. But we need assurances.

We have a strain of pig in Boston that appears unable to transmit their viruses to human cells.

If this finding holds up, concerns about infecting the transplant recipient or the public may be diminished.

Reducing Costs

As for cost, organs from genetically engineered pigs may well cost several thousand dollars. But expenses now associated with procuring organs from human donors can range from $7,500 to $25,000. Successful transplants will mean savings on dialysis and other forms of treatment of patients with end-stage organ failure.

One further development may reduce costs.

My colleagues can now induce what is known as a state of tolerance in some patients receiving a human organ transplant, which means that they require no immunosuppressive drugs after the first few weeks. We are trying to induce tolerance to a transplanted pig organ.

If this could be achieved, it would not only be greatly beneficial for the patients, as they would avoid the side effects of drug therapy, but the long-term costs would be significantly reduced.

If we never took risks with the unknown we would make little progress in medicine.

| "More than 100 foreign proteins have been produced experimentally from different organs in several animal species."

Genetically Modified Animals Are Beneficial to Medicine

Part I: Alexandre Fouassier; Part II: Manufacturing Chemist

The following two viewpoints were taken from Manufacturing Chemist, *an international trade journal. In the first viewpoint Alexandre Fouassier, a development manager at BioProtein Technologies in Paris explains how insertion of human genetic material into rabbits can force the animals to express a desired protein. The protein is then harvested from the rabbits' milk. In the second viewpoint the staff of* Manufacturing Chemist *reports that the genetic modification of cows allows for the production of human antibodies within these animals. These two viewpoints argue that the creation of "transgenic" animals such as modified rabbits and cows will be useful in quickly producing human proteins and antibodies that can be used to fight disease.*

Part I: Alexandre Fouassier, "Milking Rabbits' Protein Potential," *Manufacturing Chemist*, vol. 74, no. 5, May 1, 2003, pp. 47–50. Copyright © 2003 Polygon Media Ltd. Reproduced by permission of the publisher, www.manufacturing-chemist.info. Part II: *Manufacturing Chemist*, "Cows Offer Potential New Source of Human Antibodies," vol. 74, no. 5, May 1, 2003, p. 49. Copyright © 2003 Polygon Media Ltd. Reproduced by permission of the publisher, www.manufacturing-chemist.info.

As you read, consider the following questions:

1. According to Fouassier, what diseases has the cloned erythroprotein been used to combat?

2. As Fouassier states, what advantages do transgenic animals offer pharmaceutical companies in the production of complex proteins?

3. According to *Manufacturing Chemist*, what two factors limit the supply of immunoglobulin, an antibody used in the treatment of many immune system disorders?

Part I

Over the past few years, biotechnology has generated new opportunities for the development of human pharmaceuticals. One particular success story is the use of recombinant technologies to produce therapeutically useful proteins, such as hormones, antibodies, growth factors and antigens for vaccines. Producing these proteins in the quantities required to meet clinical needs presents a challenge, however, and manufacturers are constantly looking for new solutions. Transgenic animals provide one answer, and can offer benefits compared with traditional methods of recombinant protein manufacture. The transgenic rabbit, in particular, gives a fast, cost-effective and efficient means of producing therapeutic protein in milk.

Through advances in biotechnological techniques, scientists are able to isolate sequences of bases coding for specific proteins (genes), and insert them into the DNA of other living cells. These 'hosts' are usually rapidly reproducing cells such as bacteria, yeast or cultured cell lines, which can be grown in large volumes to express the protein of interest on an industrial scale for use in therapeutics. Naturally occurring erythropoietin, for example, is a very rare glycoprotein hormone responsible for the regulation of red blood cell production. The erythropoietin gene was cloned in 1985 and today it is routinely expressed [i.e., developed] in cultured cells. The recombinant erythropoietin harvested from these cells is used to increase the production of red blood cells in patients with anaemia caused by a variety of conditions, such as cancer chemotherapy or in association with HIV. . . .

The use of transgenic animals and plants for the production of human therapeutic proteins is a relatively new manufacturing development. Ever since the birth of 'Tracey', in 1991, the first transgenic sheep expressing the human blood clotting factor, human a-1-antitypsin, the idea of transgenic animals as protein fermentors has taken off.

Since then, more than 100 foreign proteins have been produced experimentally from different organs in several animal species. Transgenic animals have the potential to make a significant contribution to the production of biopharmaceuticals because they can produce complex proteins at high volume and with low cost.

Methods of Transferring Genetic Material

Transgenic animals can be created through two principal methods—microinjection and nuclear transfer.

In the microinjection method, freshly fertilised oocytes [eggs] are harvested and DNA constructs [foreign genetic coding] are injected into the male pronucleus (a vacuole that contains the male DNA and has entered the female egg but has yet to fuse with the egg pronucleus) using a thin glass needle. The male and female pronuclei fuse to form the nucleus, which now contains foreign DNA. The cell then divides to form a two-cell embryo and is transferred into a recipient female.

The main disadvantage of this technique is that transgene integration within the male pronucleus genome is random. The expression of the transgene can, therefore, be affected by its position in the genome, meaning that the subsequent selection of efficient protein-producing animals is required.

Nuclear transfer involves transferring the nucleus from a somatic [nonreproductive] cell into an enucleated oocyte [one that has had its nucleus removed]. . . .

Choosing the Desired Protein and Its Source

The choice of animal for commercial protein production depends on a variety of factors, including generation time, number of offspring, potential yield and susceptibility to disease. A variety of animals have been used successfully, including mice, rabbits, goats, sheep and cows.

The source of the protein is also an important consideration. Milk, blood, urine and seminal plasma can be used, as well as the egg white from birds' eggs and the cocoons of some insects.

The most convenient source is milk, however. The secretory properties of the mammary gland make it the ideal protein producer, and the milk is easy to collect. . . .

In general, the larger the animal, the greater the milk yield, but this must be balanced against longer gestation periods and the time it takes to produce a functional transgenic herd. A key factor in the use of transgenic species is the efficiency of expression of the desired protein. . . . The rabbit has emerged as a key model for protein production based on: the speed at which transgenic animal colonies can be established; good milk yields; high protein content; an ability to produce complex functional proteins; and ease of handling.

Transgenic rabbits are generally produced using the microinjection method. A female rabbit is implanted with 20 viable embryos containing DNA constructs. The founder generation are born after one month. . . .

A Cost-Effective Option

The benefits of the rabbit are particularly important in light of today's uncertain manufacturing environments. Biotechnology-derived products represent about 25% of all new medicines and it is predicted that this will increase to about 50% within 10 years.

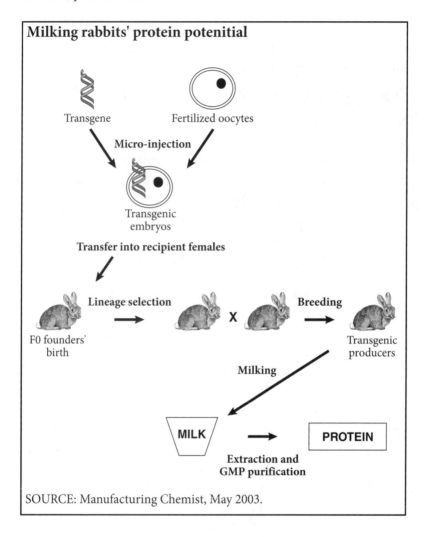

Milking rabbits' protein potenitial

Transgene   Fertilized oocytes

Micro-injection

Transgenic
embryos

Transfer into recipient females

Lineage selection   X   **Breeding**

F0 founders'
birth

Transgenic
producers

Milking

MILK → **PROTEIN**

**Extraction and
GMP purification**

SOURCE: Manufacturing Chemist, May 2003.

Current trends indicate that there is going to be a shortfall in manufacturing capacity for biopharmaceuticals. While many companies are investing in increasing their manufacturing capacity, it can take four to five years to build a manufacturing plant at a cost of US$100–500m[illion] ([euro]94.5-473m). The use of transgenics offers pharmaceutical and biotechnology companies an attractive option as a highly flexible, scaleable source of protein with a fast time to full production.

Part II

Cows Offer Potential New Source of Human Antibodies

Scientists have reported the successful application of proprietary cloning techniques to produce four calves that express a human chromosome fragment coding for the broad range of human antibodies. The research was the result of an ongoing joint effort between US company Hematech and Kirin Brewery to develop a system for the production of human polyclonal antibody-based therapeutics. This marks the first step in the development of a large-scale system for producing human polyclonal antibodies [antibodies derived from different cell lines] that could be used to prevent and/or treat a wide variety of diseases, including antibiotic resistant infections, autoimmune diseases, cancer and diseases resulting from bioterrorism.

Currently there is a substantial need for immunoglobulin [proteins secreted by plasma in the immune system], or broad-spectrum human polyclonal antibodies, for the treatment of many immune system disorders. However, the supply is limited to that which can be obtained from human donors and the application is limited because human donors cannot be optimally immunised.

'A bovine system for the production of human polyclonal antibodies would be fast and easily scalable to tons of product,' said Dr. James Robl, president and chief scientific officer of Hematech. 'A cow carrying complete human antibody genes could simply be immunised against the target disease agent and human antibodies could be collected in a couple of months.'

Meanwhile, the company has been awarded US$3.3m[illion] ([euro]3.1m) in government funding to develop a bovine system for producing human polyclonal antibodies against botulinum neurotoxins, which pose a major bioweapons threat. . . .

| "Many if not most human proteins will not be 'as they should' structurally, functionally and biochemically unless they are produced in a human milieu."

Genetically Modified Animals Are Not Beneficial to Medicine

Animal Aid

Animal Aid is a British organization that campaigns against cruelty to animals. In the following viewpoint Animal Aid asserts that genetically modified (GM) animals have not benefited medical progress. According to the organization, using GM animals as disease models has failed to yield results that can be applied to humans. In addition, the use of GM animals to produce beneficial human proteins has the potential of transmitting animal diseases to human recipients. In both cases, the suffering and harm to the animals involved also calls into question the necessity of such experiments.

Animal Aid, "Man or Mouse: Uses of, and Problems with, Genetically Modified Animals," Kent, United Kingdom: Animal Aid, 2005. www.animalaid.org.uk/viv/manmouse3.htmwww.animalaid.org.uk. Reproduced by permission.

As you read, consider the following questions:

1. According to Animal Aid, what percent of toxicity testing results done on one group of animals can be correlated by tests on other groups?
2. In Animal Aid's view, why are pharmaceutical companies investigating the use of GM animals to make human proteins when other production methods are available?
3. What is "leaky" gene expression and why does Animal Aid say it is problematic for GM animals?

If promises from those involved in their creation are to be believed, the contribution of GM animals to human life will rival that of the wheel. Manipulating the genomes of 'imperfect' animals will lead to a complete understanding of genetics and cell biology; drugs to cure all diseases; simple and reliable test protocols to determine which chemicals, drugs and foodstuffs are safe and which dangerous and in what amounts; an unlimited supply of animal organs for human transplant with no problems of rejection; animals that can act as 'drug factories,' churning out huge amounts of effective drugs in their milk. . . .

Inappropriate Models for Toxicology Testing

In recent years, transgenesis [the insertion of foreign genetic coding into an animal] has been used in what can only be considered to be a last-ditch attempt to derive some form of useful information from animals used in toxicity testing. For decades, the assessment of which chemicals, drugs, food additives and so on might pose a hazard to human health has relied heavily upon administering them to mice and rats, and examining their tissues for damage. It is now universally accepted that the correlation between results from these investigations are in the region of 5–30%, a statistic that belies claims that these tests can be in any way predictive of human response.

The FDA Deputy Commissioner Discusses the Risks of GM Animals Used for Food

The Food and Drug Administration is familiar with the risks of biotechnology. We are aware that using genetically altered animals for food raises serious safety concerns that must be addressed through rigorous, science-based analysis. Bioactive compounds are a good example. They include growth hormones, proteins that aid in resisting disease, and even proteins of pharmaceutical interest. If these proteins are present in edible tissues of transgenic animals, they might pose a food safety risk.

Allergic reactions are another concern. The risk of adverse reactions is raised whenever foods contain new proteins from genetically modified organisms, regardless of whether their source is an animal, plant, or microorganism such as yeast or bacteria.

Lester Crawford, "Genetic Kingdom:
Reaping the Bounties of Our Biotech Future,"
American Enterprise, *vol. 15, no. 2, March 2004.*

And so these mice have been transformed into new, improved transgenic animals that are now more susceptible to the harmful effects of various substances—and, it is hoped, be more predictive of which substances will poison and/or cause cancer in human beings. The reality is that transgenic animals are continuing to produce inconsistent results and be of no predictive value in such assessments, and that no single transgenic animal or combination of transgenic animals performs nearly well enough to be considered sufficiently reliable for regulatory use. For example, genetically engineered mice manipulated to investigate genes involved in cancers of the nervous system in children showed that some genes and mutations clearly associated with specific human tumours produced very different effects in mice, and that one cancer-causing genetic pathway in rats did not operate in any human tumours. . . .

The Unknown Dangers of Pharming

Human proteins are used therapeutically in the treatment of a wide range of diseases, such as multiple sclerosis, hepatitis, cancer, cystic fibrosis and malaria. These proteins have been successfully produced via a number of methods for some years, including GM [genetically modified] bacterial and yeast cultures, cultures of mammalian and plant cells, and entire GM plant crops, with each method having distinct advantages and disadvantages. Transgenic animals have been added to this list more recently, not due to necessity, but mainly because companies producing the therapeutic proteins believe that, once developed, pharmaceutical-producing GM animals can be scaled up to a huge degree and will then generate almost limitless amounts of product very cheaply.

Cows, chickens, goats, pigs, rabbits and sheep have been genetically engineered to produce therapeutic proteins in an industry known as 'pharming' or 'biopharming.' The animals are manipulated so that they produce these products in their milk, mostly, but also in their urine, blood, or even sperm. Large amounts of these proteins are then purified and processed into a final product. . . . There are some . . . problems specific to pharming. In principle, transgene expression is intended to be confined to, for example, the mammary gland in those animals engineered to produce the transgene protein product in their milk. However, 'leaky' gene expression is often detected in other tissues, and the proteins are often found in the animals' blood. This can have severe negative health consequences, causing animals to suffer from 'pathologies and other severe systemic effects', as reported by the National Academy of Sciences in the USA.

Scientific and medical concerns surrounding these endeavours include, in common with xenotransplantation, the risk of cross-species disease transmission. This risk, of course, is real, though it may be considered minor by patients relying upon a transgenic therapeutic protein to ameliorate their suffering and/or disease. In addition, it is a statement of fact that many if not most human proteins will not be 'as they should' structurally, functionally and biochemically unless they are produced in a human milieu, i.e. in cultured human cells. Some proteins are absolutely fine being produced in bacteria, for example, but others show marked differences—ranging from ostensibly inconsequential, superficial changes, to massive and catastrophic ones. Proteins in the latter class need to be produced in 'higher' cells . . . so why produce them in cow's milk instead of cultured human cells? The only answer is: profit. And to produce such therapeutic proteins in transgenic animals, with all that the process entails, when this is not strictly necessary, can be regarded as ethically abhorrent and unjustifiable, especially in cases where they could be efficiently produced using plants and other means.

> "Animal cloning . . . was initiated to seek
> fundamental knowledge for the benefit
> of humankind."

Animal Cloning Is Worthwhile

Marie A. Di Berardino

*In the following viewpoint Marie A. Di Berardino describes the
process of cloning animals and asserts that this practice promises
benefits to medicine and agriculture. As Berardino explains, biotechnology has already shown, for example, how genetically
modified animals can produce beneficial human proteins. Cloning these animals, in her opinion, could create whole herds of
protein producers. She also attests that cloning genetically enhanced livestock could similarly improve reproduction rates,
meat quality, and milk production for the agriculture industry.
Marie A. Di Berardino is a professor emerita of biochemistry at
the Medical College of Pennsylvania-Hahnemann University in
Philadelphia.*

As you read, consider the following questions:

1. What is Polly and why is she significant, in the author's
   view?

Marie A. Di Berardino, "Cloning: Past, Present, and the Exciting Future," *Breakthroughs in Bioscience*, Federation of American Societies for Experimental Biology,
n.d., pp. 1–8. www.faseb.org. Reproduced by permission.

2. As Di Berardino states, how can cloned animals be helpful to xenotransplantation?

3. How is nuclear transfer technology being used to investigate the aging process, according to Di Berardino?

Jimmy walks into the neighborhood pharmacy to fill his
prescription for a protein he was born without. He lacks the
gene for blood clotting factor IX and relies on the local drugstore for his medicine. Jimmy pulls open the bag that contains
his 90-day supply of patches, removes the old patch from his
chest, and attaches a new one. He adjusts his jersey and heads
out to meet his buddies for a game of touch football. Even
though he is hemophiliac, Jimmy isn't worried about the
bruises and scrapes he is sure to get. . . .

This is the future. It is what Dolly so wondrously has
wrought. Born July 1996, she is the first mammal successfully
cloned from an adult cell, one taken from a ewe's mammary
gland.

The Nuclear Transfer Process

Dolly was not created in the ordinary way. Typically, a lamb is
the product of natural reproduction—two germ cells, a sperm
from an adult male and an egg (oocyte) from an adult female,
fuse at fertilization. Each of these germ cells (the sperm and
the oocyte) contributes half the chromosomes needed to create a new individual. Chromosomes are found in the cell's
nucleus and they carry the DNA, which is the genetic blue-
print for an individual.

The process that produced Dolly differs from ordinary reproduction in two major ways. First, body (or somatic) cells
from an adult ewe's udder (this is the donor) were placed in a
culture dish and allowed to grow. The nutrients were then removed from the culture, which stopped the cells' growth. One
of these non-growing cells was then fused (by electric jolts)
with another ewe's oocyte from which the nucleus had been

previously removed (i.e., enucleated, so it had no chromosomes). This procedure is known as 'somatic cell nuclear transfer'. Within a day the fused cells began to divide in the culture dish. After several divisions, the early embryo was transferred to the uterus of a surrogate mother and allowed to develop.

Second, unlike the sperm and the egg, each of which contributes half the number of chromosomes at fertilization, each body cell contains twice the number of chromosomes in each germ cell. So fusion of a sperm and an egg forms an individual whose full genetic composition is unique to that individual. On the other hand, the embryo cloned from somatic cell nuclear transfer begins development with the diploid (double) number of chromosomes, all derived from one somatic cell (adult udder) of a single individual. This embryo has the same nuclear genetic composition as the donor of the somatic cell. . . .

Transgenic Protein Producers

Imagine herds of female sheep, cattle, and goats producing large quantities of human proteins in their milk, an ideal place for those proteins to be harvested and used to treat patients like Jimmy, the hemophiliac, whose blood cannot clot. We can realize this dream today—one step at a time, because the process that produced Dolly also can be used to produce the transgenic (one species carrying another species' genes) clones.

Scottish scientists first removed cells from a fetal lamb and grew them in a culture dish. Multiple copies of fragments of DNA (deoxyribonucleic acid, which holds genetic information) containing the human gene for blood clotting factor IX were added to the dish and coaxed into the cells. Some cells incorporated the human DNA into their chromosomes, thus becoming 'transgenic cells', or cells containing a transferred gene.

These transgenic cells were then separated from those without human DNA and used to create Polly, the transgenic sheep that today produces the human clotting factor IX in her milk. Purposely, scientists genetically designed the transgenic sheep clones so that the human gene would function only in the mammary gland.

It will soon be possible for the human clotting factor IX protein to be routinely harvested and purified from the sheep milk. . . .

The importance of the transgenic clones is that biotechnology is now being extended to produce different human proteins like insulin (diabetes), interferon (viral infections), clotting factor VIII (hemophilia), and tissue plasminogen activator (dissolving blood clots). In other words, female clones of such animals as cattle, sheep, and goats are being genetically designed to be dairy/pharmaceutical producers, a virtual living bio-pharmaceutical industry. Transgenic clones of mammals are a major advance in biotechnology because they can synthesize, in large quantities, complex molecules critically required for patient care. . . .

Other Benefits of Clones

While these advances are on the horizon for us, beneficial applications to agriculture are already being implemented. Transgenic cloning can be used for the genetic improvement of livestock related to milk production, quality of meat, growth rate, reproduction, nutrition, behavioral traits, and/or resistance to diseases. This cloning process simply accelerates the older, slower, and less predictable methods of crossbreeding and hybridization. . . .

Transgenic clones can be directly beneficial to humans, other animals, and agriculture in additional ways.

- They may be developed for tissue and organ transplantation. Although not yet a reality, there is promise that large animals can be genetically designed and cloned so

Sexual reproduction (A) and somatic cell nuclear transfer (B) in sheep

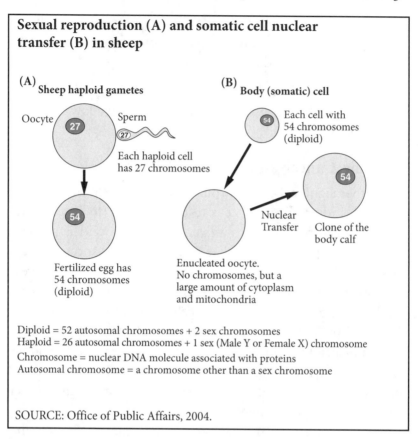

Diploid = 52 autosomal chromosomes + 2 sex chromosomes
Haploid = 26 autosomal chromosomes + 1 sex (Male Y or Female X) chromosome
Chromosome = nuclear DNA molecule associated with proteins
Autosomal chromosome = a chromosome other than a sex chromosome

SOURCE: Office of Public Affairs, 2004.

that their tissues and organs will not trigger immunological responses in the recipient and cause them to be rejected. Recently, muscle rigidity and tremors in parkinsonian rats were improved by transplanting cloned transgenic bovine neurons into their brains. This research, called xenotransplantation, is one of the many avenues being pursued in an attempt to alleviate the desperate shortage of human tissues for transplantation.

• Domestic animals can be genetically designed to express a certain human disease and therefore serve as models for the study and treatment of human illnesses. Although many mouse models of human diseases are available today, such models in large domestic animals physiologically more similar to humans are sparse and critically needed.

- Somatic cell nuclear transfer might help preserve endangered species such as pandas that have low reproductive rates.

Fighting Cancer and the Aging Process

Two other significant gains from clones are worth mentioning.

First, inducing cancer cells to differentiate [to mature into a specific cell type, such as a liver cell or skin cell] is a useful type of therapy. We know that many types of cancer cells are less specialized than their normal counterparts. For this reason investigators suspected that the precursors of cancer cells could be immature cells or stem cells that fail to complete differentiation. If this is so, then by using information gained from nuclear transfer technology, we may be able to induce the cells to mature and stop making tumors. Previous studies have demonstrated that we can control at least some cancer cells by using the differentiation process.

Second, aged cell nuclei can be rejuvenated. People and other organisms change as they age. Environmental insults and diseases cause these changes; others are intrinsic to the organism. Studies using cell culture have shown that body cells grow and divide normally in culture for awhile, but eventually stop dividing, become senescent [become aged and lose the ability to divide and replicate], and die. An exception was seen in aged frog red blood cell nuclei (human red blood cells lack nuclei): After their transfer into enucleated oocytes, frog red blood cell nuclei were rejuvenated. They carried out the formation of tadpoles that survived almost a third of the way to metamorphosis. The oocyte cytoplasm contains an abundance of chemicals that promote DNA synthesis and cell division after normal fertilization. We believe that these substances also rejuvenate aged cell nuclei and turn non-cycling frog red blood cells into active ones. If we could isolate these substances, we might be able to alleviate—or reverse—senescence. . . .

Ethical Choices

The choices we make for the application of knowledge reside in ethical decisions by humans. Animal cloning, like other research, was initiated to seek fundamental knowledge for the benefit of humankind. In addition to expanding the knowledge base in cellular, developmental, and molecular biology, as well as in cancer and aging, cloning has now been applied to enhance medicine and agriculture. Presently, hospital committees in the United States bar attempts to clone humans because of clinical, safety, and ethical concerns. Cloning is only one of many discoveries in which society will have to choose which applications are ethical and which ones are not.

| *"Like pet cloning, the cloning of farm animals is monumentally unnecessary."*

Animal Cloning Is Unnecessary

Wayne Pacelle

Wayne Pacelle is the president of the Humane Society of the United States. In the following viewpoint Pacelle argues that animal cloning is an unneeded technological advance. According to Pacelle, the cloning of pets or farm livestock is unnecessary because there is no current shortage of these animals. Pet owners who want to clone their deceased animals are merely acting out of vanity, Pacelle maintains, while the cloning of livestock is motivated purely by profit. Before this technology moves forward, Pacelle urges that policy makers consider the risks to both humans and animals.

As you read, consider the following questions:

1. What are two of the reasons why Pacelle objects to pet cloning?

2. What impact does Pacelle predict agricultural animal cloning will have on small farmers?

3. According to the author, what animal welfare concerns are raised by animal cloning?

With the arrival of Little Nicky, a kitten cloned to duplicate a Dallas woman's deceased pet, animal cloning has moved from closed-door laboratories to commercial application. The $50,000 feline was delivered by Genetic Savings & Clone, the playfully named company catering to particularly devoted pet owners.

While the intentions of the pet owners are understandable, the practice itself is rife with hazard and requires a decisive response from policy-makers. There are many practical problems with pet cloning, not the least of which is that the genetic duplicate may turn out to act, and even look, different from its forebear. Each creature—shaped in part by life experience—is more than an embodiment of his or her DNA. A cloned animal may look much the same and bring back happy memories for pet lovers, but the creature they are looking at is not the same animal.

More to the point, with millions of healthy and adoptable cats and dogs being killed each year for lack of suitable homes, it's a little frivolous to be cloning departed pets. The challenge is not to find new, absurdly expensive ways to create animals, but to curb the growth of pet populations and to foster an ethic in society that prompts people to adopt and shelter creatures in need of loving homes.

Untold Risks Need Reassessment

Pet cloning is simply not worth repeating. Behind this one little kitten are far grander schemes to clone animals for use in agriculture and research. Before such projects become the norm, we should pause and think carefully about where it is leading—for animals and for humanity.

It was big news some years ago when scientists in Scotland announced the cloning of Dolly the sheep. This new technology marked a decisive moment in our ability to manipulate the natural world to suit our designs. Dolly has long since passed afflicted by a lung disease that typically occurs in much older sheep. Since her dramatic birth—and her pitiful decline—scientists have turned out clones for mice, rabbits, goats, pigs, cows and now cats. Cloned horses and dogs, we are promised, are on the way. But behind every heralded success are hundreds of monstrous failures.

As all of this has unfolded, policy-makers have stood idly by, failing to place any restraints of law and ethics on corporations and scientists who are tinkering here with the most fundamental elements of biology. We hear indignation and expressions of well-founded concern about human cloning. But we hear hardly a word of doubt or moral concern about the idea of animal cloning, much less about the particular animals subjected to these experiments. It won't be long before biotech companies in the hire of agribusiness announce plans to sell commercial clones as food. Cloned ham, steak, and even drumsticks may be served at retail operations in the future, and there's no law to forbid the sale of meat or milk from clones produced in a laboratory.

Like pet cloning, the cloning of farm animals is monumentally unnecessary. Farmers are already producing so much meat that they must find export markets to turn a profit. As for milk, it's cheaper than bottled water. The dairy industry recently "culled" tens of thousands of healthy dairy cows in order to depress production.

Small farmers, already put at a disadvantage by mounting debt and mechanized competitors, will be further marginalized as cloning practices become commonplace. More than ever, they'll be at the mercy of corporate factory farms to purchase their supply of clones.

Consumers face threats of a different sort. Who knows if consuming meat and milk from clones is safe? A recent Food and Drug Administration symposium addressed this issue, but

Sutton. © by Ward Sutton. Reproduced by permission.

the confident declarations that the animal products are safe didn't seem all that reassuring: Just one misstep could be catastrophic. With mad cow, foot-and-mouth, avian flu and other diseases now posing a greater threat in our globalized agricultural markets, the production of genetically identical animals would pose serious threats to food security. Genetic variation, already low from conventional breeding, would also be almost eliminated by cloning.

Animal Welfare Concerns

As for the animals in our factory farms, cloning is the final assault on their well-being and dignity. When the FDA held a public consultation on animal cloning in November 2003, researchers reported a graphic list of problems for clones and their surrogate mothers in cattle, pigs, sheep and goats—a string of developmental abnormalities and a host of deaths before, during and after birth. The animals being cloned exhibit grievous problems, such as cows with grossly enlarged udders, major leg problems and other forms of lameness. And these are the very animals trumpeted as success stories.

Of the largest group of clones yet—produced by Cyagra, which clones cattle—few embryos survived to term, and of those that did, a third then died by the age of 1 year. The FDA's report, "Animal Cloning: A Risk Assessment" put a nice spin on this when it said that "the proportion of live, normal births appears to be increasing." In other words, the situation has improved from atrocious to very bad.

It is time for Congress and the FDA and other regulatory bodies to engage in the animal-cloning debate. Many of the ethical concerns raised by human cloning apply to this reckless disregard for the integrity of animal life. Should such questions be left entirely to scientists and corporations, since they have an intellectual and commercial stake in these projects? Our government alone can stand up for the public interest in preventing this cruelty.

Cloning is a startling procedure, to be sure, and many scientists would have us view it as some inevitable stage in our technological development. But humanity's progress is not always defined by scientific innovation alone. Cloning—both human and animal—is one of those cases in which progress is defined by the exercise of wisdom and of self-restraint.

Periodical Bibliography

The following articles have been selected to supplement the diverse views presented in this chapter.

Roy Calne	"Xenografting—The Future of Transplantation, and Always Will Be," *Xenotransptantation*, 2005.
Philip Cohen and David Concar	"The Awful Truth: Cloning of Prize Animals Is Already Economic," *New Scientist*, May 19, 2001.
David K.C. Cooper	"Clinical Xenotransplantion—How Close Are We?" *Lancet*, August 16, 2003.
Simon Cooper	"The Small Matter of Our Humanity," *Arena*, June–July 2002.
Lester Crawford	"Reaping the Biotech Harvest," *Biotech Bounty*, March 2004.
Anthony Dorling	"Clinical Xenotransplantation: Pigs Might Fly?" *American Journal of Xenotransplantation*, 2002.
Economist	"Down on the Pharm," September 18, 2004.
Alix Fano	"One Man's Meat: Transplanting Organs from Pigs and Monkeys to Humans," *Ecologist*, December 2000.
Tony Gill	"The Atomic Fish: The Rising Controversy of Genetically Modified Pets," *Humanist*, September–October 2004.
Cheryl V. Hunter, Laurence S. Tiley, and Helen M. Sang	"Developments in Transgenic Technology: Applications for Medicine," *Trends in Molecular Medicine*, June 2005.
A. Ravelingien and J. Braeckman	"To the Core of Porcine Matter: Evaluating Arguments Against Producing Transgenic Pigs," *Xenotransplantation*, 2004.
Arlene Weintraub	"Crossing the Gene Barrier," *Business Week*, January 16, 2006.

For Further Discussion

Chapter 1

1. Ilana Mercer argues that animals cannot have rights because they act without conscience. In her opinion, only humans can derive rights because of their "innate moral agency and capacity for reason." Tom Regan, on the other hand, claims that humans should recognize and respect the inherent rights of animals because it is the "just" thing to do—and "justice is the highest principle of ethics." After examining these two views, decide how each author defines the source of rights. Do you think animals have inherent rights or are people the only creatures that can claim to have rights? Explain your answers while referencing the arguments given by the authors.

2. Matt Ball and Jack Norris question the notion that animals cannot possess rights equal to humans because they are simply not human. They point out, for example, that not all humans share the same rights, and therefore the matter of being human cannot be the sole deciding factor of who or what deserves rights. Ball and Norris suggest that the capacity to suffer should be the measure of whom or what can claim to possess rights. Josie Appleton, however, argues that while animals and humans both suffer, the distinction between humans and animal species has more to do with consciousness. Explain how Appleton argues her case that animals cannot attain rights because they are fundamentally different than humans. In the end, decide whether you support Ball and Norris's claim that rights belong to all creatures because humans are not of demonstrably superior value, or whether you believe Appleton's assertion that rights are apportioned by kind, not degree. Defend your answer.

3. Alex Epstein and Will Potter have opposing opinions on whether the actions of animal rights activists constitute terrorism. Epstein maintains that extremists' actions often tend toward terrorism, Potter suggests that activists' actions are often unfairly labeled as terrorism. After examining the authors' views, do you believe there are some grounds on which Epstein and Potter may agree? What are they? In your opinion, has either author been too harsh or too lenient in judging the actions of animal activists? Use examples from the viewpoints, as well as any other reported incidents involving animal activists, to support your answer.

Chapter 2

1. Adrian R. Morrison contends that it is moral to use animals in medical research because it is the duty of humans to keep their own race alive—in the same way that all species fight to continue their existence. David Thomas, on the other hand, believes that it is immoral to conduct experiments on any unwilling creature—animal or human—because the potential to cause pain and suffering forms the basis for all ethical judgments. Which author do you believe presents the strongest argument concerning the morality or immorality of animal experimentation? Do you think that either author has correctly identified the basis of human morality? If not, what other fundamentals of morality, in your view, impact the animal experimentation debate?

2. After examining the arguments of John Gray and the Scientific Steering Committee of the European Commission, how do you feel about the use of nonhuman primates in animal experimentation? Should research continue because apes are such excellent models for studying human diseases, or is their similarity to humans a reason to abolish nonhuman primate experiments? Explain your answer.

3. Considering the arguments made in all the viewpoints in this chapter, do you think there is a way for the competing camps to compromise on animal experimentation? That is, like the system proposed by Patrick Bateson, could there be a method to determine when animal experiments should be tolerated and when they should not? What would be your criteria for making such a judgment? In framing your answer, consider your opinion of the value and sentience of all life. Is conducting experiments on earthworms, for example, the same as conducting them on chimpanzees?

Chapter 3

1. The American Physiological Society (APS) cites several areas of research in which animal experimentation has aided medical progress. Christopher Anderegg and his colleagues list other examples in which animal experimentation has hindered or had no impact on medical advances. Which set of authors do you think wages a more convincing argument with its examples? The APS also gives several reasons why animals make excellent test subjects, while Anderegg provides many limitations of animal models. Which side makes the more persuasive argument regarding this issue? Explain your answers when responding to both questions.

2. Consider the arguments presented in the viewpoints of Kathy Archibald and David H. Freedman. Do you think that alternatives to animal drug testing are or will ever be as accurate as animal models? Explain why or why not.

Chapter 4

1. Joyce D'Silva argues that animal-to-human transplantation is too risky to implement because of unknown factors that include the possibility of widespread disease transmission. Conversely, the unnamed physician interviewed by Gale

Scott claims that xenotransplantation is too attractive an option not to pursue because it will ensure better and cheaper transplant organs than are available from human donors. Considering that tens of thousands of people waiting for transplants each year do not receive needed organs, do you think it is more appropriate to speed xenotransplantation or to restrict its implementation? Do you think that policies should be changed so that patients could take the responsibility for accepting animal organs regardless of the unknown consequences? Explain why or why not.

2. The viewpoints by Alexandre Fouassier, *Manufacturing Chemist*, Animal Aid, Marie A. Di Berardino, and Wayne Pacelle all contend with the pros and cons, rights and wrongs of manipulating animal genetics to aid humans. Fouassier and Di Berardino argue, for example, that creating transgenic livestock that can produce human proteins will help human patients in need of these proteins. Animal Aid and Wayne Pacelle counter that other methods are available to produce such proteins and that the creation of cloned herds of genetically modified animals is unnecessary and motivated solely by profits. Which argument do you find more persuasive? Explain why.

3. Wayne Pacelle notes a connection between the ethical issues surrounding animal cloning and those surrounding human cloning. Many who speak out against animal cloning, in fact, argue that to condone it would bring humanity one step closer to tolerating human cloning. Do you think animal cloning paves the way to human cloning, or is there a distinction (moral or otherwise) that separates the issues? In your opinion, should all cloning be condemned or condoned, or should animal cloning be tolerated while human cloning remains banned? Explain your decision while referencing some of the arguments made in this chapter.

Organizations to Contact

The editors have compiled the following list of organizations concerned with the issues debated in this book. The descriptions are derived from materials provided by the organizations. All have publications or information available for interested readers. The list was compiled on the date of publication of the present volume; the information provided here may change. Be aware that many organizations take several weeks or longer to respond to inquiries, so allow as much time as possible.

Advanced Cell Technology (ACT)
1201 Harbor Bay Pkwy., Suite 120, Alameda, CA   94502
(510) 748-4900 • fax: (510) 748-4950
Web site: www.advancedcell.com

The first to successfully clone an endangered animal by duplicating its cells and implanting them into another species, ACT also engages in animal cloning for technology development and drug screening. Its Web site contains links to reports and press releases that are published in various scientific magazines, as well as to testimonials, letters, and reports regarding the ethical issues of cloning.

American Anti-Vivisection Society (AAVS)
801 Old York Rd., Suite 204, Jenkintown, PA   19046
(800) 729-2287
e-mail: aavs@aavs.org
Web site: www.aavs.org

AAVS advocates the abolition of vivisection, opposes all types of experiments on living animals, and sponsors research on alternatives to these methods. The society produces videos and publishes numerous brochures, including *Dissection and Students' Rights*, as well as the award-winning *AV Magazine*.

American Association for Laboratory Animal Science (AALAS)

9190 Crestwyn Hills Dr., Memphis, TN 38125
(901) 754-8620 • fax: (901) 759-5849
e-mail: info@aalas.org
Web site: www.aalas.org

The American Association for Laboratory Animal Science is a professional nonprofit association of persons and institutions concerned with the production, care, and study of animals used in biomedical research. This organization provides a medium for the exchange of scientific information on all phases of laboratory animal care and use through its educational activities, publications, and certification program. Its publications include *Contemporary Topics in Laboratory Animal Science* and *Laboratory Animal Science.*

Americans for Medical Progress (AMP)

908 King St., Suite 301, Alexandria, VA 22314
(703) 836-9595 • fax: (703) 836-9594
e-mail: info@amprogress.org
Web site: www.amprogress.org

AMP is a nonprofit organization that raises public awareness concerning the use of animals in research. Its goal is to ensure that scientists and doctors have the freedom and resources necessary to pursue their work. To that end, AMP exposes the misinformation of the animal rights movement through newspaper and magazine articles, broadcast debates, and public education materials.

Animal Aid

The Old Chapel, Bradford St.
Tonbridge, Kent, TN9 1AW United Kingdom
(44) 73 236 4546 • fax: 44 (0) 73 236 6533
e-mail: info@animalaid.org.uk
Web site: www.animalaid.org.uk

Animal Aid investigates and exposes animal cruelty. The organization stages street protests and education tours. It also publishes educational packets for schools and colleges.

Animal Alliance of Canada
221 Broadview Avenue, Suite 101
Toronto, ON   M4M 2G3   Canada
(416) 462-9541 • fax: (416) 462-9647
e-mail: info@animalalliance.ca
Web site: www.animalalliance.ca

The Animal Alliance of Canada is an animal rights advocacy and education group that focuses on local, regional, national, and international issues concerning the respectful treatment of animals by humans. Animal Alliance acts through research, investigation, education, advocacy, and legislation. Publications include fact sheets, legislative updates, editorials, and the newsletter *Take Action*.

Animal Liberation Front (ALF)
21044 Sherman Way, #211, Canoga Park, CA   91302
(818) 932-9997 • fax: (818) 932-9998
e-mail: press@animalliberationpressoffice.org
Web site: www.animalliberationfront.com

ALF seeks to end worldwide animal exploitation and otherwise reduce the suffering of animals. The organization's Web site contains information on how to take action against institutionalized animal exploitation. The site also archives personal stories of animal activism, opinion articles, interviews, and profiles of noted activists. Educational materials on vivisection, animal experimentation, and toxicity testing are also available to download.

Animal Welfare Institute (AWI)
PO Box 3650, Washington, DC   20007
(703) 836-4300 • fax: (703) 836-0400
e-mail: awi@animalwelfare.org
Web site: www.awionline.org

AWI is a nonprofit charitable organization working to reduce pain and fear inflicted on animals by humans. It advocates the humane treatment of laboratory animals and the development and use of nonanimal testing methods. AWI encourages humane science teaching and the prevention of painful experiments on animals in the classroom. In addition to publishing *AWI Quarterly*, the institute also offers numerous books, pamphlets, and online articles.

Foundation for Biomedical Research (FBR)
818 Connecticut Ave. NW, Suite 900, Washington, DC   20006
(202) 457-0654 • fax: (202) 457-0659
e-mail: info@fbresearch.org
Web site: www.fbresearch.org

FBR is the oldest organization in the United States dedicated to promoting animal research in the pursuit of improving human and animal health. It therefore opposes animal activists who try to thwart the use of animals in biomedical research. The organization's Web site contains press releases and fact sheets on the value of animal research.

Fund for Animals
200 West 57th St., New York, NY   10019
(888) 405-3863
Web site: www.fundforanimals.org

The Fund for Animals was founded in 1967 by prominent author and animal advocate Cleveland Amory. It remains one of the largest and most active organizations working for the welfare of both wild and domesticated animals throughout the world. The fund promotes its message through education, lobbying, and litigation.

In Defense of Animals
3010 Kerner Blvd., San Rafael, CA   94901
(415) 388-9641 • fax: (415) 388-0388
e-mail: ida@idausa.org
Web site: www.idausa.org

In Defense of Animals is a nonprofit organization established in 1983 that works to end the institutional exploitation and abuse of laboratory animals. The organization publishes fact sheets and brochures on animal abuse in the laboratory and how to live a cruelty-free lifestyle.

Institute for In Vitro Sciences (IIVS)

21 Firstfield Rd., Suite 220, Gaithersburg, MD   20878
(301) 947-6523 • fax: (301) 947-6538
Web site: www.iivs.org

IIVS is a nonprofit, technology-driven foundation for the advancement of alternative methods to animal testing. Its mission is to facilitate the replacement of animal testing through the use of in vitro technology. IIVS provides educational and technical resources available to corporate, government, and public interests. It also makes its published articles available on its Web site.

Medical Research Modernization Committee (MRMC)

3200 Morley Rd., Shaker Heights, OH   44122
(216) 283-6702
Web site: www.mrmcmed.org

MRMC is a national health advocacy group composed of physicians, scientists, and other health care professionals who evaluate the benefits, risks, and costs of medical research methods and technologies. The committee believes that animals are inadequate models for testing medical treatments and that research money would be better spent on human clinical trials.

National Animal Interest Alliance (NAIA)

PO Box 66579, Portland, OR   97290
(503) 761-1139
e-mail: naia@naiaonline.org
Web site: www.naiaonline.org

NAIA is an association of business, agricultural, scientific, and recreational interests formed to protect and promote humane practices and relationships between people and animals. NAIA provides the network necessary for diverse animal rights groups to communicate with one another, to describe the nature and value of their work, to clarify animal rights misinformation, and to educate each other and the public about what they do. NAIA serves as a clearinghouse for information; it also publishes the bimonthly newspaper *NAIA News*.

Patients' Voice for Medical Advance
PO Box 504, Dunstable, Bedfordshire LUS 5WS
United Kingdom
(44) 58 286 7766 • fax: (44) 58 286 7766
e-mail: info@patientsvoice.org.uk
Web site: www.patientsvoice.org.uk

Patient's Voice for Medical Advance is a patients' group formed to voice support for humane research into disabling, incurable, and progressive diseases. The organization promotes the following objectives: a greater public understanding of the methods, aims, and benefits of animal research; the provision of the resources necessary for medical research to be conducted; and appropriate legislation relating to medicine and medical research. The group publishes the *Hope* newsletter.

People for the Ethical Treatment of Animals (PETA)
501 Front St., Norfolk, VA   23510
(757) 622-7382 • fax: (757) 622-0457
e-mail: peta@norfolk.infini.net
Web site: www.peta.org

An international animal rights organization, PETA is dedicated to establishing and protecting the rights of animals. It focuses on four areas: factory farms, research laboratories, the fur trade, and the entertainment industry. PETA promotes public education, cruelty investigations, animal rescue, celebrity involvement, and legislative and direct action. It produces numerous videos and publishes *Animal Times*, various fact sheets, brochures, and flyers.

Physicians Committee for Responsible Medicine (PCRM)
5100 Wisconsin Ave. NW, Suite 400, Washington, DC   20016
(202) 686-2210
e-mail: pcrm@pcrm.org
Web site: www.pcrm.org

Founded in 1985, PCRM is a nonprofit organization supported by physicians and laypersons that encourages higher
standards for ethics and effectiveness in research. PCRM promotes using animal alternatives in both research and education. The committee publishes the quarterly magazine *Good
Medicine* and numerous fact sheets on animal experimentation issues.

Uncaged Campaigns
9 Bailey Lane, Sheffield   S1 4EG
UK
(44) 14 272 2220 • fax: (44) 14 272 2225
e-mail: info@uncaged.co.uk
Web site: www.uncaged.co.uk

Uncaged Campaigns works to end vivisection and to ascribe
moral and legal rights to animals. It stages demonstrations as
well as lobbies for legislative change. The organization's Web
site contains fact sheets and an archive of news articles.

Bibliography of Books

Diane L. Beers — *For the Prevention of Cruelty: The History and Legacy of Animal Rights Activism in the United States.* Athens, OH: Swallow, 2006.

Ruth Ellen Bulger et al. — *The Ethical Dimensions of the Biological and Health Sciences.* New York: Cambridge University Press, 2002.

Peter Carruthers — *The Animals Issue: Moral Theory in Practice.* New York: Cambridge University Press, 1992.

Carl Cohen and Tom Regan — *The Animal Rights Debate.* Lanham, MD: Rowman & Littlefield, 2001.

David K.C. Cooper and Robert P. Lanza — *XENO: The Promise of Transplanting Animal Organs into Humans.* New York: Oxford University Press, 2000.

Pietro Croce — *Vivisection or Science?: An Investigation into Testing Drugs and Safeguarding Health.* New York: Zed, 1999.

Alix Fano — *Lethal Laws: Animal Testing, Human Health and Environmental Policy.* New York: St. Martin's, 1998.

Lawrence Finsen and Susan Finsen — *The Animal Rights Movement in America: From Compassion to Respect.* New York: Twayne, 1994.

Michael Allen Fox   *The Case for Animal Experimentation: An Evolutionary and Ethical Perspective.* Berkeley: University of California Press, 1986.

Julian H. Franklin   *Animal Rights and Moral Philosophy.* New York: Columbia University Press, 2005.

Temple Grandin and Catherine Johnson   *Animals in Translation: Using the Mysteries of Autism to Decode Animal Behavior.* San Diego: Harvest, 2005.

C. Ray Greek and Jean Swingle Greek   *Sacred Cows and Golden Geese: The Human Cost of Experiments with Animals.* New York: Continuum, 2000.

Anita Guerrini   *Experimenting with Humans and Animals: From Galen to Animal Rights.* Baltimore: Johns Hopkins University Press, 2003.

Harold D. Guither   *Animal Rights: History and Scope of a Radical Social Movement.* Carbondale: Southern Illinois University Press, 1998.

Andrew Linzey and Paul Barry Clarke, eds.   *Animal Rights: A Historical Anthology.* New York: Columbia University Press, 2004.

Mary Midgley   *Animals and Why They Matter.* Athens: University of Georgia Press, 1983.

Ingrid Newkirk   *Save the Animals.* New York: Warner Books, 1990.

Martha C. Nussbaum · *Frontiers of Justice: Disability, Nationality, Species Membership.* Cambridge, MA: Belknap, 2006.

Barbara Orlans · *In the Name of Science: Issues in Responsible Animal Experimentation.* New York: Oxford University Press, 1993.

Tony Page · *Vivisection Unveiled: An Exposé of the Medical Futility of Animal Experimentation.* Oxford, UK: Jon Carpenter, 1998.

Ellen Frankel Paul and Jeffrey Paul, eds. · *Why Animal Experimentation Matters: The Use of Animals in Medical Research.* New Brunswick, NJ: Transaction, 2001.

Tom Regan · *Empty Cages: Facing the Challenge of Animal Rights.* Lanham, MD: Rowman & Littlefield, 2004.

Mark Rowlands · *Animals Like Us.* London, UK: Verso, 2002.

Peter Singer · *Animal Liberation.* New York: Random House, 1990.

Peter Singer, ed. · *In Defense of Animals: The Second Wave.* Malden, MA: Blackwell, 2006.

Richard Sorabji · *Animal Minds and Human Morals: The Origins of the Western Debate.* Ithaca, NY: Cornell University Press, 1993.

Cass Sunstein and Martha Nussbaum — *Animal Rights: Current Debates and New Directions.* New York: Oxford University Press, 2004.

Donna Yarri — The *Ethics of Animal Experimentation: A Critical Analysis and Constructive Christian Proposal.* New York: Oxford University Press, 2005.

Index

The Great Gasbag

Also by Joy Behar

*Joy Shtick: Or What Is the Existential Vacuum and
Does It Come with Attachments?*

*When You Need a Lift: But Don't Want to Eat
Chocolate, Pay a Shrink, or Drink a Bottle of Gin*

An A-*to*-Z
Study Guide
to Surviving
Trump World

JOY BEHAR

The Great Gasbag

HARPER

NEW YORK · LONDON · TORONTO · SYDNEY

HARPER

A hardcover edition of this book was published in 2017 by
HarperCollins Publishers.

THE GREAT GASBAG. Copyright © 2017 by Joy Behar. All rights
reserved. Printed in the United States of America. No part of
this book may be used or reproduced in any manner whatsoever
without written permission except in the case of brief quotations
embodied in critical articles and reviews. For information, address
HarperCollins Publishers, 195 Broadway, New York, NY 10007.

HarperCollins books may be purchased for educational, business,
or sales promotional use. For information, please email the Special
Markets Department at SPsales@harpercollins.com.

FIRST HARPER PAPERBACKS EDITION PUBLISHED 2018.

Designed by Bonni Leon-Berman

Library of Congress Cataloging-in-Publication Data has been
applied for.

ISBN 978-0-06-269991-6 (pbk.)

18 19 20 21 22   LSC   10 9 8 7 6 5 4 3 2 1

Dedicated to the

65,853,216

American

voters

who knew

better.

Author's Note

In 2015, when the presidential campaigns first began, my agent called me begging, *begging* me to write a political book. I told him I was too busy. Then he called my manager and started begging him to get me to write a book. He, too, told him I was busy. Then he called my husband, who slept through the call. Ditto, my daughter. Then the sly puss called my brilliant (then-four-year-old) grandson, who took the call. But the kid was slyer than he was. He told him, "My nana's a busy woman. She's on TV every day, she does live performances and occasional film work; she doesn't have time to write a book. But I'll tell you what, if something really weird happens, like that crazy guy with the orange face wins, call us back."

Well, on November 9, 2016, the day after the election, my phone rang again. I didn't need to be begged. I didn't even need to be asked. By the time I woke up that morning, the horror of what happened the night before had already sunk in. When I looked in the bathroom mirror, instead of seeing the gorgeous punim you all see on TV every day looking back at me, I saw Edvard Munch's *The Scream*. It was time to put pen to paper.

But what to write? Given the mercurial nature of Trump and the chaos of his campaign, I knew I couldn't write a traditional book, because in Trump World, like in the Emerald City of Oz, "things around here change so quickly" that if I wrote something in the morning, it might be out of date by dinnertime.

In fact, despite all due diligence and with an eye on timeliness, I'm pretty sure that by the time you read this, some of the people I've written about will have: been fired (Sean Spicer), been reassigned (Kellyanne Conway), left the country (Melania), been jailed (General Flynn), or moved to a kibbutz in Israel (the Kushners).

What to write came to me quite by coincidence. I was sitting in a Starbucks across from *The View* studio one day, on the Upper West Side of Manhattan, when I overheard a man and a woman talking. (And by "overheard," I mean I was eavesdropping.) Since 83 percent of the people in that neighborhood are psychiatrists, psychologists, therapists, or social workers, I thought their conversation would be worth "overhearing." The woman said, "I saw an accident on Eighty-Sixth Street this morning." The man replied, "You wanna talk about accidents? Trump has the nuclear codes. He might accidentally set off a missile. So, what happened on Eighty-Sixth Street?" The woman answered, "A taxi ran a red light and hit a pole." And the man said, "You wanna talk red? Trump's in bed with the Russians! How's that for red?"

It was like word association. Suddenly, it dawned on me—Dr. Freud and the woman with the decaf latte gave me the concept for this book: an alphabetical guide to Trump World.

It's perfect for me; I used to be a New York City public school teacher. (I taught delinquents the difference between *who* and *whom*.)

So, now that I knew what the book was, I had to figure out what to call it. Choosing a title for a book is almost as important as the book itself, because if the fifteen words on the cover don't work, nobody will read the fifty thousand words inside. Think about it——If *Uncle Tom's Cabin* had been called *Uncle Tom's Condo*, do you think it would have become an American classic? Would Harriet Beecher Stowe have gotten a three-book deal and a TV movie offer from Lifetime? No. *Green Eggs and Ham* made Dr. Seuss a literary giant. I don't think *Egg White Omelet and Chicken* would have even put him on the map.

Needless to say, a lot of thought went into choosing the title for this book. I knew it was going to be subtitled *An A-to-Z Study Guide to Surviving Trump World*, but I wanted the main title to be both clever and on point. And since I'm a fan of the classics, that's where I started. Here are some other titles I considered before deciding on *The Great Gasbag*:

Moby Dickhead
Con with the Wind
Pride and Very Prejudiced
Catcher in the Lie
Not Such Great Expectations
The Age of Ignorance
Gullible's Travels
A Farewell to the Constitution
The Son-in-Law Also Rises
War and Hairpiece

Maybe I'll use one of those titles for the follow-up book. We'll see. Anyway, I hope you have as much fun reading this as

I did writing it. (And by "fun," I mean the catharsis of writing saved me a fortune in therapy bills.)

Happy reading!
Joy

P.S. My agent didn't actually beg me to write this book. That's an "alternative fact," something you can read about in the *A*s.

[Disclaimer]

Dear ~~President Trump~~ (no, I can't bring myself to do it)

Dear ~~Mr. President~~ (same thing, ucch)

Dear ~~Donald,~~ (even though I was at one of his weddings, it feels too informal)

Dear ~~Orange Devil~~ (too much, too soon)

Dear Mr. Trump (boring, but whatever),

First, let me say that I don't imagine you'll read this book because I know you're way too busy watching TV and tweeting, and also because it's not written in Russian. I also know that you have thin skin and don't react well to jokes made at your expense, so on the off chance that Kellyanne or Ivanka tells you about it, please note that *The Great Gasbag* is satire, a protected literary genre, and that I, Joy Behar, am a satirist. If you don't believe me, ask my fifth-grade teacher, Mrs. Pellegra, who called me the "Jonathan Swift of P.S. 168." (I don't know where Mrs. Pellegra is these days, but Mount Carmel Cemetery might be a good place to start looking.)

The definition of *satire* is:

A genre of literature . . . in which vices, follies, abuses, and shortcomings are held up to ridicule, ideally with the intent of shaming individuals, corporations, government, or society itself into improvement. Although satire is usually meant to be humorous, its greater purpose is often constructive social criticism, using wit to draw attention to both particular and wider issues in society.[1]

Notice how it says satire is used as a tool to improve things? That's important, not just because it explains intent, but because it means that in addition to my being a comedian, talk show host, and satirist, I'm also a giver. And if you don't believe me, ask my old Girl Scout troop leader, Mrs. Defazio. (I don't know where she is these days, but you can probably get her number from Mrs. Pellegra.)

Happy reading!
Joy

1   Robert C. Elliott, "The Nature of Satire," *Encyclopedia Britannica*, 2004.

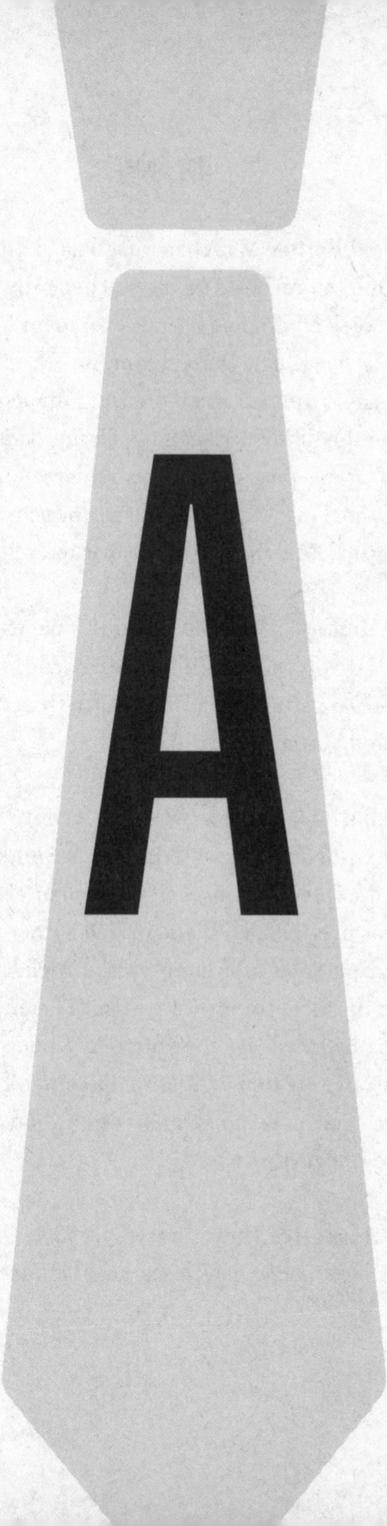
A

A **is for Acid Reflux.** Which is what 65,853,216 Americans get every time Trump holds a televised pep rally or press conference. Last week I had some friends over to my house for supper. Just as we sat down, The Donald came on TV, and all of a sudden eight stomachs rumbled and roared simultaneously—it was like listening to the flatulence scene in *Blazing Saddles*. Within two seconds of Orangeface showing up on-screen, my friends were yelling, "Gino, I'm gassy," and "Angie, the sausage and peppers are coming up." And they hadn't even eaten yet!

A **is for Alimony.** I have not seen the paperwork on any of Donald's divorces, but I'll bet he's spending a lot more on Valentine's Day gifts for Vladimir Putin than he is on alimony for Ivana and Marla combined.

A **is for All's Noisy on the Western Front.** Remember how nice and quiet things were before November 8, 2016? No chaos, no crazy, no wall-to-wall havoc. For sixteen years, the country was pretty much scandal-free. Other than George W. Bush invading the wrong country and Dick Cheney shooting his BFF in the face, things were calm. The only "scandal" No Drama Obama faced was the "birther" idiocy, which was just racist nonsense created by Trump. But since The Donald took over, we've had more noise and commotion than a Lamaze class at the Duggars' house.

A **is for Alternative Facts.** *Alternative facts* is an oxymoron, like *diet soda*, *deafening silence*, and *President Trump*. Alternative facts are lies. I prefer *lies* because "Alternative-facter, alternative facter, pants on fire," offends the Maya Angelou in me.

Some little white lies are acceptable. For example, whenever you're asked, "Does this dress make me look fat?" the answer is always, "No." (Especially if the person asking is J. Edgar Hoover.) Another example of when it's okay to lie: Last week, my grandson asked me, "Nana, how come Arnold Schwarzenegger's housekeeper's son can lift a couch over his head? And why does he have an Austrian accent?" Because my grandson is only six, and I was too exhausted that day to launch into a discussion of DNA, I simply said, "Your Mommy's on the phone; she says she wants to buy you some brand-new toys and give you one hundred dollars!" Was that wrong of me?

Trump's spokespeople are savvy enough not to own the lies themselves, so they pin them on him—and he's not smart enough to know they're doing it. Instead of saying that the president is actually lying or using alternative facts, they simply say, "The president believes . . . ," which

A is for **Alternative facts**. Alternative facts are *lies*. I prefer lies because "Alternative-facter, alternative facter, pants on fire," offends the Maya Angelou in me.

gets them off the hook for his particular brand of insanity. We've all heard his flacks say, "The president believes that three to five million illegal ballots were cast for Hillary Clinton, which cost him the popular vote," and "The president believes that Barack Obama was born in Kenya." Or, "The president believes Obama wiretapped his apartment in Trump Tower," or, "The president believes Paul Manafort had nothing whatsoever to do with Trump's presidential campaign." But those aren't the only alternative facts The Donald takes to heart. There are others.

I have a lot of friends in Washington, DC, so I did a little digging. And by "digging," I mean I got them drunk and taped our conversations without their permission. And in their vodka-induced stupors, they blabbed a lot of other ridiculous things the president believes:

- Melania married him for his looks.

- Andrea Bocelli is not really blind. He only pretends to be just to beat the rigged system and get handicapped parking spots.

- Meryl Streep is a mullah from Afghanistan. And she's an overrated mullah.

- Melania married him for his sexual prowess.

- Barbra Streisand, Madonna, Adele, Justin Bieber, Tony Bennett, Bruce Springsteen, Fleetwood Mac, Sam Cooke, Frank Sinatra, Dean Martin, and Billie Holiday sang "great" at his inauguration.

- Melania married him for his giant hands.

- Corinthians II was better than Corinthians III but not as good as the original Corinthians, or even the fine Corinthian leather in his Dodge convertible.

- Voter fraud in the 2016 election was so rampant that Vladimir Putin was cheated out of being the junior senator from the great state of New York.

- Sasha and Malia are two-thirds of the defunct singing group Destiny's Child. And Beyoncé got out because she was jealous of their Secret Service protection.

- China made Mexico pay for the Great Wall.

- Marla Maples married him for his looks.

- NASA owes him fifty million dollars because Neil Armstrong planted the flag on a plot of land on the moon that he owns.

- Angela Merkel would be a better leader if she had cheek implants and tighter abs.

- His wives Ivana and Melania were both born in Altoona, Pennsylvania. And they both speak perfect English without a trace of an accent.

- The Statue of Liberty should produce a birth certificate or be deported back to France.

- America's children are not obese; the media is using special cameras to make kids look fat, just to hurt food companies.

- Marla Maples married him because of his sexual prowess.

- We should take sand from Iraq because it will be good for the terrarium industry.

- California is a foreign country, and he plans on invading it sometime between now and his next dye job.

- Marla Maples married him because of his giant hands.

- Mike Pence is a transgender bathroom attendant from Fond du Lac, Wisconsin.

- The two hundred thousand women who "marched" in Washington were actually just standing on line to get into the restaurant in his amazing, great, fabulous, super-duper, wowee-zowee hotel.

- The national anthem should be replaced with "I've Got to Be Me."

- The publishing industry is rigged against him because *The Diary of Anne Frank* sold more copies than *The Art of the Deal*. Donald feels *The Art of the Deal* is way more touching.

- His next wife will marry him because of his looks, sexual prowess, and giant hands.

A is for Anti-Choice. The A-word is the F-word of right-wing, Republican politics. It's more important than the B-word (*business*), the E-word (*education*), or the H-word (*health care*); the only word it's not more important than is the M-word (*money*).

Republicans believe that life begins at conception. If life does begin at conception, then my daughter was actually born on November 8 . . . or November 14, 22, or 27, or January 9. (I can't believe what a horny housewife I was back then.) And she was conceived either in my house; in a Motel 6 on Kissena Boulevard, Queens; or in a Chevrolet in the parking lot of a Motel 6 on Kissena Boulevard. My ex-husband spared no expense.

If life begins at conception, then everyone in this country is actually nine months older than it says on their driver's licenses. So, I guess millions of old people are owed billions of dollars in missing Social Security payments. Wouldn't it be easier to just say that life begins when you're old enough to get Botox and you're on your third marriage?

A is for Antidepressants. Which is what 65,853,216 Americans started popping on November 9, 2016.

A is for Anxiety. Ever since Election Night, when a journalist friend texted me, "Holy shit," which told me that the unthinkable was about to happen, I have been in a continuous state of high anxiety. Could it be that for the next four years, this bloviating incompetent would be in charge of the nuclear codes? Friends of mine—the ones who are *not* normally on Prozac—suddenly were contacting psychopharmacologists on the Internet for meds. Fortunately, I have a TV show on which to rant and rave on a daily basis, so I remained drug-free. Unfortunately, all my ranting and raving is not nearly enough. In order to inform future generations of the decline of democracy as we know it, one must put things in writing. Hopefully, when millennials and Generation Z read this (or listen to it on their headphones when they're at work writing code for a tech giant), they will go to the polls and vote with their heads and not write in "Teresa Giudice" or "Kanye" or whoever is the reality star of the day. Also, I need to exorcise the intense emotional upheaval being caused by this egomaniacal con man who thought best to kick off Sexual Assault Awareness Month by defending the since-fired serial harasser Bill O'Reilly, whose idea of foreplay is using a loofah as a sex toy. What do you expect from the grabber in chief?

A is for Appalled. Which is what my grandson was when Trump was announced the winner. The boy had a stunned look on his sweet, innocent little face, and he said, "Nana! What the fuck?"

A is for *The Apprentice*. Nothing says "qualified to be president" quite like being on a reality show. Why else is Omarosa sitting in the West Wing? I doubt The Donald would have appointed Rick Perry energy secretary if he hadn't first appeared on *Dancing with the Stars*. Poor Gary Busey was hoping to be head of the Food and Drug Administration, but they were afraid he would have a relapse and steal all the drugs. Donald should put the women from *Mob Wives* in there—at least they'd know how to handle Paul Ryan and Mitch McConnell. And Ramona would bitch-slap Trey Gowdy in a New York minute.

A **is for Argentina**. Or, as Steve Bannon and Steve Miller think of it, "our weekend getaway." And I do mean getaway!

A **is for Arrested Development.** Donald Trump is seventy but acts like he's seven. Forget the tantrums and name-calling and making faces. Every time he signs an executive order, he holds it up to show everyone. He's so proud of himself, like a boy who's pulled an ouchless Band-Aid off his knee without crying. Then he flashes this giant, fake, shit-eating grin. I'm not sure if he's smiling because he thinks it's a good executive order or because he's spelled his name right and stayed within the lines.

A **is for the Arts.** Donald Trump wants to defund the National Endowment for the Arts, probably because he hates anything that's more well-endowed than he is. Next year, he plans on getting rid of Ron Jeremy and all photos of Gary Cooper.

A **is for Atlas.** Atlas is Donald Trump's doppelganger. The Big A and the Orange D have some things in common: They both had lots of children with different wives, they both have the weight of the world on their shoulders, and they both think they're gods. The only differences are that (a) Atlas really had to carry the world on his shoulders as a punishment handed down by Zeus; Trump only *thinks* he has the weight of the world on his shoulders because he's a paranoid narcissist; and (b) Atlas never called his daughter a "piece of ass."

A is for Authoritarian. All the media types keep saying Trump has "authoritarian tendencies." I disagree. Sophia on *The Golden Girls* has authoritarian tendencies. The bitch who cut in front of me on line at Chico's has authoritarian tendencies. Trump is a bombastic blowhard and a bully. Now, would they please hide the nuclear codes from him? (Ivanka, you're in the White House. Sneak in and get the codes away from him. Do it while he's tweeting; he'll never notice.)

B **is for Bankruptcy**. Or, as Trump thinks of it, business as usual. Most people consider filing for bankruptcy a sad, traumatic, life-altering, devastating process. Donald Trump considers it "Tuesday." To be fair, The Donald has never declared personal bankruptcy—don't worry, the money he bilked you out of is safe and sound—but he *has* declared corporate bankruptcy *six times*. That's a lot. Think about it: George W. Bush allowed half of Lousiana to drown only that one time, Strom Thurmond sired only one black child, and Howard Taft got stuck in the White House bathtub only once.

B **is for Steve Bannon**. What you probably don't know is that Steve Bannon is the love child of Darth Vader and Leni Riefenstahl. For some odd reason, Trump listens to him. On a scale of one to painful rectal itch, Bannon's a nine. He basically wants to destroy democracy while making sure he has lots of money and power when it's all over.

Oh, wait. I'm wondering if the "odd reason" Trump listens to Bannon is because Bannon has pictures of Trump naked in a bubble bath with a goat, a rubber hose, and a blow-up doll named Cindy. It's possible.

B **is for Base (Trump's, that is)**. Nick Kristof, the two-time Pulitzer Prize–winning columnist for the *New York Times*, says that we liberals should start a movement: We have to have more empathy toward Trump voters. We should be kinder, gentler progressives, like Bernie Bros on 'shrooms. But despite Kristof's plea, people on the left are still vicious about the

Trumpies. One woman tweeted to Kristof, "I absolutely despise these people. Truly the worst of humanity. To hell with every one of them." So much for bleeding heart liberals.

Me? I save that vitriol for the grabber in chief, Donald himself.

Having said that, I must say it's difficult to go all nicey-nicey Sarah McLachlan on some of these people, half of whom do not believe in evolution, global warming, or even that the earth is older than Larry King. Some of them have drunk the Trump Kool-Aid.

For example, Trump is okay with reintroducing pesticides into the environment, and his supporters are like, "Look, I don't have two heads and I grew up sprinkling DDT on my Cocoa Puffs." Fine, but when your granddaughter is her own twin and that "certain glow on her face" is uranium, don't come to me yelling, "What happened?"

How is reintroducing dangerous pesticides a good thing? That type of thing has to stop because I'm on this friggin' planet, too. Just because the Trumpies don't have a problem eating lettuce that has hands and feet, it doesn't mean no one else does.

As far as evolution goes, I don't really give a rat's ass what you believe, but don't start teaching creationism in my kid's school. Call me kookie, but I live in reality, and I can't say with a straight face that Noah actually had all those animals on one boat and they were paired up like they'd met on Tinder.

Many liberals think Trump voters are stupid. Be advised, we're not talking about *all* Trump voters. A lot of people who voted for Trump aren't mouth-breathing troglodytes. Many of them are probably normal(ish) and just voted for change, or because they always vote Republican, or because they'd had a three-way with Ann Coulter and Mitch McConnell. Whatever the reason, *they were conned.* No, it's the hard-core Trump base I have trouble cozying up to. I'm talking about the people who go from rally to rally waving Confederate flags, sporting swastika tattoos, and routinely punching people who've spelled their signs correctly.

B is for **Bankruptcy.** Or, as Trump thinks of it, business as usual. Most people consider filing for bankruptcy a sad, traumatic, life-altering, devastating process. Donald Trump considers it "Tuesday."

Liberals like to point out that a solid 47 percent of the Trump base thinks Frederick Douglass is still alive (and that Barbara Walters is dating him). I imagine the other 53 percent has no idea who Frederick Douglass was. But I can forgive that; I don't know everybody who fought for the slave states. But some of the other things they buy into defy logic. A lot of Trumpies still believe that Obama was born in Kenya (even after DT 'fessed up that those claims weren't true); many of them believe Obama was involved in 9/11 (even though he didn't become president until 2009); some of them actually believe Hillary Clinton used a body double to hide the fact she had Parkinson's, MS, and AIDS—at the same time. (For that to be true, her body double would have had to be David Blaine or both Penn *and* Teller.) When I hear such craziness, I shake my head and think, *What are these people smoking*?

But when I read that nearly half of them think that Black History Month should be counteracted with White History Month, I had to rethink the whole thing. First of all, it's White History Month every month, okay? So why would you need *one* month for it? Do these people not realize that if you choose one month for White History Month, then you are losing the other eleven? Okay, I'm calming down. I'm trying the Nick Kristof experiment.

B is for Believe Me. Whenever Trump says an outrageous or false thing, he usually follows it with the words "believe me." For example, "I'm going to defeat ISIS in my first thirty days. Believe me"; "I'm going to replace Obamacare with something great. Believe me"; "I may have small hands but there's no problem *down there*. Believe me." If you take away only one thing from this book, let it be "never believe someone when he says, 'Believe me.'"

Believe me.

B is for Beriberi. The only disease to be covered by the Republican health care plan. Beriberi is a thiamine-deficiency disease found almost exclusively on the island of Java. Which is why the plan covers it; no one in America gets beriberi.

B is for Bigly. Believe it or not, *bigly* is actually a word, but it's rarely used in English. Or French. Or Dutch. Or Spanish. Or even that click-click language they speak in parts of Africa. It's one of those words that you never use and avoid saying, like *obstreperous*, *antediluvian*, or *cunnilingus*. *Bigly* is an adverb meaning "largely or generously," two words rarely associated with Donald Trump. (Ironically, he uses it a lot.) There was a lot of conversation as to whether Trump was using *bigly* or was simply mispronouncing *big league*. Either way, it doesn't matter; it's not exactly soaring oratory.

B is for Blowhard. No, I'm not talking about fabulous gay weekends on Fire Island. I'm talking about nightmarish weekdays listening to Sean Hannity on the radio. Lots of media pundits have big mouths and rant and rave for ratings, but few of them have as little information as Sean Hannity. He's like an unfunny episode of *Seinfeld*: he's carrying on about nothing. Whenever I listen to him, which is when I'm trapped in a broken elevator or being held hostage in the trunk of Steven Mnuchin's car, I can't believe my ears—not just because of the paucity of facts, but because I don't know how he manages to speak so clearly with his lips attached to Trump's ass.

B is for Body Snatchers. At first blush, some of the people on Team Trump appear to be nice people, pleasant almost.

James Glover/Reuters

They seem like the kind of folks you could have a drink with or invite to the house for dinner and not have to worry about them stealing the silverware. But, upon closer inspection, you see that something is wrong with most of them, something very wrong. At first, you notice there's a slight tic or an uncomfortable hunch of the shoulders; then comes the frozen, vacant stare; and finally, the lies start spewing from their mouths like feral cats auditioning for one of those Meow Mix commercials. Then it dawns on you: this isn't just a White House press conference; it's the latest remake of *Invasion of the Body Snatchers*.

Before joining Team Trump as press secretary, Sean Spicer was a nice, albeit bland, man in ill-fitting suits. He's from Manhasset, Long Island. He has a degree in government, a wife, and two children, and he worked for the Republican National Committee. But then he got snatched up by one of the aliens from Team Trump and sucked into the pod factory of craziness. Shortly after being snatched, Spicer became a sweaty wreck, speaking in double-talk and lies, backtracking and spinning, all the while staring blankly into space. Sean, "Sleep . . . sleep . . . and be born again into a world without fear and hate!" Where's Donald Sutherland when you need him?

B **is for Breitbart News.** Another oxymoron. Breitbart has as much in common with news as Rush Limbaugh has with a twenty-four-hour fitness center. Andrew Breitbart founded the conservative website in 2007 as a platform for antiprogressive views. After Breitbart had the decency to die of a heart attack in 2012, Steve Bannon took over and declared the website a platform for the alt-right movement. Although Breitbart News is presently available in English, it's much more fun to read it out loud in a German accent.

The website is also known for its ridiculous conspiracy theories. Two of the most famous ones are that President Obama killed Supreme Court justice Antonin Scalia—his 2016 death was ruled to be from "natural causes": he was seventy-nine years old and obese—and that Obama orchestrated the "murders" of both Andrew Breitbart and, sixty days later, the doctor who performed his autopsy.

I can't wait for their next round of nonsensical theories. Maybe they'll claim that JFK's assassination was a suicide; or that Oprah is really a white Swedish boy named Anders; or that Liberace was straight.

B is for Broke. Really, really rich people never talk about how rich they are. Not once has the Sultan of Brunei ever called me to brag about the gazillion camels he owns. Which makes me think that The Donald doth proclaim too much. It's entirely possible that Trump may not be as rich as he says he is, which may be one of the reasons he won't release his tax returns. Maybe he is actually broke (in billionaire terms). He may be leveraged to the hilt and in debt up to his eyes. If that's true, how long do you think Melania will remain Mrs. Trump? I can't decide which would be more delicious, Donald not having money for health insurance right after he repeals the Affordable Care Act, or Donald living in a refrigerator box on the sidewalk in front of Trump Tower. Ahhh, a girl can dream.

C is for Cabinet. One of Donald Trump's campaign slogans was "Drain the Swamp" (along with "Build the Wall," "Lock 'er Up," "Make America Great Again," and "Obama's from Kenya"). Turns out he did drain the swamp—right into his Cabinet. Most of his Cabinet appointments were (shockingly!) old, rich, well-connected white guys, although he made sure to appoint a rich, well-connected white woman and a minority or two, either as a personal favor (Elaine Chao, wife of Mitch McConnell) or as a sop to part of his base (Dr. Ben Carson, the love muffin of the evangelical "Christians"). With few exceptions, the one thing that his Cabinet members have in common is a total lack of experience in or knowledge of the departments they're heading.

Dr. Ben Carson was appointed the secretary of housing and urban development. Apparently, his qualification was that he lives in a house. When Ben Carson was running for the Republican nomination, he said some pretty wacky things: "Obamacare is the worst thing since slavery," "Prison turns people gay," and "Joseph built the pyramids to store grain." Republicans defended his kookiness by saying, "He must be smart. He's a doctor!" I don't see the connection, but next time my bursitis erupts, I'll make sure to call my plumber.

I think Republicans love Ben Carson because he loves Jesus— which makes me think that by the end of his term, instead of housing projects, he'll have everyone living in mangers.

Then there was Secretary of State Rex Tillerson, the Marcel Marceau of the Cabinet. The man never speaks. Reporters ask him questions, and he says nothing; he just smiles at them like a puppy who's being praised for peeing on the paper. All Rex needs is white face paint and a beret and he could stand on a street corner in Paris and pretend he's walking in the wind. What qualified him to be secretary of state? Why, nothing, of course—this is Trump World! Prior to joining the Cabinet, Tillerson was the CEO of ExxonMobil, the company known for record-high prices, consumer gouging, and the huge oil spill in Alaska in 1989. Remember that? The *Exxon Valdez* was an oil tanker that ran aground in 1989 and spilled hundreds of thousands of gallons of oil into Prince William Sound. As CEO, RexxonMobil spent almost twenty years in litigation trying to minimize paying for his company's negligence. No wonder Tillerson's mute; he exhausted himself trying to explain all of ExxonMobil's fuckups.

Finally, ethically challenged crony and former Georgia governor Sonny Perdue was appointed secretary of agriculture. It's hard for me to trust a grown man named Sonny, and if I wanted a Perdue in the cabinet, I'd have chosen Frank. At least he can get me a good price on fresh chicken.

C **is for Cable TV.** Cable television is what Donald Trump watches 24/7 instead of reading. Cable news is Trump's idea of research. It's like watching *Hogan's Heroes* to learn about World War II. It scares the bejeesus out of me to think that national security is now in the hands of Tucker Carlson.

C **is for Carnage.** In his peppy little inauguration speech, Trump promised to stop the "American carnage." Does he even know what the word *carnage* means? On the very day he gave that speech, unemployment was 4.7 percent, gasoline was $2.29 a gallon, the inflation rate was 2.04 percent, and the stock market was booming. In addition, the crime rate was lower than Sarah Palin's IQ. So, where is all this carnage he's talking about? My guess? It's coming out of Steve Bannon's mouth.

C is for *Casablanca*. The other night, I was watching Turner Classic Movies with my daughter, and one of my favorite movies of all time, *Casablanca*, was on. I said, "Humphrey Bogart was sexy." My daughter was horrified. She said, "Ma, he's short, he lisps, he has buckteeth, and he spits when he talks!" I said, "He was good enough for Lauren Bacall. Who am I to say no?" She said, "Cary Grant was so much better looking." I said, "a lot of good that did me. He was interested in Randolph Scott."

Anyway, the movie ended, and I turned on the news, and right away, there was Donald Trump. Within thirty seconds, I went from Bogey to Bully. And for some weird reason (and by "weird reason," I mean three glasses of pinot noir), I thought, *What if Trump had produced* Casablanca *instead of Warner Bros.?* It would have been a completely different movie. Sam couldn't have played "As Time Goes By," because he would've quit and filed suit for not having been paid in two years; Rick's place would have gone bankrupt; Ingrid Bergman would have been alone at the airport because Trump Airlines had gone broke; and Claude Rains wouldn't have been able to walk into the fog with Bogey because all their LGBTQ rights would have been taken away.

C is for Casino. *Casino* is the Sharon Stone movie where she *doesn't* flash her cooch. Casinos are also where Donald Trump made, and lost, millions, and considered fleecing contractors and filing bankruptcies, a.k.a. "business as usual." It's hard for a casino to lose money, but somehow Trump managed to do it. Not personally, of course—he took investors' money and stockholders' money and shifted it from company to company (all the while paying himself a salary), leveraging and releveraging over and over, paying off his personal debts with corporate funds. He closed three casinos, killed thousands of jobs, and cost investors millions of dollars, all the while lining his own pockets. Turns out Trump's never been "looking out for 'the little guy.'" He's been looking out for the big guy with little hands. What better person to be in charge of U.S. fiscal policy? Alexander Hamilton is rolling over in his grave.

C is for *Caveat Emptor*. *Caveat emptor* is Latin for "Let the buyer beware." So, to the people who recently bought Donald Trump the presidency—yes, I'm talking to you, Vladimir and *Fox & Friends*—don't be surprised that it's defective. It's your fault. *Caveat emptor.* You should have seen it coming.

C is for Charlie Sheen. For years, Charlie Sheen was the undisputed Most Ridiculous Human Being in America. His diet consisted entirely of drugs, alcohol, cigarettes, and hookers. He spent more time in Betty Ford than Gerald did. But on Inauguration Day Charlie lost that coveted title. That's the day Donald Trump put his hand on a book he'd never read and swore to uphold a document he'd also never read. Forget December 7, 1941. *January 20, 2017*, is the "date which will live in infamy," because on that day, Charlie Sheen was no longer America's Top Hot Mess. The Donald was.

C is for Choice. Republicans like to talk about how their health care plan gives Americans the freedom of choice. Yes, you can choose which way you want to die, because, under their plan, you can't *afford* insurance.

Also, Republicans are a little inconsistent on the matter of choice. For example, they don't think women should be able to choose what to do with their own bodies, and they don't think people should be able to choose whom they marry, but they *do* think that churches should be able to choose which politicians they endorse (even though they don't pay taxes), and corporations should be able to choose which politicians they buy. (Maybe politicians should be required to wear the logos of the corporations who've sponsored them, like NASCAR drivers. Pence could wear a Marlboro patch on his sweater, and McConnell could wear an I ♥ THE KOCH BROTHERS on the back of his shell.)

The GOP also gives us really terrible choices in candidates to vote for: Dan Quayle? George W. Bush? Sarah Palin? Donald Trump? For a start, except for *The Pet Goat*, has any of them ever actually cracked a book? I once heard that Sarah Palin was in a library, and a passerby said to her, "What's a nice girl like you doing in a place like this?" and she demurely responded, "A library? I thought this was Home Depot." The Democrats, on the other hand, have come up with Bill Clinton, Al Gore, Joe Biden, Barack Obama, and Hillary Clinton. They may not be everyone's political cup of tea, but none of them is ignorant, stupid, or bat-shit crazy. I don't imagine Donald Trump will be up for reelection in 2020—he'll be sharing a beach house in Vladivostok with you-know-who—so who will the Republicans run? Following their criteria for presidential contenders, I have a few choices for them: Ted Nugent, Gary Busey, Franklin Graham, David Hasselhoff, Paris Hilton, Heidi Montag, Scott Baio, and Brian Griffin, the dog from *Family Guy*. I have no idea if any of them is even a registered voter, but they are all perfect for the next GOP ticket: silly, cartoonish, and free from the burden of facts.

C is for

Chris

Christ

Sorry, I couldn't fit him on one page. Chris Christie, the soon-to-be ex-governor of New Jersey—he has, as of this writing, the lowest approval rating of any governor in the history of governors, the one-man bridge-blocker, the ass-kisser supreme, was named head of the Trump administration's Opioid and Drug Abuse Commission—because who knows better about conquering addictions than a man who orders lunch by the bale? When a waitress asks Christie what he wants from the menu, he says, "Pages two through five." His three-piece suit consists of a jacket, pants, and a crockpot. The local diner offers an "All-Anyone-but-Chris-Christie-Can-Eat" Buffet.

Chris Christie became a national figure (not unlike Yankee Stadium or Mount McKinley) when Hurricane Sandy hit the Eastern Seaboard. Although, it's not clear that all the damage to the Jersey Shore was caused by Sandy—it's entirely possible that Christie jumped into the ocean to go swimming and contributed to the flooding of the one-thousand-mile-long coastline. (For all the science deniers who didn't get that joke, ask your reality-based friends about Archimedes.) When the hurricane hit, Christie did what any governor would do—he ran through the streets of Asbury Park trying to save the pizzerias, hotdog stands, and ice-cream parlors. He also met with President Obama, shook the president's hand, and accepted federal disaster aid, which is what he should have done. (One point for him!) But afterward, Republicans across the country reacted with horror—*horror*, I tell you—that he had not only met with a Democrat, but also thanked him and walked arm in arm with him on a beach. They were appalled; they would much rather have seen New Jersey turned into the Everglades.

So much for the good news about Chris Christie.

As a New Yorker, I got to know Governor Christie long before Hurricane Sandy introduced him to the rest of the country. In a 2011 town hall meeting, a New Jersey woman asked Christie why he was cutting the budget for public schools while sending his own kids to private schools. He graciously answered, "It's none of your business. I don't ask you where you send your kids to school, don't bother me about where I send mine."

Also in 2011, he got into a squabble with state senator Loretta Weinberg over a pension matter. He asked the press, "Can you guys take the bat out on her for once?" At the time, Weinberg was seventy-six. Nice!

At another town hall meeting, when a law student and former Navy SEAL interrupted him, the bloviating bully told the SEAL, "After you graduate from law school, you conduct yourself like that in a courtroom, your rear end is going to be thrown in jail, idiot." What a charmer. Anyone who talks to a Navy SEAL like that is not only rude but stupid.

But the coup de gross, of course, was the infamous Bridgegate scandal. When I first heard that Chris Christie had blocked four lanes of traffic on the George Washington Bridge, I thought, "What the hell did he do, stand in the middle of it?" Eventually, two of the Bridgegate conspirators (and Christie associates) were convicted of crimes and went to jail. But not Christie. He didn't go to jail; he went to Denny's.

For most of 2015 and 2016, Christie served as the world's biggest lapdog, standing behind candidate Trump at every rally and event, smiling and sweating, as though he'd just run the New York City Marathon. (Yeah, right.) Why? Because he knew that Trump rewards loyalty, and he assumed that, if Trump were elected, he'd be a part of the main White House team. He assumed wrong. One of the few things Trump val-

John Lamparski/Getty Images

Starting shortstop for the New Jersey Camel Toes

ues more than loyalty is optics, and faster than you can say, "I'd like another pizza, please," Corpulent Chris was gone. He didn't rate high enough on the Teutonic Tyrant's pretty meter and was soon off the team and out of sight. This was a big mistake on The Donald's part. Having Christie in the picture standing next to him would only have made him appear slimmer. I personally love to go to the Metropolitan Museum and stand next to Rubens's nudes. Much easier than joining Weight Watchers.

C is for **Chris Christie**. When a waitress asks Chris Christie what he wants from the menu, he says, "Pages two through five."

Then, in 2017, like a cyborg returning from the dead, Christie resurfaced when The Donald made him his opioids czar. Chris Christie is now the face of opioids. One thing I know about opioids is that they make you very constipated, which is apt, since Christie is full of shit.

C is for Chutzpah. Donald Trump declared April 2017 National Sexual Assault Awareness and Prevention Month. I'm not sure if that meant he intended to bubble-wrap his tiny hands and lock himself in a windowless room until May, or that, for the other eleven months, he's free to grab, fondle, and kiss women against their will. What I *am* sure of is that Donald Trump

announcing a "Sexual Assault Prevention Month" is like Bill
Cosby announcing a "Week Without Roofies."

C is for Climate Change Deniers. There are two types of
Republican leaders who deny climate change: the Craven
and the Crazies. The Craven, which is most of them, know full
well that climate change is a problem, but they've been bought
and paid for by the Koch brothers and the fossil fuel industry,
so they have to pretend it doesn't exist. Otherwise, their owners might have to spend a dollar or two fixing it. You know the
old rule: "You break it, you buy it."

The other group, the Crazies, is far more worrisome. This
is the James Inhofe, Pat Robertson, zealot wing of the party.
They seem to believe that climate change, along with every
other disaster in the history of the country, including 9/11,
is really just God's punishment for homosexuality: You wake
up in the morning and instead of finding the newspaper on
your front porch, you find the Sea of Japan—and these wackos
believe God is doing this because a couple of lesbians in Prov-
incetown exchanged commitment rings.

C is for Cojones. "Chutzpah," for my Hispanic friends.

C is for Comedians. Stephen Colbert caught a lot of flak for
a joke he told this year on *The Late Show*. The joke was "The
only thing [Trump's] mouth is good for is being Vladimir

Putin's cockholster." Complaints came from all directions: Conservatives were outraged both about the language and that Colbert had said it about Trump, and progressives were upset because they thought it was homophobic. I don't know what other words Stephen could've used to make the joke work: *Penispouch? Sausagesack? Schlongwarmer?* It's not a joke I would tell on TV, but that's not the point. (Anyway, I work in daytime.) The point is: Colbert had the right to tell the joke. And now, with Trump, the world's most thin-skinned person, going after the First Amendment—he wants to change the libel laws to make it easier to sue the media—it's more important than ever to stand up for stand-ups.

You see, it's comedians' *job* to speak truth to power, and to do it in a funny way. Not all comedians, mind you—no one expects Gallagher to stop smashing watermelons and do twenty minutes on the Taft-Hartley Act of 1947—but you get my point. These days, I try. And along with Colbert, my fellow comedians Bill Maher, Samantha Bee, Trevor Noah, John Oliver, and Seth Meyers, are doing the heavy lifting on the left. Dennis Miller serves as a counterpoint on the right. Jon Stewart was the voice of a generation of young voters. And before all of them was the great George Carlin, who said it best: "Governments don't want well-informed, well-educated people capable of critical thinking. That is against their interests. They want obedient workers just smart enough to run the machines and do the paperwork. And just dumb enough to passively accept it." I wish Carlin were still alive; he'd have been having a field day with Trump. And he would probably have had to add *cockholster* to his list of Seven Words You Can Never Say on Television.

C is for Comey. James Comey was the FBI director, a job that is supposed to be politically impartial, yet three days before the presidential election, he announced he was going to review more "possible information" about Hillary Clinton's email server, even though his prior investigation had turned up nothing. Now, in 2017, we find out that at the exact same moment he was making that "impartial" announcement, the FBI was six months into investigating the Trump campaign's ties to Russia and possible election rigging. When asked why he hadn't mentioned *that*, Comey said he wasn't allowed to comment on ongoing investigations (as he did with Hillary). Comey wants us to think he's bipartisan, but he's not bi—I think he was in bed with Trump, though Trump fired him anyway. Now I know what you call someone who says he goes both ways but really goes only one way: a Comeysexual. I hate to say it, but I think Comey may be just as bad as J. Edgar Hoover. As far as I can see, the only difference between James Comey and J. Edgar Hoover is that Hoover wore a junior petite cocktail dress, while Comey is a size 18.

C is for Con Man. There are only two big differences between Charles Ponzi, Bernie Madoff, and Donald Trump. (1) The first two aren't conning people anymore (Ponzi's dead, and

Madoff's in jail), whereas Trump is in his duplicitous prime in the Oval Office; and (2) Ponzi and Madoff both became prison bitches, and thus far Trump has not gone to jail. But if . . . er, I mean *when* Trump gets sent to Leavenworth, my inside sources—yes, I have inside prison sources; I correspond with a couple of lifers I met online; don't judge—tell me that the boys in Cell Block H would love themselves a tangerine-blond Pillsbury Doughboy. He'd be huuuuugely popular, no?

C is for Kellyanne Conway. I've interviewed Kellyanne Conway on *The View* a few times. She seems like a nice person, so I can't imagine what reasons she could have for working for Trump as his minister of propaganda, especially because, before she joined the Trump campaign, she was working on the Ted Cruz campaign. During her time with Cruz, she said a lot of nasty things about Trump. She said he was "vulgar," "unpresidential," and that he had "built his businesses on the backs of the little guy." Then, when Cruz dropped out, she immediately joined Team Trump. I guess every person has her price. (Mine is a shiatsu massage and a pair of Spanx.) What I find interesting, though, is that when she was working for Cruz, she was telling the truth about Trump. Now that she works for Trump, she can't tell the truth at all. The woman lies more than the people ducking for cover during the "Bowling Green Massacre." She made up the term *alternative facts*; she said the crowd at Trump's inauguration was bigger than Obama's; she said that "whatever the president does is presidential"; and on and on and on. But my personal favorite is when she said that our microwaves can be used as surveillance tools.

Has Trump made us so crazy that we believe our appliances are spying on us? Did I just hear my Keurig call me a bitch?

C is for Cuba. I don't want to say Trump is ignorant or ill-informed, but when he was asked what he thought about Cuba, he said, "I loved him in *Jerry Maguire*."

D is for Damage. I remember when George W. Bush became president. I thought, *How much damage could he do in four years?* Surprise! First of all, it wound up being eight years, and we're *still* trying to undo the damage he did—little things, like lying about WMD starting two wars and not paying for them, turning a surplus into a trillion-dollar deficit, causing a housing crisis, and breaking the wall between church and state. At this writing, Trump is on course to make Bush look like Nelson Mandela.

D is for *Dancing with the Stars*. On the heels of the host of *Celebrity Apprentice* becoming the U.S. president, the GOP must be scouring reality TV for its next batch of nominees. Could Bruno Tonioli win the White House in the next election, or will the Republicans have to hunt through past contestants to find someone with the right qualifications to run the country? Maybe Dennis Rodman or Suzanne Somers? How about a Vanilla Ice–Kate Gosselin ticket? Or maybe political heavyweights like Ryan Lochte and Nancy Kerrigan? How about the Countess de Lesseps, since we seem to be returning to a monarchy anyway.

D is for Darwin. I was driving to Costco the other day and I noticed the car to the left of me had a metal fish symbol on the back of its trunk. So, at a red light, I pulled up next to the driver and asked him, "What's up with the fish? Are you a Pisces?" The guy said, "No, I'm a creationist." Before I could say, "Really? So, if God created cars, why did he stick you inside a brown Yugo? Couldn't he come up with a Porsche?" the light changed, and he and Flipper drove off.

In 1859, English naturalist Charles Darwin published *On the Origin of Species*, the benchmark study of the evolution of *Homo sapiens* and other creatures. (FYI: in 2015, an original copy of *On the Origin of Species* sold for approximately $150,000. Today, you can buy a hardcover copy of *The Art of the Deal* for six bucks on Amazon. Just sayin'.) *On the Origin of Species* has been taught to, and understood by, almost everyone on the planet to be the cornerstone of biology, and therefore the basis for modern medicine. Notice I said "almost everyone." That's because a lot of religious Republicans (and religious Democrats, too) don't believe in evolution; they believe in creationism—that is, that God created everything. They cannot fathom that we evolved from apes. No, to creationists, it's much more plausible that an imaginary man in the sky made the whole shebang in about a week.

D is for **Dyson Vacuums** ... the only things that suck more than the Trump administration.

Without getting into religion—I was born Catholic, and my husband was born Jewish, so we have enough guilt already without me worrying about offending people of faith—I don't know how God could have created everything in seven days. Look, I know how to multitask. I have a job on *The View*, I'm writing a book, I do stand-up, I have a family and a grand-

Joy Behar

child, I cook, I go out, I do things. Even if God had an amazing personal assistant, I just don't know how He could have done it all in a week. What are the odds He never needed a bathroom break, or had to run to Starbucks for a Venti Latte?

I have a lot of religious friends and family, and I *love* having them over during the Christmas holidays. I decorate the tree, I wrap gifts, I cook turkey and ham, and I revel in the smile on my grandson's face when he opens his presents (and immediately figures out what he could resell them for on eBay). I just don't think faith-based Republicans should be involved with my health care. The question I pose to them is: "If God created everything . . . didn't He also create Charles Darwin?" And what about the appendix, which is about as useless as Jeff Sessions at an NAACP meeting?

D is for Deal. One of TV's longest-running game shows is *Let's Make a Deal*. It began in 1963, starring Monty Hall and the lovely Carol Merrill, whose job was to smile and point to boxes, doors, and prizes. Contestants were given a prize, and then they had to decide whether to keep that prize or to trade it in for an unknown item hidden in a box or behind a door. The fun was not knowing which deal to take. On the show, everyone, including Monty Hall, was hoping each contestant would make the right deal and walk away happy.

Thank God Donald Trump didn't host that game show. No one would have walked away happy. That's because the way you or I would define a "good deal," is not the way Donald Trump defines it. I was taught that a good deal is one in which all sides do well and walk away satisfied. Thus, the phrase "Everybody wins." Trump's idea of a good deal is when *he* does well and walks away happy, and to hell with everyone else. *Let's Make a Deal* is still on the air, with Wayne Brady as the host. Maybe Wayne can convince Trump to come on the show as a contestant.

Contestant Trump is given a fifty-thousand-dollar Rolex watch. But that's not good enough, so he decides to trade it in for what's behind door Number One. And behind door Number One is . . . voilà! A two-week stay in Cuba with Rosie O'Donnell and Hillary Clinton, who are conducting a seminar on the history of the women's movement. Guest lecturers include Elizabeth Warren, Meryl Streep, Rosie Perez, and the entire cast of Glee. *I can only dream . . .*

D is for Dear Abby. "Dear Abby" was the most famous advice column of all time. In fact, "Abigail Van Buren" (the pen name of the column's creator, Pauline Phillips) was so good that even though she's now dead, people are still writing to her. And she still answers! A recent letter has been discovered and leaked to me, and as a public service, I'm leaking it to you:

Dear Abby,

My husband, Lenny, and I live at 1601 Pennsylvania Avenue, Washington, DC. We have new neighbors, and they—mostly he—are horrible. The people who moved out were lovely. I think the husband did something in government, and the wife was always gardening and working out. They were very smart (I hear he went to

Harvard!) and had two teenage daughters and a couple of
dogs. Beyond nice!

Long story short, they moved out on January 19, and the
next day, this loud, obnoxious orange guy moved in with a
gorgeous European woman. I don't know if she's the nanny
or the housekeeper, because she was here for only a day,
and I haven't seen her since. Might've been a "date."

Then, a pretty blond girl moved in. She kept calling
him "Daddy."

Since then, a parade of creepy people keeps coming
and going. This one oily guy, Steve Something-or-other,
comes by every single day, and within minutes, it's
complete chaos, with FBI and the NSA and CIA teams all
over the neighborhood.

Lenny and I don't know what to do. We love our house,
but we can't live like this. Should we sell? Should we move?
We've tried to get the new neighbor on the phone, but his
"daughter" keeps telling us he can't talk because their
wires were tapped. We're desperate. What should we do?

Ruth, Washington, DC

Dear Ruth,

You and Lenny should be patient. Stay calm and stay
put. I have a feeling these new neighbors won't be living
there for very long.
Good luck!

Abby

D **is for Delusion**. According to Dictionary.com, *delusion* is defined as "a false belief held despite strong evidence against it." For example, Donald Trump's saying that there were three million illegal votes cast for Hillary Clinton? A delusion. Or that President Obama wiretapped Trump Tower? Delusion. Or that thousands of Muslims in New Jersey were cheering when the towers fell on 9/11? Delusion. Or that Trump's inaugural crowd was larger than Obama's? You guessed it.

Being delusional is classified as a form of mental illness. When I said on TV that Trump is mentally ill, Bill O'Reilly called me disrespectful. Now, if anybody knows how to be respectful, it's Bill O'Reilly. Is it respectful to say that all Muslims are terrorists, like he did on *The View* the day Whoopi Goldberg and I walked off our own show? Is it respectful to say that Maxine Waters's hair looks like a James Brown wig? And is it respectful as Trump himself said to "grab them by the pussy"? In the words of the great Aretha Franklin, R-E-S-P-E-C-T. Find out what it means to me.

D **is for Dementia**. Donald Trump says so many outrageous things, and contradicts himself so often, I'm beginning to worry he might have some sort of dementia. He says one thing at 2:00, something else at 3:00, a completely different thing at 4:00, and at 6:00 he denies having said anything at all.

"I met Putin once, a long time ago. We got along great."

"I've never met Putin."

"Putin and I have a very good relationship."

"I don't think I've ever spoken to Putin."

"If I've met him, I don't remember."

How could he not remember meeting Vladimir Putin? If Trump were asked, "Do you remember meeting Sol Fishman, the president of the Boca Raton B'nai B'rith?" and he couldn't remember? Fine. I'd understand. But Vladimir Putin? There's *one* Russian dictator in the entire world, and it's him, and Trump can't remember if they met? When Donald went to staff his White House, he somehow remembered Omarosa, and she was nothing more than a contestant on *The Apprentice*, and she's not even one-third as bad as Putin. (Although she was a pain in the ass the last time she was on *The View*.)

If Donald Trump *does* have dementia and can't remember what he's saying, then, for both his sake and ours, we should get him some help. If he doesn't have dementia, and he's just lying all the time, fuck him.

P.S. Twice, I think I heard him call Melania, "Mr. Watkins." Just sayin'.

D is for Denial. This is the state where most of my Blue state friends are moving to. It's cheaper than moving to Canada or Europe. It's also the state where many Trump supporters live; it's located right between Xanadu and Fantasyland.

D is for Betsy DeVos. I'm a feminist and I want women to do well—just not *this* woman. (FYI: when I say I'm a feminist, I mean I believe in equal pay, equal opportunity, paid maternity leave, etc. It also means that I've had lunch with Gloria Steinem and gone hat shopping with Bella Abzug.) Betsy DeVos is, in my opinion, the Antichrist of education. If I went through the entire U.S. phone book, it would be hard to find anyone less qualified or more wildly inappropriate for this position. The Department of Education is all about *public* schools. Betsy DeVos is all about private schools, charter schools, Christian schools, and school voucher programs. She cares less about public schools than I care about mixed martial arts. (Truth be told, I don't even know what they are. One night, my husband was channel-surfing and he stopped on a channel with two men kicking the shit out of each other. He told me it was a mixed martial arts fight. I thought it was *The Jerry Springer Show*. I still don't understand how kicking, punching, and biting are considered "arts." Does this mean ballet, opera, and decoupage are now considered "sports"?) Putting Betsy DeVos in charge of public education is like putting gravel in your lubricant: it's counterproductive and could cause permanent long-term damage.

D is for Diet. Believe it or not, Donald Trump's presidency may be very good for women's empowerment and self-esteem. Think about it: Trump admits he judges women on their appearance and weight, and ogles only women who are supermodels or skinny bitches. So, unless you want to be ogled (or, worse yet, groped) by Donald J. Trump, it's time to start packin' on the pounds. Fuck Jenny Craig. Screw Nutri-System. Get me Ben and Jerry on the line! Hurry up. I need me some Chunky Monkey!

D **is for Disaster.** *Disaster* is one of Donald Trump's favorite words, along with *me*, *I*, *I'm*, *my*, and *mine*. According to Trump, *everything* is a disaster. In March 2016, way before he was semi-elected president, the *Chicago Tribune* listed fifty things Donald J. Trump has called (mostly in tweets) "disasters." Here is a *partial* list:

- The U.S. economy
- The U.S. border
- The U.S. military
- The U.S. deal with Iran
- Mitt Romney as a presidential candidate
- Obama's executive orders
- Former New York City mayor Ed Koch
- The Electoral College
- George W. Bush
- Ken Starr
- Obamacare
- Supreme Court justice John Roberts
- The North American Free Trade Agreement
- Hillary Clinton in general

Clearly, there are other, more accurate, words to describe most of these. For example, Leona Helmsley was a greedy bitch; Ken Starr is a sleazy right-wing tool; Ed Koch was a whiny mama's boy with male-pattern baldness and child-bearing hips; George W. Bush was a bumbling simpleton who needed the Heimlich Maneuver three times a week; and Mitt Romney is a zillionaire Mormon whose sideburns wear magic underpants.

Since very few things are true disasters, Donald Trump's overuse of the word is troubling, because (1) it minimizes and diminishes the pain caused by real disasters, and (2) it exaggerates the gravity of things that are not disasters.

Here's a short list of things that really have been or are disasters:

- The *Titanic* sinking

- Pearl Harbor

- 9/11

- The AIDS crisis

- Famine

- Earthquakes

- Tsunamis

- Hurricanes

- *Godfather III*

D **is for Drinking.** There's an old adage that when people get drunk, they lose their inhibitions and say what they really mean. I'm betting this is why Trump doesn't drink. I know this adage is true because I always had a glass or two or six of white wine before I sat down to work on this book. Pence doesn't drink, either, apparently worried he might find himself in a Bloomingdale's window wearing a teddy and six-inch heels and singing "I Will Survive."

Run, they told him, Pa-Drumpf-Drumpf-Drumpf-Drumpf

A new dic-ta-tor's born, Pa-Drumpf-Drumpf-Drumpf-Drumpf

D **is for Drumpf.** By now, everyone knows that Donald Trump's original family name is "Drumpf," and that his grandfather, Friedrich Drumpf, changed it to "Trump" when he came to America from Germany. You read that correctly: Donald Trump's grandfather was an immigrant.

I don't blame Friedrich for changing the family name from "Drumpf" to "Trump." "Drumpf" is a pretty clunky name, although it could have been worse; it could have been "Dump." Then we'd have Donald Dump. And his driver's license would read, "Dump, Donald." Take away the comma, and that's a movement I can get behind.

It's not uncommon for notable people to change their family names: Cary Grant's real name was Archibald Leach, Judy Garland's real name was Frances Gumm, Tony Curtis was Bernie Schwartz, and Rock Hudson was Doris Nussbaum.

D **is for Dyson** Vacuums. The only things that suck more than the Trump administration.

D **is for Dystopia.** During the campaign (and in the early stages of the administration), Team Trump, led by Field Marshal Bannon, painted America as crumbling and collapsing. Liberals know that that's not true, that we are not living in a dystopia. Trump's base believes dystopia is either a country in Europe or a blood pressure medicine. What *is* crumbling is Trump's agenda. And what will be happening soon is they'll all be moving to Dystopia and wearing leftover outfits from *Fiddler on the Roof.*

E **is for Economy.** Trump rants and raves that he inherited an economic mess from Obama, but, shockingly, that's not true. Other than "sixty-nine" and the figures making up a winning lottery ticket, numbers are boring, but here are a few worth remembering: According to FactCheck.org, when President Obama took office, the economy had lost 4.4 million jobs in the previous twelve months. When Trump took office, the economy had *added* 2.2 million jobs over the previous twelve months, and had *gained* jobs for *seventy-five* consecutive months, a record. When Obama took office, unemployment was 7.8 percent; when Trump took office, it was 4.7 percent. And corporate growth was running at near-record levels during the Obama years. There are negatives, to be sure, such as a slow growth rate and stagnating wages, but overall, Obama left Trump a much better hand than the one W. left Obama. The one negative I'm having the most trouble with is that when Obama took office, a Starbucks Venti Cappuccino cost $3.75. Now, it's $287,000. What's up with that? (Just kidding, Howard Schultz—you are one of the good guys.)

E **is for Education.** During the 2016 campaign, Donald Trump said, "I love the poorly educated." Of course he does! They're easier to dupe, and he can fool them into helping him get what he wants (which is more money for him, basically). If Trump loves the poorly educated so much, how come he didn't appoint any of them to his Cabinet? (As noted in the *C*s, his Cabinet may be filled with terrible, awful, and possibly mendacious people, but at least they all went to college.) When he appoints CEOs and executives to head up the gazillion companies he claims to own, do you think he hires any eighth-grade dropouts to run them?

Every civilized country in the world that calls itself a democracy has free higher education. Not us. That's because, every chance they get, Republicans cut the education budget, making it harder for kids to go to college and way harder to pay for it. Why? Because they *don't want their voters to go to college*. You see, the less info voters have, the less likely they are to ask questions. Questions like: "How come our tax dollars pay for your health insurance but not ours?" or, "Do you really want my nana to eat cat food?" or "Does Congressman Louie Gohmert have to wear a helmet just to eat soup?"

The mind is a muscle—use it or lose it. I may not do sit-ups or bench presses, but I exercise my brain as often as I can. I don't mean I lay my head on the treadmill for twenty minutes—my hair would look terrible—but every morning, I read the papers, watch the news, do crossword puzzles, and write letters and emails to people who post annoying cat videos.

E is for Eeeeewww!

> Yeah, she's really something, and what a beauty, that one. If I weren't happily married and, ya' know, her father . . .

—Donald Trump, speaking about his daughter Ivanka on *The Howard Stern Show*, 2004

EEEEEWWW IS RIGHT!

E **is for Eisenhower.** Dwight D. Eisenhower was the last Republican president I liked. He was quiet, he didn't bother anybody, he was the commander of the Allied Expeditionary Forces on D-Day, and he let Mamie comb out her bangs in the sink. He also famously warned us to be very wary of the military-industrial complex. We didn't listen. Shame on us.

E **is for Elephant.** Elephants are giant, lumbering creatures that poop all over everything, so it's fitting that the elephant is the symbol for the Republican Party. But it wasn't the party's first choice. Before they settled on the meandering pachyderm they went through other options for creatures that would fairly represent them:

- **SLUG:** a disgusting thing that serves no purpose and can be killed with salt.

- **CATFISH:** a slithery bottom-feeder.

- **MOUNTAIN LION:** a vicious killer that preys on the small and weak.

- **LAUGHING HYENA:** a mammal that thinks it's hysterical when the anteater gets its tongue stuck in a log.

- **KOALA:** a marsupial that sits around all day doing nothing.

- **PRAYING MANTIS:** an insect that went to court to change its name to "praying mantis" because it was forced to by creationist caterpillars.

- **FLY:** an insect that spends most of its time dancing in pieces of poop or buzzing around public restrooms.

E **is for Eloquence.** Words matter, and contrary to what Donald Trump said in December 2015—"I know words. I have the best words"—he doesn't. He seems to know about twenty-five or thirty words, which he repeats over and over, and not always in the right order. I think my dogs have a more extensive vocabulary. In fact, according to Dr. Stanley Coren, an expert in canine communication, the average dog can understand 165 words. Border collies, which are the smartest dogs, can learn up to a thousand words. Not only that, dogs can learn in any language they're taught. Which makes me think, spare me Trump's ridiculous border wall. Just put a couple of bilingual collies on the border and let them handle illegal immigration. They won't bite, they won't rip families apart, and they won't cost twenty billion dollars. A couple of chew toys and a case of Alpo, and they're good to go.

I miss President Obama's soaring oratory. Everyone says his speeches were the kind of speeches you hear in gospel churches. I haven't spent much time in gospel churches—I was raised to listen to priests telling me not to go to Queens College because there were "Commies there."

Presidents *should* be able to give good speeches; they're supposed to be statesmen. Democrats understand that. Franklin Roosevelt said, "The only thing we have to fear is fear itself." JFK said, "Ask not what your country can do for you, ask what you can do for your country." Bill Clinton said,

"Monica, don't bang your head on the drawer." What do we get from Donald Trump? "I have big words." The last Republican who came even marginally close to speaking eloquently was George Bush Sr., and I don't exactly consider "Read my lips, no new taxes" scintillating oratory, but at least it was a full sentence. "I see a thousand points of light!" A lovely sentiment, but I had no idea what he was talking about. I thought maybe he was seeing floaters.

Republicans call Ronald Reagan "the great communicator," and compare him to Kennedy. They always cite the speech when Reagan said, "Mr. Gorbachev, tear down this wall," as though it's great oratory. It sounds like Reagan was having a Shirley Temple–like tantrum, whimpering, holding his breath, and stamping his feet: "Tear down this wall. Me mad!"

E is for Empathy. This is the one gene that Trump and his congressional Republicans seem to be missing. I think they used to have it, but somehow, over time, it mutated, evolving into a mean gene, which is ironic, since a lot of them don't even believe in evolution.

E is for English. Donald Trump says that everyone in America should learn to speak English. Ironic, coming from a seventy-year-old man who speaks English at a sixth-grade level. He says it will help assimilation, and while that's a fair topic for discussion, our foreign-born residents aren't going to wake up one morning and magically start speaking English. They'll need to be taught. And while linguistics experts say it's more difficult for adults to learn new languages than children, it can be done. Melania Trump is said to speak five languages. She can say, "I want a divorce," in English, French, German, Serbian, and Slovene. And don't forget, President Obama learned to speak English while he was growing up in Kenya.

is for Estrogen. Something the White House is in desperate need of. There's so much testosterone in the West Wing, it's like a gay bar, except without the good-looking men. Trump had a press conference touting all the women in his administration. There were four or five, depending on whether Steve Bannon is transitioning.

is for Eugenics. Can you guess when and where eugenics became a popular practice? If you said "the 1930s" and "Germany," you win the grand prize. Do you know when and where eugenics became *un*popular? If you said "1945" and "everywhere," you win again! (And again, there's no prize.) Do you know who seems to be a fan of eugenics in 2017? If you said "Donald Trump," you're on a roll. Here are some actual quotes from our Teuton in chief:

is for Evangelicals. Where in the Bible does it say, "Thou shalt grab thy neighbor by the pussy"? Is it Leviticus or Genesis?

- "All men are created equal. Well, it's not true. 'Cause some are smart, some aren't."

- "Do we believe in the gene thing? I mean, I do."
- "I have great genes and all that stuff, which I'm a believer in."

If Trump has such great and powerful genes, how come none of his kids looks like him? Ivanka and Hans and Fritz look like Ivana; Barron looks like Melania; and Tiffany? We rarely see her, so I'm stumped on that one. And by the way, how come none of them has an orange face or salmon-colored hair? Answer me that!

E is for Europe. Once, the majority of the countries in Europe were our allies, but ever since Trump took over, they're running away faster than Katy Perry at a Taylor Swift concert. Yet, Donald Trump doesn't seem to be worried by these defections. I'm not sure if it's because he doesn't know about them, or because he figures Europe will be part of Russia by the end of his first term anyway.

Think about it this way: Trump is not welcome in Europe, a continent that's more than happy to have Roman Polanski wandering the streets. I'm not sure if it's because Europeans hate his politics or his personality. He's ill-mannered, for sure—when Angela Merkel came to the White House, Trump wouldn't shake her hand. Lucky her: you never know where those little paws have been.

But he hasn't stopped at Europe. He's spreading his rudeness all over the world. You want to talk amazing? Trump has alienated Australia, of all places. How crude and nasty do you have to be to get the Australians mad at you? These people invite you to their houses the minute they meet you. (Of course, you never go: it's a bloody twenty-four-hour flight.) Mel Gibson notwithstanding, the Aussies are fabulous! All they do is drink and laugh and eat peanut butter-and-dingo sandwiches; they're beyond nice—and *they* can't stand him. I'll bet if Donald Trump goes to the North Pole, within three weeks, the Eskimos will be telling him to "Go fuck himself" in Inuit.

E is for Evangelicals. Evangelicals are Protestant Christians who have been "born again," read the Bible as literal fact, have "turned away from sin, and are devoted to spreading the Word." Born again? The first time was bad enough.

Yet, in the 2016 election, when they had a choice to support a religious woman who is a mother and grandmother, has been married to the same man for forty-one years, and has devoted her entire adult life to public service and helping children, *or* an ignorant, amoral, lying, vulgar adulterer with five children by three different wives . . . they went with the adulterer. They chose a man who alleges that he grabs women by their privates without asking, who makes fun of the handicapped, who disses war heroes, who calls women derogatory names, and who hasn't seen the inside of a church since Ivanka was a virgin. So, I ask these evangelicals, where in the Bible does it say, "Thou shalt grab thy neighbor by the pussy"? Is it Leviticus or Genesis?

Donald J. Trump   Follow
@realDonaldTrump
   Any negative polls are fake news, just like the CNN,
   ABC, NBC polls in the election. Sorry, people want
   border security and extreme vetting.

Donald J. Trump   Follow
@realDonaldTrump
   FAKE NEWS—A TOTAL POLITICAL WITCH HUNT!

Donald J. Trump   Follow
@realDonaldTrump
   Totally made up facts by sleazebag political operatives,
   both Democrats and Republicans—FAKE NEWS!
   Russia says nothing exists.

F is for Fake News. There's no such thing as "fake news"—
unless, of course, you count Fox as news, in which case, I
stand corrected. *Fake news* is the term Donald Trump invented
to describe any factual stories or journalistic reporting that is
unfavorable to him or hurts his feelings.

Last night, I had dinner at an Italian restaurant and I
ordered the Clams Casino (which, by the way, is the name I
would use if I were a stripper). The clams weren't very good—
they were overcooked and chewy—but I didn't jump up and
start yelling at the chef that they were fake clams or it was fake
food. I just didn't finish them. The end. When Trump started

going out with Marla Maples, she was quoted in a headline in the *New York Post* that read, "Best Sex I Ever Had!" Now *that's* what I call fake news.

F is for Falsehood. *Falsehood* is the word the media and cowardly members of Congress use instead of *lie* when talking about Donald Trump's penchant for saying things that aren't true. It's kind of like calling an hour with a hooker a "date."

F is for Fiddle. Emperor Nero is said to have fiddled while Rome burned. The only differences between Nero and Emperor Trump are (1) Trump doesn't play a musical instrument, and Nero did; (2) Trump doesn't live in Italy; Nero did; and (3) Trump started the fire; Nero didn't. I mean this both literally (Trump denies climate change) and metaphorically (he's torching democracy). By the way, every time I see him on TV, my eyes start to burn. He's a visual arsonist.

F is for Filibuster. One of my favorite movies is *Mr. Smith Goes to Washington*, in which Jimmy Stewart filibusters for hours on the Senate floor until he collapses. In the old days, a senator who was filibustering actually had to stand up and speak for as long as he could. Nowadays, they only have to *declare* a filibuster, and they can sit there doing crossword puzzles or listening to Pat Boone on their Walkmans while thinking of new ways to wreck the Constitution. I think if they want to filibuster like Jimmy Stewart, then they should have to stand there and talk like Jimmy Stewart. I realize that listening to Ted Cruz speak is worse than listening to a chorus of men coughing up phlegm in a stuck elevator, but look on the bright side—eventually Ted would collapse.

is for Florida. If Trump and Congress cut Social Security and Medicare, Florida is going to be really pissed off. Florida has lots of old people. The average age of a person living in Florida is "dead." Cut their benefits, and you can bet that angry seniors will take to the streets—they'll be yelling and chanting and coughing. They'll start the Million Nana March. Okay, it might not be a march. It might be more of a shuffle but they'll protest—and there's nothing scarier than a bunch of senior citizens on Viagra driving their motorized wheelchairs toward you. If they really get mad, their dentures could be used as weapons.

is for Flynn. Michael Flynn was Trump's first national security advisor. Turns out it was a temp job. Flynn is an old Irish name, meaning "Haldeman and Erlichman."

is for Foreign Relations Committee. This is what Donald Trump uses to meet his wives.

is for Foreplay. Note to Trump voters, the Trump agenda is like foreplay: promises of free health care, jobs, jobs, jobs, and low taxes . . . It's teasing and teasing and teasing, but eventually you know you're going to get screwed.

F is for Fracking. Fracking, the process of injecting liquid into subterranean rock at high pressure to force out oil or gas, is one of the resource extraction methods our *real* presidents, the Koch brothers, are in favor of—not because it's good for the country, but because it's good for *them*. They have lots of money invested in fracking. And after buying Congress, they'd like some return on their investment. If fracking were safe and regulated, it might be a good stop-gap measure until we transferred our energy sources from fossil fuel to wind and solar. But right now, fracking is tied to water contamination and . . . earthquakes. Yes, you read that right. Oklahoma is known as the Sooner State, but since they began fracking there, you'd sooner get caught in an earthquake than a tornado. According to *60 Minutes*, in 2015 there were 907 earthquakes in Oklahoma. Nine hundred seven! Tulsa shakes more than the ground under Chris Christie's feet.

F is for Foreign Relations Committee. This is what Donald Trump uses to meet his wives.

F is for Fraud. Donald "I Never Settle Lawsuits" Trump recently settled a $25 million lawsuit for fraud against Trump University. Twenty-five million dollars. That's a lot of diplomas. Apparently, Trump University wasn't actually a university, and a number of students sued for fraud. (How the students didn't know it was a scam is beyond me. The courses included Snake Oil 101, The Basics of Bilking, and Fleecing for Dummies. Not only that, but Bernie Madoff was a professor emeritus.) Anyway, Trump had to pay out $25 mill, and the "university" is no more. Trump U? FU is more like it.

Trump University Course Offerings

Making Your Mark

How to pick a sucker in less than fifteen minutes. The telltale signs that a person is a patsy. Ten easy steps to turn a dope into a dupe.

Stakes and Steaks

From rustling cattle to bankrupting the butcher, this class teaches all you need to know about opening, and closing, a beef business—in a bull market!

Fly Me to the Ground

Starting an airline is easy. Running one into the ground takes talent. This "crash" course teaches you how to turn a loss leader into a massive tax write-off.

Advanced Pandering

How to make everyone you deal with think they're happy? Learn how to tell 'em what they want to hear. Turn brown-nosing into a shit-eatin' grin.

Tweet Your Way to the Top

Build your brand by saying outrageous and crazy things in fewer than 140 characters. A must-take class for students with limited vocabularies.

You Are Your Greater Good

Find out why altruism, charity, and ethics are bad for business, and learn how to make selfishness an asset.

The Art of the Feel

This course offers the ins and outs of pussy-grabbing. Find out how even you, a nonfamous commoner, can sexually assault women and brag about it later.

How to Make John Maynard Keynes Your Bitch

The British economist's theories spawned the rise of modern liberalism in the West. Sad! Keynes bad; Milton Friedman (economic adviser to Reagan and Thatcher) good. Guest speakers include the four people who did well in the United States as a result of Reaganomics. The dean of Trump University, Donald Trump, will make a (paid) appearance.

Ten Cents on the Dollar

Why pay 100 percent of what you owe employees, contractors, or business partners when there are semilegal ways to pay ten cents on the dollar?

Preparing a Prenup

Find out how to protect your investment. Learn how to buy silence at a fraction of the market rate. Get helpful tips on how to "convince" your exes to say nice things about you.

Just Say No

Learn how to put the old adage "Rules are for losers" into practice. This course will teach you how to hide assets, open shell companies, and bury funds overseas. As a bonus, it offers free lessons in conversational Russian.

F is for Freedom. Republicans are obsessed with the word *freedom*: individual freedom, personal freedom, financial freedom, religious freedom—they can't get enough. They yell it all the time, "Freedom! Freedom! Freedom!" It's like they have Tourette's syndrome. They could be at a funeral and they'd jump up on top of the deceased and start yelling, "Freedom! Freedom! Freedom!" trying to round up a few more votes.

F **is for Freedom Caucus.** The Freedom Caucus is a group of very conservative House Republicans who get together to vote against anything that might extend freedoms to American people they don't happen to like. For example, freedom to get a doctor to remove your brain tumor without sending your entire family to a homeless shelter, or freedom to repair bridges and tunnels that are about to collapse. The members of the Freedom Caucus want the freedom to know who's peeing in the stall next to them, and if they don't approve of that person, she'll have to hold it in. They want the freedom to carry guns everywhere, and they want insurance companies to have the freedom to deny coverage because a bullet hole is a preexisting condition.

They shut down the Republican health care plan because it gave too *much* help to poor people and the elderly. Who's in the Freedom Caucus? There are about three dozen members—too many to list here, but three prominent names are the congressmen Andy Biggs, Dave Brat, and Ted Yoho. That's right, Biggs, Brat, and Yoho. Sounds like a law firm in Toyland.

F **is for Freedom Fries.** The dumbest thing I've ever heard in my entire life, and I've heard a lot of dumb things. Don't forget: I was a teacher. If you say, "Billy, what's the capital of the United States?" and he replies, "Cantaloupe," he's not going to be in Mensa, he's going to be in Congress. Which brings me to former Republican congressman Bob Ney, of Ohio. In 2003, when France decided not to support the U.S. invasion of Iraq, Ney decided that its betrayal of America was so awful and so egregious that he had to take the strongest action he could possibly take. Enraged, he grabbed his Magic Marker, ran downstairs to the basement of the Capitol Building, and stormed the cafeteria. And with one violent flourish of his Sharpie, he changed the name of French fries to "Freedom fries"! *Sacre bleu!* That'll show them.

This histrionic display reminds me of Donald Trump. Is it possible that Bob Ney is Trump's role model? Since Trump is pissed at Canada, England, and Mexico, how long will it be before we have to refer to Canadian bacon as "Constitutional bacon," English breakfast tea as "Old Glory breakfast tea," and Mexican jumping beans as "jingoistic jumping beans." I can't wait for that executive order signing ceremony.

G is for Gall Bladder. The gall bladder is like Vice President Mike Pence. It serves no major purpose other than to store bile, and we can live happily without it.

G is for GITMO. The U.S. federal prison located in Guantánamo Bay, Cuba. After 9/11, President Bush and his vice president, Lon Chaney, began imprisoning, warehousing, and torturing people suspected of being terrorists. *Suspected*, not convicted, and, in many cases, not even charged or tried. President Obama tried closing GITMO down, and failed, but Trump plans on keeping it open and filling it up, again. Is this because he thinks he's keeping America safe, or because he plans on making it the site of the next great new Trump Hotel and Casino? I can see it now: gold-plated cell doors, marble torture chambers, shiny brass leg irons, and electric chairs with gilt head attachments. Every time you pull the handle on a slot machine, it electrocutes a detainee from the Middle East. Kill one, get one free!

G is for Guns. If guns don't kill people, why do we give our soldiers guns rather than spatulas?

G is for Giuliani. At some point during the 2016 campaign, "America's mayor," Rudy Giuliani, turned into "America's maniac." He began ranting and raving and foaming at the mouth. I didn't know whether to call 9–1–1 or Cesar Millan.

ALLISTON MEMORIAL
BRANCH
NEW TECUMSETH PUBLIC
LIBRARY
DUE DATES

--- Currently Checked Out
Items ---
Title: The Predator [1 DVD
- 107 min.]
Call number: P
Item ID: 33900904095090
Date due: 07 March 2019
23:59

User ID: 23900300509191

Title: The great gasbag : an
A-to-Z study guide to survi
Call number: 973.933092
TRUMP-B
Item ID: 33900904174507
Date due: 26 March 2019
23:59

Total checkouts for session:
1
Total checkouts:2

G is for *Glee*. The TV show *Glee*, which ran on Fox for six years, from 2009 to 2015, was a send-up of teenage life in the Midwest. It tried to entertain, but also to send a message: the characters were diverse, multicultural, and of different sexual orientations. The show was a hit, but very annoying. No matter what the story line was, no matter how intense the drama, in the middle of a scene, someone would burst into song. Who needs that? Who does that? If I'm at Macy's buying a brassiere, do I need the sales clerk to burst into a rousing rendition of "Climb Ev'ry Mountain"? No. I think if *Glee* had had fewer impromptu show tunes and more acting, it might still be on the air. That said, on the day that Donald Trump gets impeached, I plan to run out into the street and burst into "Happy Days Are Here Again."

G is for God. Republican politicians *love* God. Not like or care for, but *love*. They love Him almost as much as they love loitering in men's rooms. They try to put God into every political discussion. "Well, it's God's will that ExxonMobil got a twenty-million-dollar tax break," or, "It's God's will that Betsy DeVos's brother's company, Blackwater Security, got a billion-dollar no-bid contract." So, it makes perfect sense that Donald Trump won the Republican nomination for president. He thinks he *is* God.

G is for Gold. Donald Trump loves gold. Ever been to one of his hotels? It's shocking. The glare is so bright it can cause hysterical blindness. (Not unlike when he speaks, which can cause hysterical deafness.) Or to his New York City apartment? Everything is gold: the ceiling, the fixtures, the walls, the people. It's like living in Flava Flav's mouth.

They say money can't buy happiness. Apparently, it can't buy taste, either.

G is for Gold(en Shower). There have been rumors of a secret dossier that reveals that the Russians have a sex tape of Donald Trump and some prostitutes engaging in . . . well, how do I put this nicely? The Donald witnessing the ladies "christening" a bed the Obamas once slept in.

I don't know if it's true, and I personally don't care what Trump does in the bedroom (or bathroom); it's none of my business. If he enjoys using Svetlana as a showerhead, who am I to judge? There are plenty of fetishes that are *a lot* weirder than that:

Actirasty: Becoming aroused by the sun's rays. Not worried too much about this one; Trump's already orange. (FYI: Icarus wasn't an adventurer; he was just horny.)

Agalmatophilia: Becoming aroused by statues. Better keep Donald away from the Lincoln Memorial—and from Martha Stewart.

Climacophilia: Becoming aroused by falling downstairs. Now we know why Betty Ford stayed with Gerry all those years.

Gerontophilia: Being aroused by old people. I didn't know this was a fetish. I just think Larry King is really hot. *Grrrr . . .*

Nebulophilia: Being aroused by fog. That would explain Prince Charles's attraction to Camilla.

Given all Trump's alleged ties to Russia, his getting Siberian hookers to pish on command is the least of my concerns.

G is for Golf. On at least twenty-six occasions, Donald Trump tweeted petty complaints and nasty comments about President Obama playing (too much) golf. Yet, as president, Trump himself has spent pretty much every weekend on a golf course.

Forget the hypocrisy, why was Trump so annoyed that Obama played golf? Is it because Obama is a better golfer? Or maybe it's that Obama isn't playing on *Trump's* courses? Or . . .

G is for Government. Ronald Reagan used to say, "Government is the problem." The way *he* ran it, yes; the way Bill Clinton and Obama ran it, no. It's hard for me to take anything Reagan said seriously. The man called his wife "Mommy." That is not a sign of astute wisdom or critical thinking; it's a sign of Oedipal issues and bed-wetting. In an effort to save money on school lunches, Reagan considered ketchup a vegetable. Even worse, he privately said that he considered Kleenex a dessert and spackle a salad dressing. And this, ladies and gentlemen, is the man Republicans hold up as the beacon of leadership. Oh wait, I forgot to mention government cheese.

G is for Government Cheese. In 1981, Reagan decided to help poor people—not by giving them jobs or education or opportunities, but by giving them cheese. As part of the recently passed Farm Bill, he decided to give poor people government-surplus cheese. Because nothing says "I care" like a block of Limburger. And not for nothing, cheese is binding. Those poor people were not only down on their luck and struggling, but now they were constipated, too. This may be why people say that the Republicans don't give a shit.

G is for Grandma and Grandpa. Who doesn't love Nana and Pop? Trump and his friends, that's who, since they are not counted as close relatives in his travel ban if they come from the wrong countries. They don't seem to care much about the grandparents who were born here either. In every budget proposal they put forth, they try to cut Medicare and privatize Social Security. This is not going to work. When animals in the wild get old and sick, they go off into the woods to die. Old people don't do that. They go off to Florida and play cards and undertip the waitstaff. As for privatizing, that means letting private businessmen take care of your grandparents—businessmen like Donald Trump. If that's the plan, we all might as well just give up the card games and go wandering into the woods with the other animals.

Rudy became "America's mayor" after 9/11—a nickname he milked like a dairy cow in heat. To this day, Giuliani references 9/11 every couple of minutes. If you ask him what time it is, he'll say, "Sixteen years, eighty-three days, four hours, and twenty-six minutes since nine-eleven." In bed, his safe word is *Osama*; he refers to his penis as "the Freedom Tower." Must I go on?

Listen, on September 11, 2001, Giuliani did what any mayor of a city under attack would have done—nothing more, nothing less. Do Giuliani supporters think that if David Dinkins had still been mayor on that day he would've played tennis at the Asphalt Green instead?

If all this isn't enough to explain why Trump liked Rudy, here's the coup de grace-less: women. Like Trump, Giuliani has been married three times. Like Trump, he cheated on wife number two with wife number three; and like Trump, he takes special delight in humiliating his ex-wives. This proves that, as my friend Mitch once said, "Women will go for anything."

G is for Guns. Republicans love guns more than Rush Limbaugh loves pie. They're obsessed with them (especially the pro-lifers; ironic, no?). I ran into one of my neighbors in the supermarket, and while we were comparing meats, he blurts out, "Joy, I just want you to know that I voted for Trump because Hillary and Obama want to take my guns away. I need them for protection!" I was stunned; I dropped my chicken thighs and said, "David, nobody is taking your guns away. Obama was in office for eight years. You still have your guns, right? And Hillary didn't want to take away *your* guns, she wanted to take away guns from people who shouldn't have them. And as for protection, you have three shotguns, a pistol, and an AK-47. How much protection do you need? You live in the city, not the Sudan. Who do you think is coming after you, Girl Scouts during cookie season? I assure you, Little Mindy isn't going to pull a Glock if you don't buy a box of Thin Mints."

I don't know why today's Republicans are so fascinated by weapons. I miss the good old days, when all the Republicans cared about was saving money and wearing dowdy clothes.

The GOP base is constantly yelling, "Second Amendment, Second Amendment, Second Amendment!" as though they've actually read the Constitution. (And why should they? It's not like their leader has, or even can.) Pardon the pun, but all they know are the bullet points of the Second Amendment because they've heard some right-wing nut ranting about it on the radio.

And it's not just standard firearms they think they should be allowed to have. They think the Second Amendment gives them the right to have *any* kind of weapon they want. Why stop at assault rifles? Why not have howitzers and bazookas and cannons in the garage? How about a couple of tanks or an atomic bomb in the backyard? Maybe a nuclear submarine in the pool?

Republicans love saying, "Guns don't kill people, people kill people." I beg to differ. If guns don't kill people, why do we give our soldiers guns rather than spatulas?

After the horrible school shootings in Newtown, Connecticut, at first the pro-gun contingent suggested that the teachers should be armed. Really? I was once a teacher. Forget about giving me a handgun. I had trouble working a staple gun. Terrible idea.

So, then the Republicans said we should just keep the guns out of the hands of the mentally ill and everything will be okay. This assumes that just because you haven't been diagnosed means that you're not mentally ill. Look around you. Does that sound reasonable to assume? Where I grew up, between the cat lady, the neighborhood flasher, and the guy who used to say, "Good morning, Ted," to the fire hydrant, there were plenty of people with undiagnosed illnesses. But even if you say that only the mentally ill should not have guns, why, in February 2017, did the House GOP block a measure that would have prevented the mentally ill from getting firearms? You tell me who's crazy . . .

P.S. If we didn't have guns, when Trump's sons went hunting, they'd have to strangle the lions. Now, *that's* a fight I'd pay to watch.

H is for Hair. I was born with naturally frizzy hair. For me to look the way I look on television requires curlers, straighteners, blow dryers, keratin, and a SWAT team. But when the cameras roll . . . *c'est magnifique!* Which is why I have trouble reconciling the situation on top of Donald Trump's head. He clearly spends a lot of time getting it organized, and the process appears to involve tape, glue, pins, gel, spray, staples, nails, and industrial-grade rivets. Yet, when the cameras roll . . . *mucho ridiculoso.* As we learned on *The Apprentice,* Trump loves firing people. My suggestion? He should fire not only whoever does his hair, but whoever he has on payroll telling him it looks good.

To be fair, it's not a Trump family problem. The problem is *his* hair. The others have terrific tresses. His wife . . . er, I mean, his *wives* all have great hair. Ivana, Marla, and Melania? Not a split end in sight. The daughters, Ivanka and Tiffany? Silky and smooth. And underneath the gel and mousse, Hans and Fritz have normal heads of hair. Even the little one, Barron, comes out of Supercuts looking good. The Hair Horror belongs solely to Herr Trump.

(FYI: I'm not a big fan of making fun of people's looks, but since Trump and his acolytes have no problem mocking the disabled, denigrating women, and their alleged plastic surgery I'm making an exception.)

H is for Hans and Fritz. Hans and Fritz are my nicknames for Trump's two eldest sons, Donald Jr. and Eric. They're the winners of my Most Annoying Siblings in History Contest, an amazing achievement considering the competition: Lyle and Erik Menendez, Donny and Marie, the Olsen twins, two-thirds of the Duggars, and Cain and Abel.

I know what you're thinking: "Seriously, Joy? Cain and Abel?" Yes. To me, those two are less annoying than Hans and Fritz, if for no other reason than that they supported themselves and didn't mooch off their parents. (Adam and Eve's parenting skills are a conversation for another book.)

I could handle Hans and Fritz's smugness and hair gel, but when I saw the photos of them hunting wild animals, I lost it. There they were, in Africa, smiling from ear to ear, proudly displaying the body of a defenseless leopard they had gunned down. I was disgusted but not surprised. Why wouldn't those two go after big cats? It's a family tradition: their father grabs pussies, doesn't he?

is for **Hypocrisy**. Other than acid reflux, mimes, and people whose dentures click when they chew, nothing bothers me more than hypocrisy.

H **is for Harvard**. The school that President Obama attended . . . and Donald Trump didn't. Nah nah nah nah nah!

H **is for Hawaii**. Or, as Donald Trump thinks of it, Kenya Adjacent.

H **is for Health Care.** Until recently, whenever a politician used the words *health care*, I'd fall asleep. A glass of wine and five minutes of Debbie Wasserman Schultz on C-SPAN, and I'm out like Sunny von Bülow at a slumber party.

Democrats have been talking about health care for thirty years. And for thirty years, Republican voters have ignored them and independent voters have dozed off. It's a boring topic—important, but boring. Dems use terms like *policies* and *premiums* and *copays*, and have to fight for attention. Republicans use terms like *death panels* and *government control*, and they have their voters frothing at the mouth like rabid dogs.

So, how, you ask, did President Obama get the Affordable Care Act passed? Easy. Just like in comedy, the answer is timing: right place, right time. When Obama took office, the baby boomers had just started hitting retirement age, and suddenly every politician had constituents with preexisting conditions or with twenty-something kids who needed to stay on their parents' insurance plans. For Democrats, it was a boon; for Republicans, it was a perfect storm. The Affordable Care Act was exactly that—an affordable care act. But since that sounded good, the Republicans referred to it as "Obamacare," so it would sound bad, because they had decided that anything the "Kenyan socialist" did was bad.

But now that the "Kenyan socialist" has been replaced by a rich sociopath, it's safe for Republicans to repeal and replace the Affordable Care Act with a plan of their own—a plan that will offer less help to fewer people and give more money to more companies and huge tax breaks to the rich. They can't decide if they should call their plan "Trumpcare" or "Ryan-care." I think they should call it exactly what it is: "Dying is easy. Health care is hard."

H is for Hero. During the campaign, Donald Trump said that John McCain wasn't a war hero because he'd been captured, "and I like people who weren't captured, okay?" The truth is, McCain withstood unbearable torture for his country. I'm not talking about his five years in the Hanoi Hilton. I'm talking about his two months on the campaign bus with Sarah Palin. Talk about torture. I'd rather be waterboarded.

Donald Trump is the last person in America who should be questioning John McCain's courage. Trump avoided the draft the way Mel Gibson avoids Passover Seders. Our commander in chief got five deferments to avoid serving in Vietnam, one of them because he had a sore foot. (He probably hurt it step-ping on one of his employees.) Trump also said that when he was younger he had such a busy sex life that "avoiding STDs was his Vietnam."

Wow. Maybe one of our Wounded Warriors could point out that there's a big difference between getting blown up and get-ting blown.

H is for Hillary Hypocrisy. Nowhere was Trump's hypoc-risy on display more than on the campaign trail. Trump dumped more crap on the trail than Seabiscuit at Belmont. He kept accusing Hillary of things he himself was actually doing. Here's a small tasting menu of his hypocritical hors d'oeuvres:

- Trump accused Hillary of being a bigot. Trump says he's the "least racist person you'll ever meet." And if you don't believe him, feel free to ask the eleven million nonwhite people he plans on deporting.

- During the campaign, Trump said Hillary "never talked about policy." That's *all* she's ever talked about. At her wedding, when the minister asked her, "Do you take this man to be your lawfully wedded husband?" she said, "As per page nineteen, clause seven, of the amendment to the rider to the original proposal . . . I do." Meanwhile, Trump's idea of a policy statement is "Believe me."

- Trump has accused Hillary of being "involved with Russia." If he meant that she once gave a lap dance to Boris Yeltsin, then, okay, fine. But when Trump cuts himself shaving, vodka comes out.

- Trump said that Hillary "does not have the temperament to be president." Yet, in the past few months alone, he's picked fights with Mexico, Britain, China, Australia, France, Greece, Canada, the CIA, the FBI, the NSA, the United Nations, NATO, *SNL*, the handicapped, Rosie O'Donnell, Robert De Niro, Meryl Streep, and the Freedom Caucus, a.k.a. the Tea Party.

H is for Hindenburg. The most famous blimp disaster in New Jersey that didn't involve shutting down lanes on the George Washington Bridge.

H **is for History.** "Those who don't know history are doomed to repeat it." Variations of this quote have been attributed to many people, including Edmund Burke, George Santayana (often confused with Carlos Santana), Winston Churchill, and the guy who lives next door to me, who's caught his hand in his car door so many times he's changed his name from Elliott to "Lefty." Considering that Donald Trump knows nothing of history, I'd like to recommend the following reading material before it's too late: *The Rise and Fall of the Roman Empire* (for where the country is headed), *All the President's Men* (for where *he's* headed), and *Working on the Chain Gang* (for where his surrogates are headed).

H **is for Homosexual.** Which is who Donald Trump should hire to fix his fucking hair. Do you think any sighted gay man would let him go out looking like that? Of course not. Even a blind gay man could feel Trump's head and say, "Oh no, sister! You are not leaving this Oval Office until someone with a brush or a wand works some magic on you." And let me add that since the "party" will probably start chipping away at LGBTQ rights, the chances of his mop ever, ever improving are becoming close to nil. And who suffers for that? You and me, my dears. You and me because we have to look at it for as long as it takes to impeach this guy.

H **is for Humorless.** Critics make fun of Hillary Clinton's laugh, saying it's more a cackle than a laugh. Well, at least she has a sense of humor—to this day, the woman can't walk past a cigar shop without giggling.

Donald Trump, on the other hand, almost never laughs. He's been roasted by the Friars Club and Comedy Central, he's hosted *Saturday Night Live*, and he's attended White House Correspondents' Dinners, yet I've never seen him laugh, not once. What are the odds that at shows like that, put on by the nation's best comedians and writers, not *one* thing has ever been written or said that was even marginally amusing to him?

I'm a comedian. I've done stand-up for thirty years. And in all that time, both onstage and off, I've never met anyone who doesn't like to laugh or have a good time. Even Hitler knew how to have a good time. Check out this pic of Adolf dancing a

jig with Goering at Berchtesgaden. Is it too much to ask to see a photo of Trump and Bannon twerking at Mar-a-Lago?

There are various explanations for Trump's seeming inability to laugh. A shrink friend of mine says that "laughter relieves shame," and since Trump has no shame (see: *Shame*), he has nothing to relieve, so this theory makes perfect sense. In 2012, a social anthropologist and an evolutionary biologist wrote a paper stating that people who don't laugh practice self-deception, and self-deception leads to inflated ego and outsize self-esteem. And since Trump lies to everybody, including himself, and is a world-class narcissist, this is a definite possibility. If Trump laughed, he would be responding to something funny *someone else* did or said, and that would make the laughter about them, not him, so he's unable to do it.

I'm not a shrink, but I have my own theory on the highly important subject of why POTUS is such a sourpuss. I believe that The Donald: (a) might be too dumb to get the jokes; (b) is afraid he won't get the jokes, and he'd rather look like a scowling menace than a feckless dunce; or (c) won't admit that someone else is getting attention and applause.

H is for Hyperbole. In a previous entry, I put Trump's sons in the same category as Donny and Marie. Clearly, that's hyperbolic exaggeration—Donny and Marie actually smiled (boy, did they smile). I don't think Hans and Fritz have ever smiled. I think they got the antismiling gene from their humorless father. But I'm a comedian writing a satirical book, not the leader of the free world. If I grossly exaggerate something, it's just a joke. My words won't make Syrian refugees turn around and head back to Damascus, or make Dumb Jong-un in North Korea fire off nuclear missiles. The worst that'll happen is that someone won't laugh and someone else will go online and say, "Joy Behar's a moron." (Like I haven't heard that before! Okay, I hear it every day, but usually it's from people who actually know me.)

The point is Donald Trump *always* speaks in hyperbole: everything is a disaster or carnage or a failure—rhetoric that can be dangerous, because he's the president. When he speaks like that, it paints a false picture of reality. It helped him get elected, of course, but it could also lead to serious international trouble. I don't want Iceland invading Bermuda because of some 5:00 a.m. tweet in which Trump claimed that thousands of Bermudans were laughing about exploding lava fields near Reykjavík.

H is for Hypocrisy. Other than acid reflux, mimes, and people whose dentures click when they chew, nothing bothers me more than hypocrisy—or, as I like to think of it, the Republican way of life.

Okay, class, let's start at the top of the recent hypocrisy list and work our way down:

- In 2012, Citizen Trump criticized presidential candidate Mitt Romney for not releasing his tax returns. President Trump still refuses to release his tax returns.

- In 2016, Candidate Trump said, "Hedge fund guys are getting away with murder." President Trump appointed a hedge fund guy to be treasury secretary.

- President Trump, who didn't go to public schools, nominated a woman, Betsy DeVos, who didn't go to public schools and who doesn't believe in public schools, to be secretary of education.

- Professional Christian and all-around homophobe Mike Pence accused mothers who put their kids in daycare of having "stunted emotional growth." He then voted *against* paid family leave.

- In 2012, Mitch McConnell, the Concubine of Coal, wrote a bill about the debt ceiling. As soon as President Obama agreed to sign it, Murky Mitch decided to filibuster his own bill.

And what of the GOP It-boy, Paul Ryan? I've never seen Paul Ryan's balls, and I don't want to, but I'll bet they're huge. The smarmy Speaker once announced publicly that repealing Obamacare was "an act of mercy." Really? Is there anything less merciful than letting poor, sick families suffer? Ryan doesn't think so. He probably believes that if, God forbid, the Gosselins, the Duggars, and Octomom all lost their health insurance, got sick, and died at the exact same time, such acts of mercy might get him nominated for sainthood. It could happen; Paulie's already performed at least two miracles: (1) he's convinced voters that his destructive policies are good for them, and (2) he's managed to spend time alone with Donald Trump without drinking, throwing up, or jumping off the roof of the South Portico. One more highly unlikely achievement and Ryan will end up either being canonized by the Pope or joining the R&B group Smokey Robinson and the Miracles.

H is for Hysteria. Conservative pundits and the right-wing media keep saying that liberals like me are engaged in hysteria over Trump's election. They're wrong. I'm not hysterical; I'm horrified. Hysterical is what I am when the woman in front of me at Saks gets the last pair of Junior Petite Spanx. Horrified is what I am when crazy people take charge of the country. Big difference.

Joy Behar

is for Ignorance. The old saying "Ignorance is bliss" is absolutely true—for the person who's ignorant. Everyone else is screwed. And if the ignorant person is in charge of everyone else, it's not bliss; it's bedlam.

Donald Trump isn't just ignorant, he's aggressively ignorant. Proudly ignorant. He wears his ignorance like a merit badge. But he's not alone. Ignorance is a Republican tradition, like flag waving and wearing cotton-poly blends. James Inhofe, Steven King, Louis Gohmert, Sarah Palin . . . shall I go on? Sarah Palin thinks dinosaurs roamed the earth in 1957. Unless she's referring to Strom Thurmond, she'd better check with a paleontologist.

is for Immigrant. The following people are/were immigrants to the United States:

Donald Trump's grandfather

Donald Trump's grandmother

Donald Trump's first wife

Donald Trump's third wife

Jared Kushner's grandmother

Albert Einstein

Madeleine Albright

Joseph Pulitzer

Enrico Fermi

Irving Berlin

Alex Trebek

Eight of the signers of the Constitution

William Penn

Alexander Hamilton

The Pilgrims

Christopher Columbus . . .

. . . and the most important of all . . .
Dr. Ruth.

Can you imagine how much crankier Republicans would be if they *weren't* having good sex?

is for Incidental Contact. I think of incidental contact the same way I think of diabetes—there are two types:

Type 1: You're getting ready to cross the street and you break a heel of your shoe on the handicapped ramp and bump into the person in the wheelchair in front of you. This is incidental contact—unless you knock the person into oncoming traffic, in which case it's no longer incidental contact; it's involuntary manslaughter.

Type 2: You brush up against somebody and you like it so much that, twenty minutes later, you need a cigarette and a shower. When this type of incidental contact happens on New York City subways, it's called "frottage," which comes from the French word *frotter*, which means "to rub against a stranger." To some people, it may be a prelude to pussy-grabbing. I've been on crowded subways a million times and not once have I ever been groped, grabbed, or fondled. Then again, I've never been on the subway with Donald Trump or Bill O'Reilly.

is for Incomprehensible Demoralization. One of my Twelve Step friends—I work in television; it's a union rule that everyone who works in show business has to have *at least* three friends in rehab, two in AA, and one with an electronic ankle bracelet and live-in sobriety coach—tells me that when addicts and alcoholics reach their bottom, one of the things they deal with is the feeling of incomprehensible demoralization. I've had that feeling since the 2016 election. Does this mean that in order to get over it, I have to start drinking like an alcoholic? If so, I'd better stop writing and run to 7-Eleven for a six-pack of Schlitz.

is for India. Trump keeps saying he's going to bring jobs back to America from foreign countries. Manufacturing? Technology? Not likely. Call centers, perhaps? That would be a huge gain. When is the last time you called a customer service department or an airline and spoke to someone who wasn't living in Mumbai? So, is Donald #ImmigrantsBad Trump planning on bringing 3.2 million Indian workers here? And if so, would he have to lift his own travel ban to do so?

Slightly off point, but why do the call centers make the operators take on American names? You call to make a flight reservation, and you hear a man say, in a very thick Hindi accent, "Hello, this is Kevin, can I help you?" It's ridiculous. I know his name's not Kevin, and *he* knows I know his name's not Kevin, and I know he knows I know his name's not Kevin, so what's the point? I'm perfectly happy speaking with Vijay or Lakshmi or Subramanian. Just get me a friggin' aisle seat on American Airlines.

If Trump really wants to bring American jobs back home, maybe he should stop making his ties and suits in China (and Ivanka should stop making her clothes in Hong Kong and Vietnam) and open factories here. (And maybe Hans and Fritz should stop killing elephants in Africa and go on safaris in New York City and shoot the rats in the basement of Trump Tower.)

is for **Iran**. Forget a nuclear holocaust—if Trump screws things up with Iran, how will I be able to buy Persian rugs? I have my priorities.

is for **Insomnia**. Lack of sleep can lead to physical, psychological, and emotional problems. In my case, it can lead to five extra pounds, because if I'm awake at three o'clock in the morning, so is my refrigerator. According to *Psychology Today*, lack of sleep can lead to impaired brain activity, disorganized thoughts, cognitive dysfunction, moodiness, memory problems, and bursts of irrationality. Apparently, it can also lead to insane tweeting in the middle of the night.

It's possible that Trump's biggest problem is that he hasn't slept since 1997. Have you seen what time he likes to tweet? Maybe all the man needs is a good nap. Can you imagine if all we needed to fix this hot mess were a prescription for Ambien? (Our luck, he'd be one of those rare people who experience side effects from Ambien. Some people unconsciously sleep-walk, others mow the lawn or make a meatloaf. He'd probably drop a bomb on Canada.)

is for Intolerant. The opposite of *intolerant* is *tolerant*. I hate those words. *Tolerant* means you're willing to grudgingly put up with something. Teenagers are professional tolerators. They are amazingly skilled at rolling their eyes, shrugging their shoulders, and making sucking sounds with their teeth to express their disgust. (Or is that just me on *The View*?) Whenever asked to do something, they do it grudgingly, if at all. This is typical teenage behavior, not a national political party platform. Most teenagers outgrow it, but apparently the GOP has not.

After Obama beat Romney in 2012, the Republican leadership decided they needed to appear more "tolerant" of minorities, gays, and other people who don't usually vote for them. Who are they to "tolerate" anybody? You tolerate lactose or barking dogs or the unexplained success of Sean Hannity—you don't "tolerate" people just because they don't contribute money to your PAC.

The minute a minority group gains some rights, Republicans send Rick Santorum or Mike Pence to the grave of Jesse Helms to suck some meanness out of his bones to infuse back into the party.

(I have to stop writing this entry. It's making me crazy. I just can't tolerate intolerance.)

is for Iran. During the campaign, Donald Trump said that the Iran nuclear deal President Obama had signed was "a horrible deal; disastrous." He must have meant it was a bad deal for him, because he wasn't making any money off it. The Iran nuclear deal was signed by the five permanent members of the UN Security Council—China, France, Russia, the United States, and the United Kingdom—*and* the European Union. Mathematically, what are the odds that every single one of these nations was duped into making the same terrible deal, but that a reality TV show host knows better? I'm not an arms expert, nor do I play one on TV, but I think we have to keep the Iran deal in place. Forget a nuclear holocaust—if Trump screws things up with Iran, how will I be able to buy Persian rugs? I have my priorities.

is for Iraq. There are only a handful of people who think that invading Iraq in 2003 was a good idea: Dick Cheney, George W. Bush, Dick Cheney, Donald Rumsfeld, and Dick Cheney—oh, and whoever is profiting off the war and occupation—probably a certain person who is related to Betsy DeVos.

We've been in Iraq for almost fifteen years, and we don't

seem to be leaving it anytime soon. In fact, Trump's just requested an increase in troops and funding. It's no longer an occupation; we've moved in. Time to redecorate. I have a bunch of 20 percent–off coupons from Bed, Bath & Beyond. Where do I send them?

is for IRS. Trump says he wants to rewrite the tax code. I don't believe that for a second. He doesn't pay his taxes now, why would he change anything?

is for Israel. Israel has always been one of America's strongest allies. This is important to me because, my whole life, I've always gone out with Jewish guys and I'm married to a Jewish guy.

I know that not everyone who lives in Israel is Jewish (in the same way I know that not everyone who lives in the Keebler Forest is an elf), but it *was* created as a Jewish state. There are different reasons that everyone in America—and every U.S. president—cares about Israel. For some evangelicals, it has to do with the Rapture. (According to the New Testament's Book of Revelation, after the Battle of Armageddon, Jesus will take all believers up to heaven, and all nonbelievers—I wonder who they could be—will, *poof*, like magic, be gone.) For others, it's because Israel's the only democracy in the Middle East; for still others, it's because Israel is our eyes and ears on the ground in the region. Republicans ranted and raved that Obama didn't like Israel because he and Bibi Netanyahu didn't get along. They didn't get along because Obama is a center-left conciliator and Netanyahu is a right-wing hawk. Trump likes Israel, too, but for a completely different reason, and I don't think it's because the Kushners are Jewish, or because he loves gefilte fish. I think it's because he's having a bromance with Bibi—if for no other reason than to make his main squeeze, Vladimir, jealous. Either way, it doesn't sound kosher to me.

is for Ivana. Ivana Zelnickova was the first woman to say, "I do," to Donald Trump. Of course, she said it in Czech, so who the hell knows what she really said? It could have been, "Shove that prenup up your ass, you orange-hued motherfucker. In a couple of years, I'll have half of everything you own." I'm not sure how they met—maybe she was starring on *Prague's Got Talent* or the sitcom *Hot in Ostrava*—but they had a whirlwind romance and a huge wedding in New York City. They had a few kids, and everything was going fine until, one day, The Donald decided to play Hide the Kielbasa with Marla Maples. He cheated on Ivana publicly, and faster than you can say, "Don't get mad, get everything," she filed for divorce. She reportedly walked away with twenty million bucks and, because she's the only woman he seems intimidated by or afraid of, I'm guessing pictures of Donald in a compromising position (like blow-drying his hair). You go, girl!

is for Ivanka Danka-Doo. Ivanka Trump is America's youngest First Lady. I know, technically she's not the First Lady, but she *is* the only woman related to Donald Trump who has an office in the West Wing. His actual wife has an office on QVC and sleeps in Trump Tower whenever she can get away

Getty Image News/Getty Images

[Merkel] I am the chancellor of Germany, I was a research scientist, and I have a doctorate in physical science.
[Ivanka] My father thinks you're a two.

from DC and DT. Now that Melania has moved into the White House, will she be known as the First Lady or, because she's his third wife, as the Third Lady? Or should we call her the First Trophy? It's very confusing.

I don't know Ivanka Trump. She seems smart and composed and poised. Of course, compared to her father, the guy from the movie *Jackass* seems smart and composed and poised.

Is it just me, or do the daughters of most Republican presidents seem smarter than their fathers? Jenna and Barbara Bush are clearly smarter than W. (Although, truth be told, I don't think the bar was set too high for them.) Patti Davis? Definitely brighter than Ronnie. Was Susan Ford smarter than Gerald Ford? Duh. Even the Nixon girls might have been smarter than their dad. At least Tricia knew enough to shave off her five o'clock shadow before going on television.

Ivanka Trump grew up in the public eye, so fame is nothing new for her. She started out as a model and appeared in lots of fashion magazines and runway shows. I'm not sure if she was a model or a "supermodel." I don't really know the difference. Do supermodels leap tall salad bars in a single bound, or pop laxatives with the speed of a locomotive?

Ivanka went to Georgetown for two years, then transferred to the Wharton School of Business, where she graduated cum laude. (The Donald also went to Wharton, and even though he can't stop telling us how smart he is, he didn't graduate with honors, he didn't get an MBA, and he may have gotten in only due to familial influence and wealth.) Ivanka took what she learned at Wharton and brought it to the business world. She's lucky she didn't go to Trump University; she'd have brought what she learned there into an unemployment office or a courtroom.

Ivanka's having an MBA from Wharton definitely makes her qualified to run a business—but to negotiate international trade agreements with Angela Merkel? I don't think so. How much do you think the Republicans would have carried on if

President Obama had sent Malia to Cuba to renegotiate the embargo with Raúl Castro?

White House "insiders" say Ivanka has her father's ear, and he'll actually listen to her every now and again. (And by "insiders," I mean the people who haven't been fired yet because they forgot to compliment Donald.) Apparently, Ivanka can talk her father out of following his worst instincts. And considering the mess he's already created, can you imagine what she's talked him out of?

Things Ivanka Has Talked Her Father Out Of

- Referring to British prime minister Theresa May as the Brexit Babe;

- Drilling for oil in Johnny Depp's hair;

- Selling Hawaii to Kenya;

- Naming Bruno Mars the head of NASA;

- Giving a Kennedy Center Honor to Chachi;

- Changing "Stop and Frisk" to "Stop and Punch in the Fucking Face"; and

- Building a wall around Rosie O'Donnell's house.

J is for Andrew Jackson. Steve Bannon, Newt Gingrich, and Rudy Giuliani—and they wonder why women WANT to become lesbians—have all compared Donald Trump to Andrew Jackson. The Donald must be so proud. While there *are* some similarities (they both ran as outsiders and as populists), Jackson was a statesman while Trump is . . . actually, I don't know what the fuck Donald Trump is, but he's definitely not a statesman. Trump has more in common with Michael Jackson than Andrew Jackson. Michael Jackson had clingy, leechy adult siblings; Donald Trump has clingy, leechy adult children. Michael's hair caught fire; Donald has a warning sign on his comb-over that reads, DANGER: HIGHLY FLAMMABLE.

J is for Jared-of-all-Trades. When speaking about his son-in-law, Jared Kushner, Donald Trump turns into a reverse Sally Field—"I like him, I really, really like him!" (And I say "like," not "love," because the only person, place, or thing Donald Trump truly loves is Donald Trump.)

I'm not sure if The Donald likes The Jared because he is the scion of a rich New York City family, because he went to a good school, or because he's sleeping with Ivanka (and we all know how much Daddy loves Ivanka). Regardless, Kushner has enormous power in the White House.

Jared's White House duties—none of which he's qualified to perform—include the following: negotiating peace in the Middle East; heading the White House Office of American Innovation; modernizing the Department of Veterans'

Affairs; assisting Chris Christie in solving the opioid crisis; reforming the criminal justice system; serving as a liaison to Mexico; serving as a liaison to China; and serving as a liaison to the Muslim community—because who better to smooth over Trump's xenophobic, anti-Muslim rhetoric than an Orthodox Jew? That's like sending Sean Hannity to run Al Franken's campaign.

You must be thinking, "Is there anything Jared Kushner *can't* do?" The answer is he can do anything and everything! The man wears more hats than conjoined septuplets. My sources tell me that Daddy-in-Law-Dearest has quietly given Jared lots of other responsibilities, in addition to the ones I've just listed. Here are a few of them:

- Recovering lost gold from the *Titanic* and the *Lusitania*;
- Taking over as lead male dancer for the American Ballet Theatre;
- Chairing a new Republican activist group, Black Lives Sorta Matter;
- Explaining to his father-in-law why the Holocaust was bad;
- Playing shortstop for the New York Yankees;
- Serving as head of Cardiology at Mount Sinai Hospital;
- Locking up Hillary Clinton with James Comey;
- Getting Ivanka's handbags and belts back into Nordstrom; and
- Changing the name of the White House to Don-a-Lago.

J **is for Jazz.** I feel about jazz the way I feel about moderate, normal Republicans who voted for Donald Trump. I want to understand and I want to like them more than I do, but I'm completely baffled by the whole thing. At least with jazz, you're usually listening to it in a hip club with a cocktail in your hand. How do you sit down and drink with people who agree with Ben Carson that the pyramids were used to store grain (did King Tut know this?), that dinosaurs roamed the Earth along with people (maybe just Strom Thurmond?), and that Satan walks among us (Dick Cheney is still alive)? Maybe there's hope yet to sit down with more moderate Republicans, if you can find any. Maybe they're hiding in the pyramids with the grain?

J is for **jellyfish.** A jellyfish is a dangerous spineless creature that can cause severe and debilitating pain in unsuspecting innocent people. Sorry—my mistake. That's not a jellyfish, that's Mitch McConnell.

J **is for Jefferson Beauregard Sessions.** At one point in 2017, Attorney General Sessions said, "I am really amazed that a judge sitting on an island in the Pacific can issue an order that stops the president of the United States from what appears to be clearly his statutory and constitutional power." By "island in the Pacific," Sessions was referring to Hawaii. Excuse me? *Guam* is an island in the Pacific; *Tahiti* is an island in the Pacific; *Bora Bora* (named for Charles Krauthammer) is an island in the Pacific. Hawaii has been the fiftieth U.S. state since 1959, and the *real* birthplace of the last president of the United States—you know, the one who *doesn't* Snapchat with Vladimir Putin.

Jeff Sessions is from Alabama, a state that in 2014 was ranked forty-seventh in education—the third worst in the nation, beating only Mississippi and the District of Columbia. (It somehow edged out Louisiana.) Poor little Jeff Sessions, who was thirteen in 1959, never got the lesson that Hawaii became a state. And here he is today, with the same lack of knowledge about the country that he claims to love so much. Maybe he needs to start watching cable TV like his boss, so he can learn something. But, not to worry. I'm sure our brilliant secretary of education, the woman whose brain is always in reverse, Betsy Devour, will straighten him out at the next Cabinet meeting. I hope she's wearing a lei.

J is for Jellyfish. A jellyfish is a dangerous spineless creature that can cause severe and debilitating pain in unsuspecting innocent people. Oh no, I'm sorry. My mistake. That's not a jellyfish. That's Mitch McConnell.

J is for Jerusalem. One of Trump's first suggestions as president was that the U.S. embassy in Israel be moved from Tel Aviv to Jerusalem, because why leave well enough alone when you have the opportunity to create chaos, division, and religious resentment in one of the most violent and volatile regions in the world? Why? I'm guessing because there's a possibility of building a Trump Tower in Jerusalem, that's why.

J is for Jesus. This is a very tough one for Trump. When someone asks him about Jesus, he doesn't know whether to suck up to his evangelical base or deport his gardener.

J is for JFK. The president, not the airport. In 1963, President Kennedy, who, by the way, won a close election without the help of the Russians or James Comey (although a call from mobster Sam Giancana didn't hurt) went to Berlin to speak about democracy and freedom as counterpoints to communism. This was shortly after the Berlin Wall had been erected (and I must say, it was quite an erection). A few great quotes came out of that speech—which Kennedy delivered in full sentences, never once using the words *bigly*, *best*, or *pussy*. Kennedy had two main talking points in the speech: freedom and unity. He talked about the wall that separates families and divides countrymen; he praised the mayor of West Berlin and the chancellor of West Germany; and his most famous quote was: "Two thousand years ago, the proudest boast was 'civis Romanus sum' [I am a Roman citizen]. Today, in the world of freedom, the proudest boast is 'Ich bin ein Berliner!' . . . All free men, wherever they may live, are citizens of Berlin. And, therefore, as a free man, I take pride in the words 'Ich bin ein Berliner!'" (We'll ignore the fact that *Ich bin ein Berliner* literally means "I am a donut.")

Fifty-four years later, we have a president who says, "We're going to build that wall, and Mexico is going to pay for it"—which is, of course, ridiculous. Mexico is not going to pay for any wall; if there's going to be a wall, we'll have to build it and pay for it. The good news? Given Trump's history of stiffing contractors, it's quite possible that no one will pay for it—it will end up in bankruptcy court. How fabulous would it be to see the Orange Amigo ending up on the wrong side of the wall, standing in Tijuana, yelling, "Ich bin ein Mexicano"? Will he even realize they speak Spanish in Mexico?

J is for Jimmy Hoffa. Mobbed-up Teamsters leader Jimmy Hoffa vanished in 1975. He went to meet a "friend" at a restaurant outside Detroit and was never seen again. (How bad could the food have been?) Seriously, his disappearance is one of the great mysteries of the world, along with the building of the pyramids, the Shroud of Turin, and why the white tiger ate Roy but didn't so much as lick Siegfried. Every few years, someone comes up with a new theory as to where Jimmy Hoffa is buried. One theory is that he was under the end zone in the old Giants' Stadium in the swamps of New Jersey's Meadowlands. (My husband says if that's true, he would have been found years ago, if only the Giants had scored more often.) Another story goes that his body was thrown into the Florida Everglades, where it was probably eaten by alligators.

My theory is that it doesn't matter: we'll never, ever find Jimmy Hoffa's body because he was buried in a coffin along with Donald Trump's tax returns.

J is for Job. These days the poor thing is a total wreck. Even he can't take the constant drama. He's had to stop watching Rachel Maddow and Keith Olbermann, he's cancelled his *New York Times* subscription, and he's deleted the *Huffington Post* app from his iPhone. Since November 8, Job has been living on Xanax and vodka. If Job, the most patient guy in history besides Wolf Blitzer, can't take it, how do you think the rest of us feel?

J is for Job Application. We've all filled out job applications, and we've all fudged a little bit. For example, years ago, before I got into show business, I applied for a job as a receptionist at ABC. I fudged my résumé a little. Where it asked for "previous experience," I put down, "Translator at the UN." That wasn't exactly true—what *was* true was that I once yelled at a Croatian cab driver for slamming on the brakes and almost knocking my teeth out. I thought he didn't speak English, so I gave him the finger, which he clearly understood. He told me to fuck off. Voilà! International translator!

　　Anyway, I got the job at ABC. (It didn't last long; they fired me—something about my having a "bad attitude." Who, *moi*?) But if you want a job in the Trump administration, is lying on your application a bad thing or a requirement?

TRUMP ADMINISTRATION
JOB APPLICATION

Name _____

  Alias _____

  LLC Name _____

  Bogus LLC Name _____

Legal Address _____

  Illegal Address _____

  Bank Address _____

  Offshore Bank Address _____

  Offshore Shell Company Bank Address

_____

Name(s) of Lawyer(s) _____

  Name(s) of Bankruptcy Lawyer(s)

_____

Previous Nonrelated Job Experience

_____

_____

If Hillary Clinton were on fire, I would:

a. Put her out

b. Call 9–1–1

c. Ignore her

d. Pee on her

If Donald Trump were on fire, I would:

a. Put him out

b. Call 9–1–1

c. Lock Hillary Clinton up

d. Pee on him (he would like that)

Keep your friends close and your enemies:

a. Dead

b. In your basement/crawl space

c. In Russia

d. I don't have enemies; everyone loves me.

_____ is next to Godliness:

a. Great wealth

b. A uuuuge brain

c. Power

d. A woman with big hooters

Have you read the Constitution?

a. No

b. No

c. No

d. What's the Constitution?

Donald Trump won the popular vote by:

a. Three million votes

b. Three hundred million votes

c. Three billion votes

d. Too many votes to count, but close to a gazillion

How important is loyalty to the ~~king~~ leader?

a. Very important

b. All-consuming

c. It's everything

d. I'd give up my children for him

Which percentage of your children do you like?

a. 80 percent

b. 66 percent

c. 50 percent

d. Only the pretty ones

Should the Bible be replaced with *The Art of the Deal*?

a. Yes

b. Duh

c. What's the Bible?

d. We doesn't reed

Cabinet officials should come from:

  a.   Right-wing think tanks
  b.   Right-wing radio
  c.   Right-wing websites
  d.   TV shows that feature Omarosa

How many women have you grabbed?

  a.   A lot
  b.   To many too count
  c.   A gazillion
  d.   If you're famous, they let you

Please submit this form to:

Whoever is in charge of things at the White House this week
1600 Pennsylvania Avenue
Washington, DC
United States of Make America Great Again

J **is for Joe Biden.** In a 2017 *New York Times* interview, one of the few not totally insane Republican senators, Ben Sasse of Nebraska (who loathes Trump), said Joe Biden would've clobbered Trump in the general election. We'll never know, but he might be right. Joe Biden is like Sara Lee: nobody doesn't like him. Biden is one of those rare career politicians who is liked and respected by both parties and has been able to work across the aisle for years. He's a patriot, and his personal story is so compelling that even the most craven, cold-hearted Republicans have a soft spot for Joe. That said, I disagree with Ben Sasse. Yes, a lot of Republicans like Joe Biden, but they would never have voted for him for president, because two things about him render him unelectable to a certain tranche of Republican voters: he's qualified for the job and he's a Democrat.

J is for Joe the Plumber. The Republicans began their formal drive for the undereducated, bigoted, disenfranchised white voter in 2008, when they made "Joe the Plumber" their cartoonish mascot. Turns out he was the perfect choice.

For starters, he's a liar: (a) he was not a licensed plumber in the state of Ohio, and (b) his name isn't Joe; it's Sam. His full name is Samuel Joseph Wurzelbacher. (Maybe he uses his middle name instead of his first name. It's entirely possible, but kind of unusual, no? I don't remember anybody calling Richard Nixon "Milhous," or John Kennedy "Fitzgerald," or Dwight Eisenhower "Big Dave," do you?)

Secondly, he's a gun nut. After the horrible 2014 shootings in Isla Vista, California, Sam/Joe wrote an open letter to the parents of the kids who were killed in which he said, "[Y]our dead kids don't trump my constitutional rights . . . We still have the right to bear arms." Nice, huh? He's also made some "unusual" Holocaust references. In 2012, when Sam/Joe the Not-Actual-Plumber decided to run for Congress, he made a progun campaign video that claimed that "in 1939, Germany established gun control. From 1939 to 1945, six million Jews and seven million others unable to defend themselves were exterminated." Call me crazy, but I don't think the Luftwaffe, the SS, and the Third Panzer Division could have been stopped by Rivka wielding a pistol. And finally, while appearing at a political rally in Arizona, he said, "Put a damn fence on the border, go into Mexico, and start shooting."

Sam/Joe is not the kind of person Republicans want running for Congress—he's the kind of person they want running for president. He's a total crackpot, but he might actually be able to drain the swamp. Don't forget, he's a plumber (not!).

J is for John Gotti. Donald Trump made his fortune (at least the part of it his daddy didn't give him) in the real estate development business, building primarily hotels and casinos. Given the nature of the construction business, what are the odds Donald Trump never dealt with, worked with, associated with, or paid off any members of an organized crime family? (Although, truth be told, if Trump were seriously involved with organized crime, it would no longer be organized.) I wouldn't be surprised if, one morning, he wakes up with a horse's head in his bed. And why not? Melania wakes up every morning with a horse's ass in hers.

J is for the Joker. An evil, erratic, cartoonish villain with crazy hair and bizarre makeup. Recently moved from Gotham City to the White House.

K **is for Kansas.** In 2005, journalist Thomas Frank wrote the best-selling book *What's the Matter with Kansas?*, which takes a look at why the people of Kansas (and other states) lurch to the political right and vote against their own self-interest. For example, why vote against universal health care, why vote against public education, why vote against clean air and water, why vote for tax cuts for the one-percenters, and why identify with a rich orange guy from Queens?

I'd rather look at what's great about Kansas. First on my list: wheat. Kansas is the number one state in wheat production, and I love bread. Without bread, I'd have to eat corned beef and pastrami on tofu, and I don't see that happening in this lifetime (or the next, or the next, or the next one after that—I put that in just in case Shirley MacLaine is reading this book). Second, aviation manufacturing is a big industry in Kansas. Without it, we wouldn't have planes, and as much as I hate flying, it's much better than other kinds of schlepping. I get carsick just going the twenty blocks from my apartment to work. I can't imagine spending eighteen hours on a Greyhound from New York to Miami sitting next to Ratso Rizzo, who wasn't exactly known for good hygiene. And third, and most important, *The Wizard of Oz.* Without Kansas, there's no Dorothy; and without Dorothy, there's no Judy Garland; and without Judy Garland, there's no fabulous conversation with my fabulous gay friends at their fabulous gay dinner parties. Yes, we could talk about Bette versus Joan, or who was the best Dolly Levi on Broadway, or how it's possible that anyone could still think John Travolta is straight. But, ultimately, it would all come back to Judy Garland. As well it should. What can I say, I ♥ Kansas! Even if they did vote for Donald Trump.

K is for Kardashian. I love the Kardashians. Why? Because they're fascinating? Certainly not. I've interviewed them a number of times, on both *The View* and my show on HLN, and while they're all very nice, they don't make for scintillating interviews (although Khloe can be funny in a kind of "I drank a fifth of lunch today" kind of way). I love them because *they* are the actual biggest international stars of reality TV, *not* Donald Trump. If you doubt this, feel free to travel around the world and speak to girls everywhere, and see whom they'd rather be like, Kim Kardashian or Donald Trump. I rest my case.

The Kardashians got famous because Kim made a sex tape with a rap artist named Ray J and it was leaked all over the Internet. I haven't seen the tape, and I have no desire to. If I want to hear a reality star moaning, I'll watch Val Chmerkovskiy try to lift Sherri Shepherd on *Dancing with the Stars* (apologies to my girl Sherri).

K is for Kevorkian. You can't have a doctor pull the plug just because you're having a bad hair day, though if I were a judge I might pull the plug on anyone who showed up in court with a mullet.

Anyway, while the Kardashians themselves might not be interesting, their choice of spouses is fascinating. First of all, there's the interracial thing, which I love. They also marry athletes and celebrities: Kanye West, Kris Humphries, Lamar Odom, Bruce Jenner, and Robert Kardashian. When it comes to marriages, though, the family matriarch, Kris Jenner, is the bomb. Donald Trump may have married a few European beauty queens, but Kris married a lawyer who defended the world's most famous accused murderer (O.J. Simpson) and a famous athlete who became the world's most famous woman. Take that, loser!

K **is for Dr. Kevorkian.** In the 1990s, Dr. Jack Kevorkian became famous for promoting and practicing euthanasia on terminally ill patients (with their consent, of course; he didn't break into nursing homes and smother unsuspecting widows). Even though he went to jail, he made the issue of physician-assisted suicide part of the national conversation.

I think one of the reasons he got in trouble was his methodology. First, he advertised in local papers. "Fed up with coughing, sneezing, and wheezing? Sick and tired of being sick and tired? Call Dr. Jack and make a onetime appointment now. You'll never need a follow-up! Have your caregiver dial, 1–800–555-DEAD." Dr. Kevorkian also did some of his euthanasia work from inside his van, which became known as a Death Mobile. Even though I believe in physician-assisted suicide, dying in traffic is not for me. If I want to die in a van, I'll go for a ride with Barbara Walters. The woman is a menace behind the wheel. Was it my imagination, or did she try to run down Diane Sawyer on Madison Avenue once?

Five states (California, Colorado, Montana, Oregon, and Vermont) plus Washington, DC, have legalized physician-assisted suicide, passing legislation with names like the Death with Dignity Law. (I'm a big fan of death with dignity. No way do I want to be found in an undignified manner like David Carradine was: naked in a broom closet wearing a horse collar and chaps. I don't have the shoes for that.) The laws are stringent; you can't have a doctor pull the plug just because you're having a bad hair day—although, if I were a presiding judge, I might personally pull the plug on anyone who showed up in court with a mullet. Naturally, congressional Republicans, led by the always craven Jason Chaffetz, are against physician-assisted suicide. They do not believe in euthanasia. They think people should die naturally, you know, after getting sick with no health insurance, or by getting shot forty times by a mentally ill person with an assault rifle.

I think we should start calling this congressional-assisted suicide.

K is for KKK Sera Sera. During the 2016 campaign, Donald Trump received the endorsement of David Duke, the former leader of the KKK. Now, I don't even like being bothered by AARP let alone the KKK, and all AARP wants to do is sell me walk-in bathtubs and long-term-care insurance.

When Trump was asked about this dubious honor, at first he said he didn't know anything about David Duke (which, of

course, wasn't true), but then, in response to criticism from
both political parties, he disavowed the endorsement. A lot
of people were annoyed that it took Trump so long to distance himself from Duke. I didn't care about that. What I care
about is that Trump has never walked away from his belief
system, which frighteningly aligns with David Duke's. They
both champion nationalism, populism, and anti-immigrant
stances; they traffic in outlandish conspiracy theories; and
they're usually seen only in the company of white men. Trump
may have disavowed Duke's endorsement publicly, but privately, I don't think the crabapple falls far from the tree.

K is for Korea. As Donald Trump would say, in his *elegant* way,
South Korea good, North Korea bad; Donald Trump getting
involved in either Korea, worse. Since the end of World War II,
the United States and South Korea have been close allies, and
when the Russian-backed North Koreans invaded the South in
1950, the United States (along with sixteen other UN member
states) came to its aid. The United States and South Korea have
been close economic, military, and cultural partners ever
since. In 2013, President Obama cited the musical artist Psy's
hit song "Gangnam Style" as part of South Korea's growing
cultural influence. We returned the favor in 2016, with President PSYchotic's "Gangster Style" platform being cited as part
of America's growing political craziness.

   I don't love everything about Korean culture. For example,
I've heard that they eat dogs. Somebody please get me Anthony
Bourdain on the phone—I'd like him to verify whether in

Pyongyang a BLT is a "bacon, Lassie, and tomato." If true, I find this quite upsetting. I have no interest in eating Kung Pao Collie. If I go to South Korea, will I find chain restaurants like Kentucky Fried Corgi, or IHOP: International House of Poodles? I hope not, because unless Trump blows everything up, I might just go to South Korea. I'm not kidding. The 2018 Winter Olympics are in Pyeongchang, and while I care nothing about sports, I find the two-man luge kinda kinky.

K is for Krispy Kreme. I rarely see a very thin person walk out of a Krispy Kreme donut shop. (I'm not saying that only overweight people go there; it's entirely possible that chubbettes volunteer to go to the store for the whole family because they consider donut shopping exercise. Who am I to say?) But, to me, the consumption of Krispy Kremes is a metaphor for Donald Trump's hardcore base voters. They know they're buying something that, in the long run, may not be good for them, but they can't help themselves, so they buy it anyway. The big difference is if they gorge themselves on sugar and glaze and gain eighty pounds, it doesn't ruin *my* life, but their voting for Trump does.

Joy Behar

L **is for Liar.** There are at least thirty-four different types of lies, apparently. I won't list them all here, because I don't have the time—I'm due at Mount Sinai Hospital in ten minutes to start my shift as head of Cardiology.

Okay, you caught me. I'm lying—and that would be a lie of fabrication, i.e., just making shit up. Some of the most common lies are lies of: disinformation, omission, fraud, dissembling, defamation, cover-up, and my favorite, the bald-faced lie. Why is that my favorite? Because of its etymology. An eighteenth-century British term, it was originally *bare-faced lie*, because it was believed that men without beards were more transparent. It eventually morphed into *bald-faced lie*, and then into *Boldfaced lie*, which is when a man has no beard but has covered his face with laundry detergent. (Okay, that's silly, but so what—who cares?)

There are a few types of people who routinely lie, especially children and politicians.

Young children don't usually lie very effectively, as lying is an acquired skill. For better or worse, little kids are painfully honest. If you ask a six-year-old, "Isn't Aunt Immaculata pretty?" and she's not, he'll say, "No, she's ugly."

(FYI: not all six-year-olds would be so crass. I'm bragging here, but my grandson is far too brilliant to say something like that. If I asked him, "Isn't Aunt Immaculata pretty?" he'd say, "Not particularly, Nana. She has heavy-lidded eyes, a protruding brow, and a weak chin. To say nothing of her upper lip, which is in desperate need of a cream depilatory. And don't forget her provolone legs.")

As children get older, they learn to lie to protect themselves from getting caught doing something wrong. For example, my neighbors Paul and Amy Nussbaum have a nine-year-old daughter named, let's call her Bella. (They named her Bella because they think she's beautiful. Don't ask my grandson if *he* thinks she's beautiful.) I stopped over there one night to watch *Celebrity Jeopardy*. (I love that they dumb down the questions for the stars, so they don't look like idiots.) Right before they started Final Jeopardy—the category was "Celebrities Appearing on *Jeopardy* Tonight"—Bella came out of the kitchen with pistachio ice cream all over her face. Amy said, "Did you eat the ice cream I told you not to eat?" Bella looked her right in the eye and said, "No, the cat ate it." It was clear Bella was lying, not because of the evidence all over her face, but because the Nussbaums don't have a cat.

By now, Bella has probably grown out of making stuff up because, for most children, lying is a phase, and with time, maturity, and proper parenting (assuming the parents aren't the Madoffs), most children outgrow it.

Not so much with politicians. All politicians bend the truth, tell people what they want to hear, and offer promises they know they can't fulfill.

During the 1928 presidential campaign, Herbert Hoover promised "a chicken in every pot and a car in every garage." How did he see that happening? For starters, in 1928 the U.S. population was 120,500,000 people. Assuming an average of two people per household, where was Hoover going to find 60 million chickens? On a Mormon chicken farm? And how did he plan to deliver them to every home, pink and fresh and ready for eatin'? A flying coop the size of Noah's Ark? And as for a car in every garage, I grew up in Brooklyn; we lived in a tenement building. What was Hoover going to do, park a Buick on the stoop? While technically Hoover was lying, I'm assuming he said the chicken-pot-car-garage thing as a metaphor for American prosperity, not as an actual promise he couldn't keep.

In 1992, George Bush Sr. famously said, "Read my lips, no new taxes," and then raised taxes. That lie famously cost him the election.

In 1997, Bill Clinton said, "I did not have sex with that woman," which, of course, was a lie. What he should have said was, "I did not provide dry-cleaning services for that woman."

Perhaps the most famous (infamous?) lie of all came in 2003, when George W. Bush started the war in Iraq because "there were weapons of mass destruction" there. There weren't; it was a lie. (Unless, of course, he believed it and, fifteen years later, he's still

is for **Liar**. In 1997, Bill Clinton said, "I did not have sex with that woman," which, of course, was a lie. What he should have said was, "I did not provide dry-cleaning services for that woman."

looking for them, in much the same way O.J. is still looking for Nicole's real killer).

Those political lies stand out because they were aberrations, not the norm. Donald Trump lies so often and so frequently that the *truth* stands out—or at least it will, if he ever tells it.

Donald Trump tells all kinds of lies. He tells lies of defamation (that Ted Cruz's father was involved in the JFK assassination, for example); lies of dissembling, which is lying by posing as someone you're not (Trump used to call journalists and pretend he was his own publicist); lies of deception (he fired Comey because of the "way he handled the Hillary email investigation"; even *Trump* didn't believe that one!); lies of fabrication (he said Muslims in New Jersey were cheering on 9/11); and my favorite, bald-faced lies (for example, about the size of the crowd at his inauguration, in spite of aerial photos proving that what he was saying was patently false).

The truly fascinating thing is that Trump lies when it's unnecessary and for no apparent reason. To this day, he carries on about how he was at the top of his class at Wharton Business School, a lie that (a) is not true, (b) was about something from fifty years ago, and (c) *nobody* cares about. If I said I was the Queen of Sweden from 1963 to 1964, it would clearly be a lie, but would you give a flying fuck? No. You'd just wonder why I would lie about something like that.

Which brings us to the real problem with Trump's lying: credibility. If he's lying about inconsequential things, how will we know if he's telling the truth about big things, like a nuclear attack or a health pandemic or whether he's hung like a horse, as he claims? It's hard to trust someone who lies constantly. The philosopher Friedrich Nietzsche said it best: "I'm not upset that you lied to me, I'm upset that from now on I can't believe you." (He was deep.)

Donald Trump is like an adult version of the character in Aesop's fable "The Boy Who Cried Wolf." The boy lied and lied and lied about the wolf coming for his sheep, and then, one day, the wolf really did come, but nobody helped the boy fight the wolf off because they no longer believed him. In the end, the boy was eaten by the wolf. I think that if Trump keeps on compulsively lying, sooner or later no one will believe him, and he'll get eaten by the wolf. And so will we, even though we have not been the ones doing all the lying. And that pisses me off.

M **is for Alicia Machado.** Alicia Machado was 1996's Miss Universe, the one Trump called "Miss Piggy" because she gained a few pounds after winning the title. He also called her "Miss Housekeeping," because she was from South America. (She was Miss Venezuela.) This all came to light during the campaign, when Hillary Clinton mentioned Alicia and the degrading things Trump had said about her.

I wouldn't be surprised if, when Trump is in the Situation Room (the one in the White House, not the one with Wolf Blitzer) with his national security team—ignoring all the generals as they try to give him strategic intel on urgent issues involving Iran and ISIS—he's thinkng about Alicia Machado and how she should be contacting Jenny Craig.

M **is for Mainstream Media.** *Mainstream media* is the term Republicans use to denigrate any news outlet other than Fox, Brietbart, or Infowars—in other words, any actual, real news outlet. When people say, "I don't know what publications to believe anymore," I tell them, "Breitbart was established in 2005 and Infowars started in 2004, which was when the Internet and fake news were coming into their own. Compare that to the *New York Times*, which started publishing in 1851, and the *Washington Post*, in 1877." If those two publications had been giving us "alternative facts" all that time, I doubt that they would still be in business. Whom are you gonna believe: Woodward and Bernstein, or Conway and Bannon? I rest my case.

M **is for Mar-a-Lago.** Mar-a-Lago is Donald Trump's vacation mansion in Palm Beach, Florida. If you're not familiar with Palm Beach, it's where rich, old, white people go to get some sun and eat watercress sandwiches. And if you're not familiar with Mar-a-Lago, it's the Playboy Mansion with six fewer germs in the hot tub. For years, Donald Trump has been going to Mar-a-Lago every weekend, to relax, play golf, and buy and/or con other rich people. And up until January 21, 2017, he paid for those weekends himself. Now we, the taxpayers, pay for them—because why spend money feeding poor people or helping sick children when we can use that money to make sure that a handful of foreign billionaires have clean towels and fresh fruit on the lanai?

Mar-a-Lago was originally built by socialite and billionaire Post cereal heiress Marjorie Merriweather Post. She envisioned it as a winter retreat for American presidents, and after she died in 1973—she was buried in a beautiful bowl of Grape-Nuts and strawberries—MMP willed the estate to the nation. Seven years later, the nation gave it back, saying, "What, are you crazy? This place costs a fortune to run." In stepped Donald Trump, who made a ridiculously lowball offer for the property, which the Post family turned down. But rather than letting go and moving on with his life, Trump decided to be a petty, vindictive, small-minded prick (and by that, I mean "himself") and bought a strip of land between Mar-a-Lago and the beach. He threatened to build a high-rise that would block Mar-a-Lago's view of the ocean, and thus lower its value. Needless to say, he bullied his way into getting Mar-a-Lago on the cheap. He would call that a good deal; most people would call it extortion. And finally, in 2017, Marjorie Merriweather Post's dream of having Mar-a-Lago serve as a winter White House has come true—as has Donald Trump's dream of having other people pay for it.

M **is for Marco Rubio.** During the 2016 campaign, Candidate Trump kept insulting Rubio by calling him "Little Marco." Was that because he was short? So what? Paul Simon is short (he writes great songs), Tom Cruise is short (which allows him to jump up onto couches easily), and Danny DeVito is really short (but funny and adorable). So, was "little" actually a reference to a certain body part? (Remember, Trump bragged about not having "any problem in that area, believe me." Okay, we believe you. Feel better? Again, so what? Gary Cooper was known to be well endowed—just ask Patricia Neal—and he was a pretty good actor, but could he run a country? Probably not.) Either way, the intent was to diminish Rubio in the eyes of the electorate. So, what can we learn from this? When it comes to being president of the United States, it's better that the country be well run than that the president be well hung.

Republicans *love* Marco Rubio. They think he's perfect for the future of the party—very conservative, very religious, under ninety years old, and hetero. I think he's perfect for them, too, but for different reasons: he's terrible with money, and he lies. Rubio used GOP credit cards for personal use, had a home facing foreclosure, had to liquidate a retirement account, and put family members on his payroll. He also lied about when his parents came to America. Over the years, Rubio told everyone a heartfelt story about how his parents fled Cuba in 1959, when dictator Fidel Castro took over. The truth is, they came to America in 1956, three years *before* the revolution. And contrary to what Marco says, they flew to Miami on a plane; they didn't swim here disguised as porpoises.

M is for Marriage(s). Donald Trump has been involved in 3,500 lawsuits (3,502 if you throw in his divorces). Whatever. Who's judging? The point is, when The Donald says, "I do," he *doesn't*. Maybe he just should replace "I do" with "perhaps" or "maybe" or "I'll get back to you."

Marriage is the last thing (okay, one of *many* last things) Donald Trump should be allowed to weigh in on, yet, as president, he can and does. Same-sex marriage is still a hot-button issue for Republicans. Some of them can't fathom two men or two women falling in love; some of them are buttinsky religious zealots; and some of them just don't want neighbors who have better taste than they do.

Trump has flip-flopped on the issue of same-sex marriage regularly. While he's never been pro-same-sex marriage, in a

M is for **Melania**, the first First Lady who is actually the president's third lady.

2000 interview in *The Advocate*, he said marriage equality was an issue for the states. (If you're not familiar with *The Advocate*, ask your husband's boyfriend what it is.) More recently, in a November 2013 interview on *60 Minutes* with Lesley Stahl, he said the matter of marriage equality had already been "settled" by the Supreme Court. Yet, shortly after taking office, he overturned a transgender rights bill and said he would appoint very conservative Supreme Court justices—his first turned out to be Neil Gorsuch—who would likely overturn the same-sex marriage laws if a case came before the court. I don't know what Trump actually believes, but then, no one does. He's like the offspring of the Sphinx and the Riddler. But standing *right behind him* is the Anti-gay Whisperer, Mike "the Top" Pence. This guy wants to use conversion therapy to turn gays straight. (Interestingly, no one ever wants to use conversion therapy to turn straights gay. Why is that?)

M is for Mars. Donald Trump has ordered NASA to go to Mars in his first term, even though he originally signed a bill directing that it get there by the 2030s. What's his hurry? Is he afraid that fellow billionaire Elon "Big Fingers" Musk or Richard "Huge Hands" Branson will beat him to the punch and get there first? Does Trump know something we don't know? I'm kidding. What are the odds of that?

But Trump *could* have some secret information—like how he's planning to destroy the earth and build a bunch of gaudy Mars-a-Lago on the Red Planet. Or he wants to open a couple of mines and bring coal back from Mars (after which he can take credit as a "job creator" and blame Obama for the high unemployment rates on other planets). But because his record so far on climate change has been horrendous, I'm guessing he's planning a getaway before Mar-a-Lago turns into Chernobyl.

Maybe Trump wants to go to Mars to host some brand-new reality shows up there, like *Dancing with the Aliens* or *Mars's Top Chef* or *Martian Apprentice*. He could sit there and vote people off the galaxy. Talk about an ego trip.

The whole Martian thing is tedious. I couldn't even sit through the Matt Damon movie. But I'll tell you something, if Trump ever gets a second term (God forbid), I'm on the next spaceship outta here!

M is for Masturbation. In 2007, Ted Cruz was working for the Texas attorney general, Greg Abbott, who is now that state's governor. On Abbott's behalf, Cruz filed a brief with the U.S. Court of Appeals, requesting a ban on "dildos, vibrators, and other obscene devices." Cruz said that Americans have no right to masturbate. The Dutch, *ja*. The French, *oui*. The Italians, *sicuro*. But Americans, *nyet*. Cruz actually said, "There is no substantive due-process right to stimulate one's genitals for non-medical purposes unrelated to procreation or outside of an interpersonal relationship." Needless to say, Cruz lost the lawsuit. Thank God, otherwise no more sitting on the washing machine for my aunt Immaculata. (FYI: in those days Cruz was known not as "Lyin' Ted," but "Blue Balls Cruz.")

Ironically, Ted Cruz is one of the biggest dildos out there.

M **is for Media**. President Bannon—I mean White House "advisor" Bannon—has declared the media to be "the enemy of the people." Ironic, in that the guy sitting in the Oval Office got there only because of his ability to manipulate and use the media for his personal gain. Donald Trump doesn't hate the media. In fact, in a weird way, he loves them. (Not as weird as the way he loves his daughter, but weird nonetheless.)

Trump loves the media because, without them, he's nothing. Take away the TV coverage, newspaper headlines, and magazine covers, and he's just another invisible rich guy who made a career off his daddy's money—kind of like Hans and Fritz are doing now. What Trump wants is for his *base* to hate the media.

The media are the friends of the people. If it weren't for the media, Nixon might still be in the White House (he'd be dead, but he'd be there), the Vietnam War might still be going on, and the Kardashians would just be Armenian American girls with generous derrieres and thick eyebrows.

M **is for Melania.** Melania Trump is not only beautiful, but she is also a lot of "firsts." She is the First Lady. She is the first First Lady from Slovenia. She is the first First Lady who has a jewelry line. She is the first First Lady who is actually the president's *third* lady. And she is the first First Lady to tell her husband, "Do whatever the fuck you want" in five different languages.

M is for **Meryl Streep.** When Meryl Streep made an impassioned anti-Trump political speech at the 2017 Golden Globes (though she never mentioned his name), the president-elect did what any president-elect would do: he made nasty, petty, childish remarks about her on Twitter. At least, that's what any president-elect of a middle school class would do. Any other president-elect *of the United States* would have done something entirely different—most likely nothing. But no, the Tangerine Tornado took his phone out of his Miley Cyrus backpack and tweeted, "Meryl Streep, one of the most over-rated actresses in Hollywood, doesn't know me but attacked me last night at the Golden Globes. She is a Hillary flunky who lost big."

Meryl Streep is a lot of things, but overrated isn't one of them. She has won 156 awards for her work in film, television, and music. In 2011, she received a Kennedy Center Honor, and in 2014 she was awarded the Presidential Medal of Freedom. I also hear she'll be up for Most Valuable Player in the National Hockey League in 2018. But Meryl's got these serious character flaws: she hates bullies, she tells the truth, and she speaks her mind. The Tweeting Tyrant can't tolerate such horrific attributes. Knowing Meryl as well as I do—every other Wednesday, Mer and I go to the local Y, swim a couple of laps, shoot some hoops, and wax our legs—Trump's tweets didn't bother her at all. Not because they were petulant and inane, but because they weren't really personal. Sure, they were about her, but he sends out nasty tweets about anybody who hurts his feelings. I think all those UV rays from the tanning booth have penetrated his thin skin. There are other high-achieving famous people whom Donald Trump may have called overrated:

- **Noah:** Over-rated. No taste. He thinks THAT'S a boat? Ha. No casino, no lounge. No wonder only animals would book this "cruise."

- **Sir Edmund Hillary:** Climb a mountain on foot? No way. I'd take my private helicopter to top of Everest. I have money. Climbing over-rated. #Sad!

- **Nelson Mandela:** A black John McCain. He got JAILED. I like people who don't get jailed. #BlackLivesOver-rated.

- **Winston Churchill:** Bigly over-rated. Would've lost wars if not for Patton. Fatties can't lead a charge.

- **Gandhi:** Skinny loser. Wears white after Labor Day. But not at Mar-a-Lago. He'll never be invited.

- **The Pope:** Stole my first name, THE. I've been THE Donald way longer than he's been THE Pope. And Francis is a girl's name. #nicedress

- **Albert Einstein:** Genius? I don't think so. Didn't speak English good. I have better brain #JewsNotThatSmartExceptJared #over-rated

M is for **Miranda Warning.** I watch a lot of crime and police procedural shows on Discovery ID. I first got hooked in the '90s, watching *NYPD Blue.* Remember Dennis Franz's tush? I sure do. Hot. Anyway, one of the most important rights we have as citizens is that if we get arrested, the police have to read us our Miranda rights: "You have the right to remain silent, you have the right to counsel . . ." But in 2016, the Supreme Court weakened the Miranda rights, making it okay for police to use evidence obtained in an illegal search, and it created loopholes for police to get into your house without a formal warrant, among other things. I know, I know—you're thinking, *But, Joy, if you didn't do anything wrong, why would you care about the police coming into your house?* My answer is: Because what if I haven't vacuumed, or there are dishes in the sink, or my Spanx are hanging over the shower curtain rod to dry (or, worse, I'm wearing Spanx and nothing else)? That's why. No one should see that. We need to keep the Miranda warning in place. If they want to change it, how about they change it just for Donald Trump? Every morning, a police officer goes into the Oval Office and tells him, "We have a right for *you* to remain silent." I just pray they don't take away the Carmen Miranda warning: "You have the right to wear bananas on your head no matter how crazy everyone thinks you are."

M **is for** *Mishpocha*. *Mishpocha* is Yiddish. It means "extended family." So, when my three hundred Catholic relatives came to our house for Easter dinner, my mother would say, "Joy, make sure we have enough linguini. The whole *mishpocha* is coming over." (Although my mother was Catholic, she would hook on to an apt Yiddish word when she heard it.) We've never seen Donald with his whole *mishpocha*. We've seen parts of his *mishpocha*. We've seen him with his wives, Ivana, Marla, and Melania. We've seen him with his kids (especially the two and a half he likes), and we've even seen him with Mr. Ivanka, Jared Kushner. Yet, we've hardly ever seen Hans's and Fritz's wives. I know both sons are married; I've seen wedding bands on their fingers in those photos where they're holding up the dead animals they've gunned down. So, what's the story? Are the wives Mexican? Are they Muslim? Are they men? Or, most important, are they still under warranty? I'm joking, of course. Truth be told, Hans and Fritz's wives fit the Trump mold precisely: they're blonde amazons who look like they could step on you at Neiman Marcus and never even notice it.

M is for Miss Universe Pageant. Putting the predator in chief in charge of a beauty pageant is like putting George W. Bush in charge of an English class—nothing good is going to come out of it. Trump brags about sexually assaulting women; he shouldn't even be allowed to attend a beauty pageant, let alone own one.

In 2011, I was a judge for the Miss America Pageant. It was a lot of fun. The women were smart and thoughtful and beautiful. And I can tell you for a fact—a real fact, not an alternative one—that there's no way the people who ran Miss America would insult or disparage any of the contestants. Yet, that's what The Donald routinely did to the contestants in *his* pageants—that is, when he wasn't wandering into their dressing rooms unannounced. And he didn't even need to do that; he could have had the microwaves spy on them.

M **is for Mistake.** George W. Bush once famously (infamously?) said he couldn't recall making any mistakes. I guess saying mission accomplished, blowing up the deficit, destroying the economy, and creating a housing crisis slipped his mind. Donald Trump is the same—he never apologizes for anything because he doesn't think he makes mistakes. There is a clinical psychological term for a person who believes he never makes mistakes: *liar*.

M **is for Moron.** Donald Trump and his Merry Band of Misfits don't seem to know much. In fact, they might be morons—which is something of a backhanded compliment, because there is an actual medical scale of stupidity, and "moron" is *not* at the bottom. The scale is based on standardized IQ testing. There are specific terms to describe various levels of intelligence. For example, an imbecile is smarter than an idiot. And a moron is smarter than an imbecile. So, Donald, when it comes to the stupid scale, be proud! You're a moron! Don't ever, ever, ever let anyone call you an idiot! That word is saved for Rick Perry. And Dan Quayle. And Michelle Bachmann. And that crazy ex-governor Annie Oakley from Alaska.

M **is for Mr. Magoo.** When I was a little girl, *Mr. Magoo* was one of my favorite Saturday morning cartoons. Magoo was a little old man who wore glasses with triple-thick Coke bottle lenses but was basically blind. Every week, he would drive all over town, almost crashing his car or driving off a cliff. Even though he couldn't see anything, he always came away unscathed. Everyone around him, however, was scared to death and in constant peril, yet Magoo kept right on driving, knocking things over everywhere he went. Now, with Trump, I think life is imitating art—if you replace the glasses with bad hair and tiny hands.

M **is for Mussolini.** It's become very trendy to compare Donald Trump to Benito Mussolini. They have a similar scowl, neither one is ever seen laughing, neither speaks English, and both walk like they're carrying a Genoa salami in their pants. There is one big difference, however. Mussolini made the trains run on time. Trump shredded the Amtrak budget so the trains may not run at all.

N **is for Nancy Reagan.** When Nancy Reagan started out as First Lady, she was not very popular. People saw her as a cold, calculating, entitled Hollywood diva. (Kind of the same way Republicans see me, except that I live in New York and I don't gaze at my husband like a dog looking at a pork chop. More on that in a minute.) At the same time that President Reagan was declaring, "Let them eat ketchup (as a vegetable)," Nancy was playing Marie Antoinette of Washington, spending a fortune on new china for the White House. She had two sets of dishes at all times, which begs the question: was Nancy Reagan kosher? She also used to give Ronnie policy advice, but only after she'd consulted astrologists instead of experts. How crazy was that? I don't want our national security based on someone's moon being in retrograde. I want it based on someone's ass being in a library.

But then John Hinckley Jr. shot Reagan because he wanted to impress Jodie Foster so she'd go out with him—that's delusional on so many levels—and public opinion toward Nancy began to change. And when Reagan developed Alzheimer's disease, people's opinion of Nancy softened even more. I felt bad for her; I wouldn't wish that on anyone, but I also know that she didn't go up against Republican dogma and speak out in favor of stem cell research until *after* it affected her personally. But at least she finally did get it. Unlike Mitch McConnell, who had polio as a child and was treated at Warm Springs, for free, but now wants to cut medical benefits for the indigent. Some people never learn. Let's just say he's an ingrate with a short memory.

And as for the gazing thing—I've never gotten over that. Nancy would look at Ronnie with this creepy, glazed stare, like she'd just gotten off the bus from Stepford. Look, I love my husband, but if I ever sit there and stare at him for hours on end without blinking or moving, it won't be because I'm wildly in love, but because I'm dead.

N is for Neo-Nazis. Not to be confused with the old, original Nazis. No, these are new and improved Nazis! The old Nazis were subtler than the new ones. For starters, the neo-Nazis have lots and lots of tattoos; the old Nazis rarely had tattoos, and if they had, they would have been small, maybe a petite I ♥ ADOLF on one ankle. The neos have tattoos all over the place: on their hands, their heads, their necks, their faces. If you see a guy with a swastika on his lips, you're not going to have to think, *Geez, I wonder what that's about?* Old Nazis, though, would discreetly try to find out if you were in their corner. A Nazi official would walk up to a woman on the street and say, "Hello, Fraulein, what are your plans for . . . Chanukah?" And she'd say, "What's a Chanukah?" and then they'd both laugh and laugh and march down the street to an Oktoberfest party, even though it was only April.

The Trump administration only semi-tries to distance itself from the alt-right neo-Nazis. And I say "semi-try" because they never really come out and say, "We don't want your crazy-ass, hateful, racist, anti-Semitic votes," because they *do* want those votes. Team Trump needs that part of the base to come out and vote, so they say just enough to appear not okay with neo-Nazis to appease their nonracist constituents, but not enough to alienate the neo-Nazis themselves.

My question is: Why are the hate groups and neo-Nazis drawn to the Republican Party? Do they prefer elephants over donkeys? Do they look better in red than blue? You don't see an army of skinheads and neo-Nazis at Democratic Party events, do you? Why is that, I wonder?

N is for Nepotism. It's not unusual for presidents to have trusted family members give them advice in the West Wing. Bill Clinton put Hillary in charge of health care, and George W. Bush used to call on Jeb all the time, primarily to ask him how to pronounce the big words. And of course, JFK appointed his brother Robert to be attorney general, which caused Congress to write the anti-nepotism law in 1967 in reaction.

There is some debate over whether the law applies as high up as the White House. This has prompted Trump to appoint his son-in-law, Jared Kushner, to be a senior advisor. He also named his daughter Ivanka "special assistant to the president," without a salary, to skirt the law. (No matter—it's been reported that the Kushners are worth 740 million buckaroos, in any case.) Ivanka will have an office in the White House near the Oval Office, so that Daddy can check her out when she's not looking. They're waiting for Barron to hit puberty so they can make him secretary of energy. In that case, I don't mind. The kid is probably smarter than Rick ("Oops") Perry.

N is for **New Mexico.** The country Trump plans to wall off as soon as he builds his big, beautiful wall across Old Mexico. And he's going to make New Mexico pay for it.

N is for **Newt Gingrich.** Has there ever been a sleazier human being? I think not. Oh, sure, he's mean-spirited and hypocritical, but like they say on infomercials, "Wait, there's more!" Newt has also been married three times, and served his second wife with divorce papers while she was being treated for cancer. At least he eventually acknowledged that he was cheating with a congressional aide during the time he was leading the impeachment proceedings against President Clinton. Enough said.

N is for **Nikki Haley.** The former governor of South Carolina was named the U.S. ambassador to the United Nations. Compared to other Republicans, she's a breath of the fresh air we're running out of—meaning, she's relatively bright and appears to be sane. Unless the Republicans skew even farther to the right—in which case, they'll fall off the end of the earth (you know at least a handful of them still believe the earth is flat)—she may be the future of the Republican Party. Her parents were immigrants from India, and even though she's tough on illegal immigration, she doesn't want to build a wall across the Atlantic and Indian Oceans. She was against the anti-transgender bathroom bill, which is good for the LGBTQ community. On the downside, she's rabidly anti-abortion, which is not good for women. But she also has more balls than the Republican men in Congress in that she stood up to Donald Trump. She said that Trump should release his taxes and that his ban on Muslims was "un-American and un-Constitutional." And when the child in chief began tweeting nasty things about her, she sweetly and condescendingly replied, "Bless his heart." But I'll bet, under her breath, she was mumbling, "What an asshole."

N is for Richard Nixon. I never saw anyone sweat like Richard Nixon did, and I've been line-dancing with Louie Anderson. Every State of the Union speech, there Nixon was, behind the desk, sweating like a pack animal carrying a load across the Andes. For three years, I thought the Oval Office was located in a sauna. Nixon could schvitz in an igloo in January. Check out the Kennedy-Nixon debates—you won't believe your eyes. There was Kennedy, happy, smiling, handsome, looking like he didn't have a care in the world. And there was Nixon, sweating so much it looked like he'd swum to the studio. The most irritating thing is that Nixon had these beads of sweat on his upper lip. I wanted to grab a Kleenex and put my hand through the TV screen and wipe him off. Why was he sweating so much? Was it because he knew he was a liar and a crook?

We can't call Nixon a sociopath; at least he had a clue about himself. I've never seen Trump sweat—seems like lying comes so easily to him it's almost like breathing. That ad that says,

"Never let them see you sweat"? Wrong. When they see you sweat, they know that you know you're a liar.

N is for No One Knew. Shortly after taking office, Trump said, "Nobody knew health care could be so complicated." *Everyone* knew. Only *he* didn't. A few months later, after meeting with Chinese leaders to discuss the North Korean situation, he said, "I realized it's not so easy." Again, *everyone* knew. *He* didn't know.

Look, no one expects the president to know everything, but how he did not even know these things were complex? Did he assume that every president, elected official, and expert for the past fifty years were total idiots and couldn't figure these things out, or that they were all dawdling and doing crossword puzzles when they should have been working?

One would think that over the course of an eighteen-month campaign season, Donald Trump would have learned

N is for Nukeleheads. Donald Trump has the password to our nuclear codes, and I wouldn't trust him with the password to my Amazon account.

something about the issues at hand, or at least the complexity of them. But one would be wrong. He seemingly learned nothing. I don't know much about splitting the atom, but I'm betting it's not as easy as making a lasagna. I don't know advanced calculus, but I'm pretty sure it's more complicated than balancing my checkbook. One would assume that even if Trump didn't know that these things were complicated, he'd at least be smart enough to keep his mouth shut about it. Again, one would be wrong. It turns out that there are other things The Donald didn't know were complicated:

- Renewable energy
- Rocket science
- High-tech agriculture
- Rising seawater levels
- Combating infectious diseases
- Talking to Siri and Alexa
- Salting a margarita glass
- Working the remote
- Buckles and snaps
- Putting his pajamas on with the fly in the front

N is for Nukeleheads. I'm scared—Donald Trump has the password to our nuclear codes, and I wouldn't trust him with the password to my Amazon account.

North Korea has been testing missiles with the apparent goal of someday getting them to reach the United States. Trump has reacted to these tests as expected—with bluster, bravado, and a "my missiles are bigger than yours" attitude. Since he didn't want to interrupt his golf game at Mar-a-Lago, he sent the whitest man in America, Mike Pence, to the Demilitarized Zone, the area separating North from South Korea, to deliver a "stern warning." Pence stopped praying long enough to say, "We will defeat any attack." North Korea bad, we good! Tarzan love Jane.

All I could think of was *Not this again*. I spent junior high school hiding under my desk (and I didn't even want to be a White House intern). I remember how scared I was during the Cuban Missile Crisis, waiting for Castro to drop atomic bombs on Queens College. I kept screaming, "I don't want to die a virgin!" The fact that I was still a virgin in college tells you how assiduously I avoided any incoming missiles, nuclear or otherwise.

Tensions were so high back then that a lot of suburban homes actually had bomb shelters in case of nuclear attack. (Today, those bomb shelters would go for $2,700 a month: "Subterranean studio apartment, lead walls to guarantee quiet, very private. Romantic underground oasis. If you think the mushroom cloud is hot . . .") The Cold War was terrifying, but I always thought we'd get through it. Why would any country start a nuclear war? Surely the leaders knew that they would be vaporized along with the rest of us. When JFK was president, I assumed he knew what he was doing, and in fact, he did. He made a secret deal with everyone's favorite shoe banger, Nikita Khrushchev, and the missiles pointing directly at Queens College campus went away.

Which brings me to the present.

Khrushchev and Kennedy have been replaced by Kim Jong-un and Donald Trump. Smart albeit tough political adversaries have been replaced by a couple of guys out on a day pass from Crazytown. Kim Jong-un, the leader of North Korea, is a total whack job. Everyone in the world agrees he's irrational, unpredictable, and belongs in a looney bin—if for no other reason than the hair and the outfits. No sane person who looks in the mirror and sees *that* staring back at him says, "Love it. I'm good to go." We, in turn, have Donald Trump, who's not as whacko as the Korean cracko, but he's on the A-Team of Ignorance. Do we trust Trump to get us through this in one piece? I'm afraid he might bomb North Dakota by accident. Does Trump even know who Kim Jong-un is? He seemed to get him mixed up with his father, Kim Jong-il, who's been dead for six years. It's entirely possible Trump thinks General Tso is the president of China and that the Queen of England is a cross-dressing dancer called Dave.

I can't go through the nuclear nonsense again. I don't want

to be afraid, and I have no interest in hiding under my desk, praying that those in charge know what's happening (my teachers sure didn't) and will fix things. The only good thing about being sent back to Queens College is that I'd be a virgin again. At least it would give me something to look forward to.

O **is for Ohio.** As John King and Steve Kornacki and Wolf Blitzer and every other newshound "manning the map" on Election Night tell us over and over and over again, "No Republican has ever won the White House without winning Ohio," and, "As Ohio goes, so goes the country." Does this mean I have to be mad at Ohio for the next four years? I hope not. I like Ohio. Some of my favorite people are from Ohio: Erma Bombeck, Gloria Steinem, Dean Martin. Clark Gable was from Cadiz, Ohio (his ears were from Wisconsin); astronauts Neil Armstrong and John Glenn were from Ohio; as were writers Zane Grey, Toni Morrison, and James Thurber. Steven Spielberg is from Cincinnati, Rob Lowe was raised in Dayton, and Paul Newman was from Cleveland. What I'm saying is that I can't hold a grudge against Ohio. Yes, they fucked up in 2016 by voting for Con Man the Vulgarian, but they also reelected the Democratic senator Sherrod Brown, so I'll look away and call it a draw. But if they do it again, in 2020, I'll never set foot in Ohio again, not even to go to the Rock and Roll Hall of Fame—unless I'm voted in.

O **is for Opioid Crisis.** I love saying "Big Pharma"; it reminds me of a lesbian Phys Ed major from Bangladesh I knew in college.

O **is for Oil.** If you want to know how Trump got to the White House, think about the Watergate story and "follow the money." What business are the Koch brothers in? The oil business. What does the Dakota Access Pipeline bring from Canada? Oil. Who will make money off the Dakota Access Pipeline? The Koch brothers. Who will make money having Trump in the White House? The Koch brothers. Whom should we never see nude oil wrestling? The Koch brothers. Truth be told, the only oil I'm interested in is Oil of Olay. Because if Trump does bring us to the point of Armageddon, why not go out with nice, silky smooth skin?

O is for O.J. Simpson. If you're thinking, *Joy's connecting Trump and O.J. because one was nicknamed the Juice and the other is the color of juice,* you'd be wrong. Apparently, the two were friends. O.J. was at Donald's wedding to Marla Maples, along with Don King, Rosie O'Donnell, and me. I don't know what I'm more creeped out about—that I met O.J., or that I was at one of Trump's weddings. All I know is there wasn't a wet eye in the house.

O is for Olfactory Senses. Or, Trump sniffing. During the presidential debates, Donald Trump kept sniffing and making these creepy snorting sounds. At first, I thought he was doing cocaine, but then I remembered that he didn't even drink, so that couldn't have been it. Then I thought maybe he had allergies—maybe he was allergic to Hillary's pantsuits or, more likely, her impressive résumé, but that didn't seem likely. (He's spent his whole life being around people much smarter than he, and this sniffing thing is new.) And then I thought maybe one of those violent Mexican thugs he talks about snuck over the border and used a shiv to punch a hole in his septum while he slept. But that, too, seemed far-fetched. Finally, though, after much contemplation (i.e., two glasses of white wine), I realized that Trump simply had heightened olfactory senses, and he wasn't so much sniffing as smelling. And after even more contemplation (I switched from white to red), I realized that what he was smelling that was so foul it made him sniff and snort was the bullshit coming out of his own mouth.

O is for Opioid Crisis. It was a shock for me to learn that the largest opioid consumption in America is going on in the Red states. That's right, the states that voted overwhelmingly for Donald John Trump. This means that in addition to Russia interfering to help Trump win, and FBI director James Comey perfectly timing his scathing, yet frivolous announcement that the Bureau was reopening its investigation into Hillary Clinton's emails, it looks like a lot of the people who pulled the lever for DT could have been high on drugs on Election Day.

In the 1960s, bored housewives began going to their local Dr. Feelgood to get "diet pills" that would help get them through their days. Fifty years later, the diet pills have been replaced by opioids (heroin, the Oxy twins, etc.), and instead of getting people through their days, they're getting them through rehab. There are a few schools of thought as to why we're in an opioid crisis, but one is that depression and a bleak outlook have led people to escape through drugs. How does it help these people to have Trump keep saying how bleak the situation is, that there's carnage everywhere? Americans need to feel uplifted; we don't need Debbie Downer telling us that the country is on the brink of annihilation (especially when it's not true).

A second possible reason for the opioid crisis is that a deregulated pharmaceutical industry has run rampant selling prescription meds. No more need to buy illegal drugs in a back alley from Shaky or Johnny B. Now you can buy them legally from the pharmacist at CVS (usually a guy named Ned who wears a blue smock with a name tag and a pocket protector).

Big Pharma—I love saying, "Big Pharma"; it reminds me of a lesbian Phys Ed major from Bangladesh I knew in college—keeps running ads for drugs that treat diseases I didn't know existed and conditions I didn't know I had. Last night, I was watching *Hoarders*—I love that show; it makes me feel better about my own housekeeping—and at the dramatic turn in the episode ("How was I supposed to know Mama had three dead cats, a compost heap, and a '67 Buick LeSabre in the bathroom?"), they naturally went to a commercial break. And what I got were back-to-back sixty-second ads asking me if I had restless legs or a dry vagina. Well, I don't have restless legs or a dry vagina. I have dry legs and a restless vagina. Do they have drugs for that?

O is for Oprah. There has been talk of Oprah Winfrey running for president. That would be great; she'd win in a landslide. Everyone would vote for her. She checks every box: She's a woman. She's a celebrity. She has a man. She might have a woman. She has an Oscar. She has a network. She has a book club. And most important, she has a weight problem. What's not to like? Oh, and she's rich. Even Trump might vote for her.

O is for Orange. In 2011, Melania Trump was a guest on my show on HLN. As we know, she's beautiful and, even more important, she has style. Her hair and makeup are perfect—not a split end or a splotch in sight. Which makes me wonder: how can she be married to a man who looks like he passed out in a bag of Doritos? Does she not notice that his face is as orange as the Great Pumpkin from the Charlie Brown Halloween special? Or maybe when she hears his voice first thing in the morning, she goes into such a panic that she suffers from hysterical blindness and all she can see coming toward her are those dinosaur arms and tiny hands. He needs a makeover. Maybe Tiffany can start a national Take Your Father Shopping Day, and she can drag him to her favorite makeup counter at Bloomingdale's. Even better, she should take him to Nordstrom, just to piss off Ivanka. Talk about a win-win. Or maybe Hans or Fritz could mention in passing that Dada needs to stop buying his makeup at Sherwin-Williams. Glossy latex enamel is for suburban houses, not human skin. His face clashes with itself.

But worse than the color is the premise: Why does Donald Trump even wear makeup? He's not on *The Apprentice* anymore, so that can't be the reason. In fact, since he took office, he almost never appears in public, and when he does, everyone holds their breath, praying he hasn't started World War

III. The straight men I know wear makeup only if they're on television or onstage. I have a gay friend who wears makeup only to provide contour, because he lives with the delusion that if he appears two pounds thinner, George Clooney will leave Amal and go out with him. (I can relate.)

So, the man and his makeup—yet one more unexplained thing about our president . . . along with his IQ; his tax returns; his mental diagnosis; his foreign, domestic, *and* economic policies; and his "fondness" for Vlad the Impaler.

O is for Overtime. Overtime is what employers should pay their workers if they work more hours than they're required to. Donald Trump and his minions disagree. When Donald drained the swamp, he took the bottom-feeders he found and put them in his Cabinet and his inner circle. Now those soulless, bloodthirsty vultures—oh, I'm sorry, I meant "business-friendly corporate executives"—are looking for ways to allow employers not to have to pay overtime to their employees, usually by cutting hours or changing their employment status. Trump is lucky *he* doesn't work at an hourly rate. Considering how much time he spends vacationing at Mar-a-Lago, we'd only have to pay him two bucks a week.

O is for Oxycodone. A strong, highly addictive opioid painkiller, or as Rush Limbaugh thinks of it, lunch.

O is for Oxycontin. A strong, highly addictive opioid painkiller, or as Rush Limbaugh thinks of it, dinner.

P is for Palin. Not just Sarah, but the whole family: Todd and Bristol and Willow and Azalea and Crabgrass and Trig and Tripp and Track and Trick or Treat.

I love Sarah Palin—not as a human being of course, but as a punch line. She's a comedic jackpot, a modern-day version of slipping on a banana peel or drinking from a dribble cup. The humor keeps flowing, like a urinary tract infection. FYI: I think "Tract" will be the name for Bristol's next kid.

Speaking of Bristol, how great was it that, after constantly getting pregnant out of wedlock, she became the spokesperson for abstinence? Bristol has spent so much time in the backseat of pickup trucks, she should have a Confederate bumper sticker tattooed on her ass. Spokesperson for abstinence? If she were any more unqualified for a job, she'd be a member of Trump's Cabinet.

P.S. I think "Truck" will be the name for Tract's twin brother.

P is for Paranoia. Republican politicians like to traffic in fear, creating a sense of paranoia among their faithful (and, if we're not careful, the rest of us). "Obama is coming for your guns"; "The Chinese are taking your jobs," etc. None of it is true. Last time I checked, Sarah Palin still has her Uzi to mow down moose, and I have yet to meet a disgruntled white guy who lost out to a minority for a job delivering egg rolls and wonton soup to my apartment on a bicycle or coming up with an app for my iPad.

Team Trump has convinced his base to be afraid of Mexicans, African Americans, lesbians, gays, transgender people, Muslims, liberals, Jews, intellectuals, brown people, all sorts of foreigners, CNN, MSNBC, the *Washington Post*, and of course the *New York Times*. Truth be told, I'm more afraid of Team Trump than of any of them. Especially Mike Pence; she scares the hell out of me.

P is for Pence. Creepy Veepy has more issues than *Life* magazine's back catalogue. Mike Pence is fooling no one with all the hateful antigay rhetoric. Pence spends more time obsessing about gay sex than all the members of the Village People combined. Pence's anti-LGBTQ record is so bad that when he went to see the Broadway show *Hamilton*, at the end of the play the cast called him out from the stage. Most of the cast members were black and Hispanic, and some were definitely gay. When the show ended, "Aaron Burr" (wearing a lovely muumuu) stepped forward and, in front of the entire audience, asked Pence if the incoming administration would please be fair and tolerant of *all* Americans, not just the ones it liked. It was a stunning moment. I only wish Pence had gone to see *Avenue Q*. It would have been fun to see a hand puppet tell him to go fuck himself.

Pence also says he won't have lunch or dinner alone with a woman other than his wife. (Notice he doesn't say anything about brunch?) I'm not sure if this is out of some misguided, fake-Christian respect for his wife or because he is *sooooo* darned heterosexual he's afraid he wouldn't be able to control himself and he might leap across the booth at the Olive

Garden and grab him a piece-o-puss like his boss man brags about. What if he were having the Never Ending Pasta Bowl and Mother Teresa, exhausted from washing the feet of the poor, walked in and plopped herself down at his table? Would he spit out his linguini and make a handsy lunge at the Saint of Calcutta?

But in spite of (or maybe because of) his flaming homophobia, mainstream Republicans seem to like Pence. I think it's because, compared to Trump, Pence seems reasonable and normal. Of course, compared to Trump, *Mad Money*'s Jim Cramer seems reasonable and normal. Mike Pence presents well; he's like a pit bull at the Westminster Kennel Club Dog Show. When he's being paraded in front of cameras and judges, he looks pretty and acts nice, but the minute he's backstage, he's harassing poodles and humping dachsunds.

And he's the *perfect* VP choice for Trump. Here's why:

- He has normal hair. It's a silver, close-cropped "Welcome to 1953" style. Makes him look like a drill sergeant in the army.

- He provides cover for Trump with the evangelical base. In their heart of hearts, the evangelicals *must* know that Trump is a malevolent, cheating, womanizing heathen. They're much more comfortable with a malevolent, faithful homophobe, as long as he's against abortion.

- He knows how to defend Trump when he lies. For example: In a December 2016 interview, George Stephanopoulos asked

Pence about Trump's penchant for lying. Pence said that Trump's speaking his mind was "refreshing" to the American people. Really? I'm an American people and I don't find it refreshing. The only kind of lying I find refreshing is lying by the pool on a lounge chair with a glass of white wine while Jon Hamm fetches me grapes and gives me a pedicure.

P **is for Pets**. Nearly every president in modern history has had a First Dog, you know, one that runs around the White House, plays in the Rose Garden, and poops in the Blue Room. The Obamas had Bo, the Bushes had Miss Beazley, the Nixons had Checkers, the Clintons had Bill. Donald Trump is such a narcissist I don't know if he's capable of caring for a dog, but if he is . . . he'd probably get a Chihuahua. Not because they're small or cute, but because when he gets bored, he could just deport it back to the shelter it tunneled out of in search of a job at Taco Bell.

P is for **Pussy Grabber**. How do you grab a pussy? Easy. Walk up to Paul Ryan, take him by the collar, and say, "Get over here, you, spineless little twit!"

P **is for Plagiarism**. Or, as Melania calls it, writing. When I watched Melania's speech at the Republican National Convention, I was quite impressed. It was well written, on point, and beautifully delivered—and familiar! DUH. (Truth be told,

Melania has a better command of the English language than Donald does, which *is* surprising, given that she's from Slovenia and he's from Queens. But I digress.)

The day after her speech, we all discovered that part of it had been lifted directly from Michelle Obama's 2012 speech at the Democratic National Convention. Melania plagiarized a Democrat, meaning they're not just stealing our money; they're also stealing our words.

To be fair, it's not like Melania had written the speech herself—all high-end political figures have speechwriters. But shouldn't they also have fact-checkers? Or at least alternative-fact-checkers, if that's what they're more comfortable with. Instead, they let the poor woman go out and hang herself in front of the whole country. Maybe that's why she has barely left Trump Tower since Shavuos (a Jewish holiday that sounds funny, even though it's not the one where a guy blows the shofar).

P **is for Prenup.** For the record, I became a believer in prenups when Anna Nicole Smith had to fight for money after her two-hundred-year-old billionaire husband died and his adult children battled her for his fortune. A rock-solid prenup, with special competency clauses in place, would have prevented such ugliness. My own personal feeling is that if Anna Nicole could go down on that withered schlong, she was entitled to every nickel the old goat had.

I know for a fact that Donald Trump always has strong prenups in place, which, given how often he gets married, is a good idea. What I don't know for a fact are the details of the prenups, but given the public statements his ex-wives have made, they must include things like "She'll only say how wonderful I am," "She'll say I'm great in bed," and "I get full custody of the bobby pins and White Rain hair products."

P is for Purell. Donald Trump suffers from mysophobia, an unnatural fear of germs. (Although, he probably doesn't think he suffers from it; he probably thinks *I've got the best phobia. Nobody has phobias as good as mine. I'm a great phobic.*) Trump doesn't like to shake hands with people, but, to be fair, neither does another famous germaphobe, Howie Mandel. Which explains why, when Howie and The Donald met, instead of shaking hands, they engaged in a deep, slow tongue kiss, complete with moaning and tingly feelings in their stomachs. Just kidding—I like Howie and wouldn't wish this on him.

P is for Pussy Grabber. How do you grab a pussy? Easy. Walk up to Paul Ryan, take him by the collar, and say, "Get over here, you, spineless little twit!"

Actually, how *do* you grab a woman by her pussy? Not sure. It's not like the puss sticks out like a penis—or like Rick Perry in a bookstore. Unless a woman is a freak of nature, and has looser lips than Julius and Ethel Rosenberg, the puss is almost impossible to grab onto—then again, if the man has extremely tiny hands . . . (See: *Tiny Hands.*)

Q is for **Queens**. I don't mean Elizabeth or Beatrix or Latifah. I mean the New York City borough where Donald Trump was born. For those of you not familiar with New York City, it's made up of five boroughs: Manhattan, Brooklyn, Queens, Staten Island, and the Bronx. To give you context: the Bronx is where the Yankees play; Queens is where the Mets play; Brooklyn is where the Dodgers used to play; Staten Island is where no one plays; and Manhattan is where Patti LuPone and Bette Midler play.

When Donald Trump was born in 1946, Queens had a population of approximately 1.9 million people, and it was 83 percent white (especially *his* neighborhood, Jamaica Estates, which is the fancy-schmancy part of Jamaica). As of 2010, Queens had a population of approximately 1.6 million and was 57 percent white. See where I'm going with this? Trump's taken the old "there goes the neighborhood" adage and applied it to the whole country. He's brought his anti-immigrant, anti-minority philosophy from Queens to Washington.

is for **Quickie**. In the past, the word quickie was usually used to describe a short sexual escapade. Now it's used to describe the length of Donald Trump's attention span and, probably, the longest sexual escapade he's ever had.

If you doubt this, don't forget that his and Daddy's real estate companies were sued twice (in 1973 and 1982) for racial discrimination in housing. Both times, the Trumps settled with the plaintiffs, even though they were not forced to admit any wrongdoing. (My question: why pay out millions of dollars if you didn't do anything wrong?) Anyway, Trump tried to prevent his buildings from becoming melting pots, and now he's trying to do the same with our country. I hope he fares about as well now as he did then.

Q is for Questions. I have so many questions and so little time, but these are the questions I would like answered *today*:

1. **(To the press)** When Trump lies, how come you never stop him and say, "Hey, that's a lie"?
2. **(To Ivanka)** Are you inviting Steve Bannon over for Rosh Hashanah?
3. **(To Bill O'Reilly)** What's your obsession with killing famous historical figures? And who told you falafel is a lubricant?
4. **(To Reince Priebus)** Is that collagen in your lips or are they swollen from kissing Trump's butt?
5. **(To Sean Spicer)** Are you physically afraid of April Ryan?

Q is for Quiche. Remember that book *Real Men Don't Eat Quiche*? It's not true. My husband loves quiche and he's a real man. And to prove it, he eats his quiche with a side of concrete. In my opinion, real men don't insult women, don't make vulgar remarks about their own daughters, don't spend nine hours constructing their hair or wear orange makeup. And now I have to go dig up the driveway; I'm making quiche for lunch.

Q is for Quickie. In the past, the word *quickie* was usually used to describe a short sexual escapade. Now it's used to describe the length of Donald Trump's attention span and, probably, the longest sexual escapade he's ever had.

Q is for QVC. For those of you who were heartbroken when Nordstrom, Bloomingdale's, and Neiman Marcus stopped carrying a lot of Ivanka Trump's clothing, jewelry, and accessories (because they were appalled by the administration's divisive policies and language), cry no more. In fact, perk the fuck up! The Ivanka brand is on the QVC TV network! Now you never have to leave your house. You can get any kind of schmata, handbag, or belt you want. You can buy the earrings, necklaces, and bracelets of your choice. And someday, in the not-too-distant future, you may even be able to buy handcuffs and leg irons that are exact replicas of the ones Ivanka's husband will be wearing in Leavenworth. (Talk about Jared the Jeweler!)

Joy Behar

R is for Raging Bull. Robert De Niro is a tough interview. He's not a big talker—he gives mainly monosyllabic answers—but Donald Trump has transformed De Niro into Patrick Henry on steroids. De Niro has said of Trump, "I'd like to punch him in the face, he's blatantly stupid, he's a punk, he's a dog, he's a pig, he's a con, he's a bullshit artist, he's a mutt who doesn't know what he's talking about, he doesn't do his homework, doesn't care, he thinks he's gaming society and doesn't pay his taxes."

This is the longest sentence De Niro has uttered since he was in *Mean Streets* in 1973. As Patrick Henry might have said (if he were alive, like Frederick Douglass), "Give me liberty or I'll break both your legs."

R is for Random Acts of Helpfulness. The Honda car company has come up with a new program called Random Acts of Helpfulness. People call in or write to Honda and tell them some personal story, and Honda steps in and helps them. It's kind of like *Extreme Makeover*, only with cars. For example, a mother from Pomona called up and said her son was in music school, but his instrument had broken and they couldn't afford to replace it. And the Honda guy said, "We're here to help. We're going to buy your son a new clarinet." And the mother gets all emotional and cries, and all the listeners think, "Aww, isn't that sweet?" (Of course, you never hear the mother say, "That's awfully nice, but he plays the piano.")

Anyway, I would like a Random Act of Helpfulness from Honda: "Dear Honda, this is Joy from New York. My head hurts and my heart is broken, but unlike Russia and the Koch brothers, I can't afford to buy an election. It would be so great if you could help me out and get me a new fucking president."

R is for Reaganomics. When David Stockman was the director of the Office of Management and Budget (OMB) from 1981 to 1985, he was known as the "Father of Reaganomics." (This must have been very confusing to Nancy because, as I mentioned earlier, Ronnie called her "Mommy.") Reaganomics is supply-side economics, or the infamous "trickle-down theory," which basically means if you give the wealthiest people in the country even *more* money, eventually it will trickle down to everyone else. (Stockman also hoped this would curtail the "welfare state." As nasty as that sounds, it's still better than the GOP's current plans to curtail the welfare state: deporting people and starving the poor, elderly, and infirm.) Rumor has it that the first time Tip O'Neill heard about Stockman's economic theory, he laughed so hard he felt something trickling down his leg.

And thirty-seven years later, that may be the only thing that has ever trickled down. The Reagan tax cuts for the rich did not help the middle class. They *did*, however, grow the national debt from $79.0 billion to $2.3 *trillion* by the end of Reagan's first term. And since Reaganomics didn't work for anybody but the wealthy the first time, guess what the Republicans are trying to push again in 2017? If you said, "Same bullshit," you'd be right. And how do they get away with it? See: "B is for Base."

R **is for Regis Philbin.** A lot of the nonracist, non-crazy people who voted for Donald Trump were voting for change. They didn't want another politician in the White House; they wanted an outsider. I can appreciate that they were tired of politics as usual, but considering that the field *is* politics, wouldn't it have been a good idea to hire a person with *some* experience in it, or at least rudimentary knowledge of how government works? When I go for my annual endoscopy, I go to a gastroenterologist, not an outsider, like my dog walker or the neighborhood auto body guy. I want someone who actually knows what he's doing.

R is for Republicans. Republicans should stay away from my uterus. Whether I use that space to house a fetus or store a winter coat, it's none of Newt Gingrich's business.

According to the most recent UN Census estimates, the population of the United States stands at 326,111,903. Think about that: 326,111,903 people, and the Republicans couldn't find *one* outsider who wasn't racist, misogynistic, xenophobic, or mentally ill to run for office?

If I want an outsider in the White House, I'd go for Regis Philbin. I love Regis; everybody loves Regis. He'd be perfect. He'll appeal to Republicans because he's an old, straight white guy with no governmental experience. He'll appeal to Democrats because he's smart, thoughtful, and lives in New York. He's always in a good mood—he's even friendly early in the morning!—he's a great listener, and on top of that, he was able to deal with the perkiness of Kelly and Kathie Lee for all those years without losing his temper or his lunch. Do you really think Kim Jong-un is going to rattle his cage? Not only that, but Regis can sing, and he has a great stage act. He won't waste a million dollars a day of taxpayer money schlepping to play golf at Mar-a-Lago. He'll grab an Uber and do a show at the Westbury Music Fair. A hundred and eight bucks, door to door. What's not to like? Regis in 2020!

R is for Reince Priebus. The first time I heard the words *Reince Priebus*, I thought it was a skin condition, like shingles or eczema. Turns out, I was right. Every time I see him I start to itch.

"Reince" is an unusual name. According to his family members, their heritage is German and—shockingly!—Russian. Not only is "Reince" an unusual name, but it's hard to pronounce. "Reince" rhymes with "Heinz" (and "Priebus" rhymes with "Ass-Kissing Sycophantic Party Hack"). If my family name were "Priebus" and I had a child, "Reince" wouldn't be on the short list of baby names. It wouldn't be on the long list, either. In fact, it would never cross my mind. I understand and appreciate ethnic pride, but you know what I appreciate more? Common sense. You know full well that every single day of Reince Priebus's life, when he's been introduced to someone, he has had to spend five minutes saying, "No, it's pronounced

Reinz," or, "No, my parents didn't drink," or, "No, I'm not joking," or, "Yes, fine, whatever. It's okay to call me Bob. A lot of people do." Takes the starch right out of that opening conversation, doesn't it?

When Reince was in middle school, he probably had his lunch money stolen at least three times a week. When he was born, his parents should have thought ahead and named him Joey or Steve or Peter. "Peter Priebus" would have made him popular; it sounds vaguely Spiderman-ish.

My parents were Italian—my father was actually born in Italy, but at no point did he and my mother consider naming me "Pinocchio" or "Ismerelda" And they definitely wouldn't have named me "Reince."

I have to take a break now and get some Benadryl. My Reince Priebus is starting to itch and I want to stop it before it spreads to my Orrin Hatch.

R is for Repeat. During the 2008 campaign, Katie Couric famously asked Sarah Palin what newspapers she read, and the Wit from Wasilla was left speechless. I'm not sure if Sarah was stunned because she didn't read newspapers or because she didn't even know what newspapers were. Either way, she was baffled, and referred to it as a "gotcha question." (To me, a gotcha question is "What was the mathematical formula Robert Oppenheimer used to invent the atomic bomb?" or, "If there were sales at both Chico's and Talbots, which store would you go to first?") During the debates, when Trump was asked a gotcha question (which is any question that requires actual knowledge of anything), he either ignored the question or gave a response that had nothing to do with the question asked. And the moderators let him get away with it.

"Mr. Trump, do you have any plans on how to resolve the conflict in Syria?"

"I like soup."

"Thank you, Mr. Trump. Next question . . ."

What they should have done is ask the same question over and over and over again until he answered it, and not ask a different question until he did. Just keep repeating the question. For example, "Mr. Trump, would you or any of the voices in your head be willing to undergo a mental health test to see if you're fit to hold office?"

R is for Reporters. Contrary to what Reichsmarschall Bannon and his boss say, the press is not the "enemy of the people." It's the *voice* of the people. Reporters are *supposed to* ask questions of the government on our behalf, and to hold truth to power. (FYI: I hate the expression "truth to power"; it's so annoying. It's like TV commercials that use the expressions "tasty nougats," "new and improved," or "that not-so-fresh-feeling.")

I put "supposed to" in italics for a reason: it's because during the 2016 presidential campaign, some of the reporters didn't ask the questions they should have or do their jobs as well as they could have. Had they done so, maybe Donald Trump would still be living in New York, shopping for wife number four, and bilking students, vendors, and contractors out of their hard-earned money instead of living in Washington setting our precarious democracy on fire.

For all Trump's bluster about how much he hates the media—he *doesn't*. He needs press coverage the way Dracula needs blood. Maybe if we make him look in a mirror, or go outside on a really, really, really sunny day . . .

I remember one of the first press conferences Trump held early on in the campaign. It was shortly after he started calling Mexicans thugs and rapists. Univision reporter Jorge Ramos stood up to ask him a question about those remarks, and rather than answer the question, Trump had Ramos thrown out of the press conference—he literally had security pull him out of the room. (Afterward, Trump said he had no idea who the security guard was who grabbed Ramos. That, of course, was a lie; the security guard was part of Trump's team.) What happened next was even more appalling: nothing. The press conference went on as though nothing had happened; as though Ramos hadn't been accosted and free speech quashed. In my not-so-humble opinion, every reporter in that room should have gotten up, walked out, and left Trump standing there by himself talking to folding chairs. I'm a comedian, not a journalist, but if I can walk out on Bill O'Reilly—okay, maybe I needed the exercise—certainly they could've mustered the backbone to walk out on Trump when he had their colleague accosted. And they should have walked out of every other subsequent event, rally, and speech when Trump started insulting them, disparaging them, and implying that violence against them was acceptable. Not out of spite, but out of self-preservation. The only thing a narcissist craves is attention. Take attention away from the narcissistic bully, and watch him come crawling back. (I would've liked to see him try to throw Oprah out of a room. Gayle would have kicked his ass from here to Mar-a-Lago.)

R is for Restiva. The drug Restiva apparently cures "dry eye." This must be for those times when Visine, onions, horse-radish, and a knee in the nuts for men just won't do the trick. The only person I ever met who had chronically dry eyes was the lady down the hall from me in apartment 7F. She'd had so much plastic surgery she couldn't blink anymore. (She also couldn't smile, frown, sneeze, or cough.) That woman was practically mummified.

The thing that bothers me about Restiva is that the actresses who play the eye doctors in the commercials are all super-model gorgeous. I'm not saying this doesn't happen in real life, but my ophthalmologist, Dr. Bernstein, is bald except for the hair in his ears and the hump on his back. In all the years I've been going to him, not once have I ever thought, *Thank God I don't have dry eyes. Otherwise, I wouldn't be able to fixate on Dr. B's tight abs and ample package.*

But the most upsetting thing about the Restiva situation (as well as the restless leg meds) is that if the Republicans get their new health care plan in place, probably none of those drugs or doctor's visits will be covered. Which means I'll be sitting in a restaurant surrounded by people shaking their legs and rubbing horseradish in their eyes. Very hard to enjoy chicken marsala with Blinky and Shaky crying and rattling all the other tables.

R is for **Restless Leg Syndrome.** Restless leg syndrome is a disorder that creates an urge to move one's legs. That's not a disorder, that's walking. Complications are daytime sleepiness, irritability, and depression. I thought that was menopause.

How is this a syndrome? Maybe some people are just fidgety. When I was teaching, half the children in the class shook their legs and squirmed around. Usually they had to go to the bathroom, or they'd forgotten their homework, or they were appalled that I'd given them *Portnoy's Complaint* as a reading assignment. Whatever. They didn't have a syndrome; they were just being children.

Now, in 2017, I find myself squirming around and shaking my legs every time Donald Trump appears on TV or opens his mouth. I don't have a syndrome; I have Trumpophobia, a fear that the president might pick up the wrong device and, instead of tweeting, press the nuclear button. I'm pretty sure there's no medication for that.

R is for **Revenge Porn.** Over the past few years, a new phenomenon called "revenge porn" has, pardon the double entendre, popped up. This is when a couple breaks up and one of the exes gets so mad he posts nude pics or sex tapes of the other one online.

I find this quite shocking. First of all, unless you're a Kardashian or a model with a rare skin rash posing for a medical journal, what kind of person would let someone take nude pictures of her, let alone videos? In order for a man to see me naked, I have to be in his will. And what kind of a spiteful jerk would get so upset over being dumped that he'd post those pictures and videos online?

Donald Trump would, that's who. He engages in revenge porn without the porn. (I pray that's actually true—the sight of Donald Trump naked is one of those things you can't unsee, like an autopsy photo or Mitch McConnell naked.) Trump is the most spiteful person I've ever seen, and I've seen *a lot* of spiteful people. I've been on *The View* for twenty years, don't forget. I think one of the real reasons Trump fired James Comey is because Comey wouldn't file criminal charges against Hillary Clinton and "lock 'er up!" Trump hates Hillary because she beat him in the popular vote, so he wants whatever revenge he can exact. Yes, Trump has the job, and yes, Republican gerrymandering gave him the Electoral College vote, but he knows full well that she beat him. And he can't let go of it. I just pray that none of his wives ever lets him walk into the bedroom wearing nothing but a camera around his neck.

R **is for Right to Life.** Republicans say they believe in the right to life, but that's not true. They believe in the right to life only for the *un*born (might-possibly-grow-up-to-be-a-Republican-voter-someday), not for the *already* born. They can't cut funding fast enough for prenatal care, postnatal care, maternity leave, health insurance, after-school programs, Head Start, and on and on and on. They're not that keen on living *adults*, either. They oppose the American Jobs Act and want to get rid of labor unions; they oppose most veterans' benefits; they oppose LGBTQ hate crimes and worker protection legislation; they oppose universal health care . . . and on and on and on. The minute you come out of the womb, they drop you like a hot rock.

It also drives me crazy when the Republicans refer to liberals as being "pro-abortion." Nobody I know is "pro-abortion." We're prochoice, and it's not the same thing. I have yet to meet the woman who wakes up in the morning and can't decide whether to go to Costco, take a Pilates class, or have an abortion. I am prochoice, and I choose to have Republicans stay away from my uterus. (Yes, I'm past my childbearing years, but that's not the point. Whether I use that space to house a fetus or store a winter coat, it's none of Newt Gingrich's business.)

R is for Right-Wing Radio. In the 1980s, I had my own talk show on WABC Radio in New York. WABC was a right-wing talk station then—believe it or not, my show was on the air every day right before Rush Limbaugh's show. My office was to the left of his—or should I say "far left"? Anyway, Monday through Friday, I'd go on the air and drive WABC's right-wing listeners nuts. I'd do crazy things, like cite facts to support my opinions. This made them furious. Then Rush would come on with his propaganda and soothe the savage beasts. In hindsight, I think Rush owes me a big thank-you for his ratings, because I got the WABC base so angry that when he came on, it was like make-up sex. And everyone likes make-up sex.

Okay, maybe not with Rush Limbaugh, but you get my point. So, Rush, you're welcome.

There is no real left-wing counterbalance to right-wing radio. It's been tried. For a few years, Air America attempted to fill the void on the left, but it never gained support. I think I've finally figured out why. According to *Forbes* magazine, it's all to do with demographics. Most right-wing radio listeners are old white guys with nothing to do but complain. The liberal base is not only much more diverse (with a choice of diverse radio stations to listen to), but most of *our* old, white guys are doing things—volunteering, engaging in social activism, holding their wives' pocketbooks in front of shoe stores in the mall. Whatever pursuit they choose, or have chosen for them, the result is that they're too busy to sit around listening to crabby loudmouths on the radio.

R is for Eleanor Roosevelt. Eleanor Roosevelt was our country's longest-serving and most influential First Lady. (And I say that with all due respect to Jackie Kennedy, Betty Ford, Michelle Obama, and Martha Washington, who not only was our *first* First Lady, but spent almost every night for four years picking splinters out of her thighs.) Eleanor Roosevelt became a spokesperson for human rights and women's rights, championed the plight of the poor, and was a beacon of strength during World War II and the Great Depression. (I hate calling that period of American history the "Great Depression." To me, it's an oxymoron. It's like saying, "excellent emphysema" or "pretty polyps.")

Eleanor wrote daily news columns and hosted radio shows; she was ahead of her time. In fact, if Eleanor were alive today, she'd be all over Instagram and Snapchat, and she'd be tweeting Trump right off Twitter. I think Eleanor would have been horrified by Trump. Trump makes fun of the disabled; FDR was disabled. Also, when Trump cheated on his wives with a new girlfriend, an ugly divorce ensued. When Franklin cheated on Eleanor with a new girlfriend, she didn't divorce him; she just got a new girlfriend, too. (Allegedly.)

R is for Rose Garden. The White House Rose Garden, which borders the Oval Office, is one of the most iconic places in the country. It has been the site of so many important events—JFK welcoming home the Mercury astronauts, Tricia Nixon's wedding, the 1994 Israel-Jordan Peace Treaty signing, and, most recently, the installation of a secret trap door that leads to the tunnel to get to the Kremlin.

R is for Rosie O'Donnell. You'd think Donald Trump and Rosie O'Donnell would get along. They're both New Yorkers, they're both TV stars, and they both have five children with three different women. But no, Trump hates her.

You may recall that, back in the day, and on *The View*, Rosie made fun of Trump's hair, his finances (or lack thereof), and his adulterous behavior. This sent The Donald into paroxysms of vituperative insults. He called Rosie every name in the book—a "slob," "disgusting" with a "fat, ugly face."

This is known as an ad hominem attack, meaning it's personal, not political, and looked upon as a low blow and not becoming of a mature person. Let's remember that Trump is the king of ad hominem. Trump called Marco Rubio "dumb," Ted Cruz was "lyin' Ted," Bernie Sanders was "crazy," and Elizabeth Warren, "goofy." But it seems that The Donald has a special hatred in his heart for Rosie.

Why? My opinion is that she is a *woman* who spoke the truth and mocked him in front of millions of people—yes, *The View* has millions of viewers, and good ratings—and Tiny Hands's fragile ego could not deal with that. I've noticed that he becomes particularly unhinged when women go after him (Megyn Kelly, Carly Fiorina, and of course that "nasty woman" Hillary Rodham Clinton). It's been ten years since that infamous exchange between him and O'Donnell, but in May 2017, after he fired FBI director James Comey, he tweeted, "We finally agree on something, Rosie." (Apparently, Rosie had been in favor of firing Comey because of the way he'd handled the Clinton email debacle.)

Let's pause here to absorb the fact that the leader of the free world, the man who complains that he cannot get his agenda going because of ongoing investigations, is obsessing over Rosie O'Donnell. He's too "busy" to go to briefings or read up on history, yet he apparently took the time out of his sleepless nights to wander around the West Wing in his bathrobe, searching for Rosie's tweet about Comey, and then post it, as if this validated his decision to fire the FBI director.

Now I'm waiting for Trump to locate something that *I've* tweeted to validate a decision he's made. I could be responsible indirectly for World War III. His tweet will say, "Joy Behar finally agrees with me on something, so let's just take out North Korea."

R is for **Russian Hacking**. The first time I heard "Russian hack" on TV, I thought, *Is Yakov Smirnoff still working?* But then I realized they were talking about a foreign power breaking into our secure computer networks, and I felt so much better.

The issue of Russia hacking into our computers became a huge talking point during the debates between Secretary of State Clinton and game show host Donald Trump. Clinton pointed out that the Russians hacked our computers to help the Trump campaign because Putin wanted a puppet in the White House. In response, Trump started whining, "I'm no puppet, you're the puppet. You're the puppet!" I'm betting that Trump *is* Putin's puppet—it would certainly explain why he has Putin's hand up his ass. If I'm wrong, however, then Trump's not Putin's puppet; he's Putin's bitch. Either way, at least now he's prepped for a colonoscopy.

R is for *To Россия with Love*. I don't understand Trump's obsession with Russia. I find it more confusing than Sudoku. I don't know much about Russia (which, of course, would qualify me to be Trump's ambassador to Russia), other than that they make good vodka, fur hats, and great pairs figure skating teams. I *do* know, however, that Russia and the United States have not been allies since the end of World War

II. Tensions ramped up during the Cold War, and we've been monitoring their nuclear capabilities for decades. Oh, I also know that Vladimir Putin is an authoritarian, and that a lot of his political enemies (real or perceived), including the press, tend to wind up missing or dead. Not exactly a Tinder profile I'd swipe right on.

Yet, Trump seems to love both Russia and Putin. He says Putin was a better leader than Obama. He says Putin is strong and tough. Trump has said Putin is a "tough guy," "he's 'brilliant.'" He even claimed that Putin had complimented him and called him "a genius." Who could resist that? Trump told right-wing radio mouthpiece Michael Savage that he met Putin "a long time ago . . . and we got along great, by the way." Sounds like quite a first date.

So, Donnie, why all the props for Putin? Do you and he share a love that dare not speak its name? Is he really Vlad the Impaler? And more important, does Mike Pence know?

I'm kidding of course. I don't think Trump and Putin are lovers. (I've seen Vlad half-naked on a horse, and I doubt he'd be into the Pillsbury Doughboy.) I think Trump is just impressed with unquestioned, unbridled dictatorial power, which would also explain his bizarre man-crushes on the strongmen leaders Recep Tayyip Erdogan of Turkey, Xi Jinping of China, Rodrigo Duterte of the Philippines, and Abdel Fattah el-Sisi of Egypt. I don't think he's having affairs with any of them, either. (Although, if they compliment him enough, who knows?) I just think he has lust in his heart (with sincere apologies to Jimmy Carter). He's attracted to the idea of total, uncontested power with no obstacles or pesky Constitutions annoying him. He had all that on his reality show, and he now thinks the Oval Office is the "boardroom" on *The Apprentice*.

The other reason for Trump's obsession with the Head of Red is green. I was watching CNN today, and it seems that when it comes to money, The Donald and the Kremlin are closer than cousins in West Virginia. Trump acolytes Carter Page, Paul Manafort, and Michael Flynn—or, as I think of them, the Nuclear Triad—are all very closely connected to Russia in that they seem to have had shady relationships with shady people who are all shadily connected to Putin.

This does not seem to bother Trump's diehard supporters in the least. But it should. Let's get something straight here: Russia is not a friend of the United States. We're not even frenemies. You know that type of rich woman with the stretched skin, who gives air kisses when she runs into an "old friend" at a restaurant and says, "OMG, Marion, you look great. We'll have to get together soon," when in fact she's been schtupping Marion's husband in the pool house for six months?

What upsets me even more than Trump's dry-humping our enemies is his antagonistic treatment of our allies, including England, Germany, Australia, and even Canada, for God's sake. How do you pick a fight with Justin Trudeau? He's the kind of man you hope your daughter will marry. He's the kind of man you hope your *son* will marry. God forbid anything ever happened to my husband. Once I got over my grief, I'm pretty sure I'd be heading up to Ottawa for a little *voulez-vous* with Monsieur Trudeau.

S is for Sad! When The Donald is in his tweeting mode (usually in the middle of the night), his favorite word seems to be *sad*. Here are just a *few* tweets, sent during the first two months of the 2016 campaign:

Mar. 3

@realDonaldTrump

Because of me, the Republican Party has taken in millions of new voters, a record. If they are not careful, they will all leave. Sad!

Feb. 28

@realDonaldTrump

@fairess369: It is a sad commentary little boy Marco Rubio can't win in his home state. Floridians despise him as a opportunist phony.

Feb. 24

@realDonaldTrump

The polls show that I picked up many Jeb Bush supporters. That is how I got to 46%. When others drop out, I will pick up more. Sad but true

Feb. 22

@realDonaldTrump

Ted Cruz should be disqualified from his fraudulent win in Iowa. Weak RNC and Republican leadership probably won't let this happen! Sad.

Feb. 20

@realDonaldTrump

> I wonder if President Obama would have attended the funeral of Justice Scalia if it were held in a Mosque? Very sad that he did not go!

Feb. 13

@realDonaldTrump

> I am the only one who can fix this. Very sad. Will not happen under my watch! #MakeAmericaGreatAgain

Feb. 12

@realDonaldTrump

> Lightweight @JebBush is spending a fortune of special interest against me in SC. False advertising-desperate and sad!

Feb. 8

@realDonaldTrump

> Now that Bush has wasted $120 million of special interest money on his failed campaign, he says he would end super PACs. Sad!

Jan. 23

@realDonaldTrump

> The only reason irrelevant @GlennBeck doesn't like me is I refused to do his failing show—asked many times. Very few listeners—sad!

Jan. 22

@realDonaldTrump

National Review is a failing publication that has lost it's way. It's circulation is way down w its influence being at an all time low. Sad!

Jan. 21

@realDonaldTrump

So sad that @CNN and many others refused to show the massive crowd at the arena yesterday in Oklahoma. Dishonest reporting!

Jan. 21

@realDonaldTrump

Wacko @glennbeck is a sad answer to the @SarahPalinUSA endorsement that Cruz so desperately wanted. Glenn is a failing, crying, lost soul!

Jan. 13

@realDonaldTrump

Sadly, there is no way that Ted Cruz can continue running in the Republican Primary unless he can erase doubt on eligibility. Dems will sue!

Jan. 7

@realDonaldTrump

The @TheView @ABC, once great when headed by @BarbaraJWalters, is now in total freefall. Whoopi Goldberg is terrible. Very sad!

Jan. 2

@realDonaldTrump. @JebBush is a sad case. A total embarrassment to both himself and his family, he just announced he will continue to spend on Trump hit ads!

You know what's really sad? That a seventy-year-old man is awake at all hours of the night, tweeting mean things about more well-adjusted people who are probably sleeping. You know what's even sadder? The fact that a seventy-year-old man doesn't own a thesaurus. Here are some synonyms for *sad*:

Unhappy (your wife Melania)

Miserable (your disposition)

Dismal (your legislative record, so far)

Despicable (your sons' hunting trips)

Tragic (your administration)

Unfortunate (your election)

Cheerless (your personality)

Morose (your PR staff)

Sorrowful (your voters)

Bitter (you)

Deplorable (ask Hillary)

S is for Santorum. Aside from Mike Let's-Do-Conversion-Therapy-Even-If-They're-Not-Gay Pence, Rick Santorum is possibly the most homophobic politico in the country. My favorite Santorum statement is "I have no problem with homosexuality. I have a problem with homosexual acts."

Okay, here's the deal, Ricky. Liza Minnelli is a gay act. A blow job is just a blow job. Are we clear?

S is for Science. Republicans in Congress hate science. They much prefer to use God, Jesus, miracles, or magic to explain things—or not to pay for things. For example, anytime a piece of environmental legislation comes up that might cost their corporate donors a dollar, Republicans in Congress like to say, "Well, I'm not a scientist, so I don't know that that's true." Climate change? "Well, I'm not a scientist . . ." News flash: I'm not a scientist, either, but I go outside sometimes. And when it's six hundred degrees in March, there are so many tornadoes that Kansas is now in Virginia, hurricane season is twelve months long, and it hasn't rained in California since the gold rush, I don't need a degree in physics or meteorology to know there's a problem—all I need is a window.

Marco Rubio and Rick Scott love to point out that they're not scientists. They're not Olympic swimmers, either, which might be problematic when Florida's underwater in a few years. Vice Homophobe Mike Pence is another big science denier (shocking!). He's not sure about evolution, he doesn't believe in climate change, and in 1998 he wrote an op-ed piece in which he said, "Despite the hysteria from the political class and the media, smoking doesn't kill." Yo, Mikey, the hysteria didn't come from the middle class and the media. It came from the surgeon general of the United States, fifty years ago. (FYI: Pence has received more than one hundred thousand dollars from the tobacco industry in his political career, and gutted as much antismoking legislation as he could when he was governor of Indiana. So, he may not be a doctor or a scientist, but that doesn't stop him from standing by his "alternative facts." Question: is he investing in inhalers and respirators? Just askin'.)

S is for Scott Baio. Thank God for Donald Trump. There, I've said it. As a result, my tongue is swelling and my throat's closing, so I'd better explain before I get cast as a corpse on *Criminal Minds*. For years, I've been beside myself worrying about what happened to Chachi. I can't tell you how many mornings I'd wake up with this dark cloud hanging over me. My husband would say, "Joy, are you okay?" I'd say nothing, and he'd look at me knowingly and say, "Chachi, again?" And I'd just nod and start weeping gently, wiping my tears on the Slanket I bought on QVC for $29.95.

S is for **Secrets.** This White House keeps more secrets than a Scientologist returning to the mothership after a weekend on Fire Island.

The last big thing Scott Baio did was *Charles in Charge*, which went off the air in 1990. I know, I know, he's done a bunch of guest roles on TV and had a series on Nickelodeon, but it's not the same. I realize that following a seminal piece of theatrical work like *Charles in Charge* isn't easy, and Nickelodeon is better than playing Biff in a dinner theater production of *Death of a Salesman* in Sheboygan, but still, we're talking about Scott Fucking Baio here.

Then, along comes Donald Trump, and out of oblivion comes Scott Baio. I don't know if Trump had any idea who Scott Baio was, but since he was having trouble getting celebrities to endorse him, suddenly Donnie Loves Chachi. (Trump couldn't even get an endorsement from the chair that Clint Eastwood spoke to.)

Lo and behold, Scott Baio gets a speaking role at the 2016 Republican National Convention. When he walked onstage, the crowd went wild—apparently, just like me, they, too, had been worried about him, not having seen him in years. (There was even a rumor that he had fallen down a well like Baby Jessica, but that nobody in Hollywood wanted to look for him.) I was thrilled to see my Scottie, but then . . . he began to speak. And it turns out, just like his Trump, he doesn't know anything. He thinks "Make America Great Again" is a policy plan, not a slogan on a hat. He said he thought President Obama was either dumb or a Muslim. He said Donald Trump made him proud to be an American again.

I turned off the TV and went back to bed, gently weeping.

And when my husband said, "Chachi, again?" I said, "Yes." But this time, not because I didn't know what had happened to him, but because I did.

S is for Secrets. This White House keeps more secrets than a Scientologist returning to the mothership after a weekend on Fire Island. There are only three real reasons for secrecy: (a) you're doing something wrong; (b) you're throwing a surprise party, or (c) you don't want to hurt someone's feelings. We know it's not *c*. I can't imagine it's *b*, because what are the odds Trump would throw a party for anyone but himself? Which leaves us with *a*, "you're doing something wrong," or, in Trump's case, *everything* wrong. He won't release his taxes, he won't tell us his plans for combatting terrorism, he launches strikes and drops bombs without consulting Congress, he issues mini-nonstatements about meetings with world leaders, he releases a vague tax "plan" that's shorter than my grocery list, and on and on and on. All presidents keep some things secret—President Obama closed the drapes when he was smoking cigarettes; President Clinton closed the drapes when Monica was smoking him; President Reagan shut the door when he was trading arms for hostages; President Cheney sealed the windows when he was ginning up the war in Iraq. But given Trump's history of deceit—Trump U, anyone?— his level of secrecy is both expected and appalling at the same time. As an American citizen, I'd like some explanations for what he's doing—or at least some alternative explanations.

S is for Seriously versus Literally. Trump supporters say he should be taken seriously but not literally. So, if, for example, Trump casually says, "I'm going to drop a nuclear bomb on One Hundred Thirty-Sixth Street and Amsterdam Avenue, right by City College in Upper Manhattan," are we not supposed to take that literally? Should the students just shrug it off with a wry smile and an "Oh, that Donald, what a kidder"? If we don't take him literally, does that mean it might not be a nuclear bomb, but just a garden-variety napalm bomb? Or does it mean he's not going bomb 136th Street, but might bomb 134th Street, or maybe just some other block in the neighborhood? I take Trump both literally *and* seriously. But what I'd like to do is take him to Russia . . . and leave him there.

S is for Shame. Last week, my husband and I had some friends over to our house for dinner, and eventually the conversation turned to Trump. And by "eventually," I mean, during the appetizers. My friend Susie couldn't even wait until the chicken cutlets were served to start in. That day, like nearly every other day, Trump had said something crude, vulgar, mean-spirited, and patently false. Susie was upset by it, and after two cocktails and a crab cake—she's gluten-free, of course—she was outraged. "The man ought to be ashamed of himself," she yelled. My friend Larry replied, "That would imply he has a sense of shame, but apparently Trump was born without that gene."

An example of something that causes shame: Your doctor

tells you to lose fifty pounds, and at your next checkup, he notices you've gained eight pounds and you have an entire brisket stuck between your teeth.

What has Donald Trump done that should have caused him to feel shame? Let me count the ways:

- Publicly cheated on his wives
- Defrauded people out of money
- Bankrupted business associates
- Bragged about sexually assaulting women
- Defamed his opponents
- Made false claims about his predecessor
- Denigrated a war hero
- Insulted the Pope
- Mocked the disabled
- Lied about mocking the disabled

. . . and yet, he's not ashamed of any of it. So, he either doesn't know those things are wrong, or he doesn't think he did them. Either way, does this sound like someone who should be in the White House? This isn't someone I'd let in my house—although, if I did, I'd make sure Susie was there, too, just to watch the fireworks over dessert (which would contain no carbs and would be gluten-free, of course).

S is for Social Conservatives. I refuse to refer to the self-righteous, ultra-tight-ass wing of the Republican Party as "social conservatives." People who don't like the way other people live their lives and try to deny them the same rights that they freely enjoy aren't social conservatives; they're intolerant. You want to talk social conservative? My aunt Viola, now *she* was a social conservative. She wore a bra and panties under her bathing suit when she went to the beach, so "men wouldn't look." (Not for nothing, but my aunt Viola weighed four hundred pounds—the only man looking at her longingly was the ice-cream vendor.) A social conservative is a guy who stubs his toe and says, "Oh, fudge," instead of "Fuck me. How did I not see that chair?" A person who says, "I don't want to bake cakes for gay people," isn't a social conservative; he's a lousy businessman.

S is for Sociopath. My friend Terry is a practicing clinical psychologist. She's listened to more people complain than a customer service rep at the DMV. She's convinced that Donald Trump displays classic signs of sociopathy. Some of the characteristics of being a sociopath are: a disregard for the feelings of others, a lack of shame or remorse, a huge ego, compulsive lying to achieve one's goals, manipulative behavior, and making statements that may incite violence. Now, I'm no psychiatrist, so I'm going to make like Fox News: I present the facts; you decide. And if your conclusion scares you, I'll give you Terry's number.

S is for Son of Sam. In 1976 to '77, New York City was paralyzed with fear by a maniac known as the Son of Sam, a serial killer who was traveling around the five boroughs randomly shooting young couples. Berkowitz became known as the Son of Sam when, after his arrest, he told the police that he was killing people under orders from his neighbor Sam's dog. I don't know if the dog actually spoke to him; I don't even know if the dog even spoke, but if it did, I hope that dog is still alive, because I'll call Simon Cowell and put him on *America's Got Talent* and collect me a nice little finder's fee. (On a side note, why is that when people hear voices, those voices always tell them to kill? How come those voices never say things like "Mow the lawn" or "Take out the garbage" or "Buy Joy a lovely bracelet at Neiman Marcus"?)

Berkowitz killed six people and wounded seven others because he took advice from "someone" ill-equipped to give advice: Sam's dog. Donald Trump has put someone equally ill-equipped to give advice to run the Department of Energy: Rick Perry. The Department of Energy is responsible for our nuclear arsenal. Prior to being named secretary of energy, Rick Perry (a) had no idea what the department actually did; (b) said he wanted to dismantle it when he was running for president himself in 2012; and (c) appeared on *Dancing with the Stars*. The only differences between Rick Perry and that pooch who spoke to David Berkowitz is that Rick Perry is housebroken *and* he's in a position to end a lot more than six lives.

S is for Spine. Years ago, a very funny comedian named Marvin Braverman was sitting in a crowded cinema watching the premiere of the movie *The Elephant Man*. In a pivotal scene, the Elephant Man, John Merrick, twisted and disfigured, finds himself at a tailor's, trying on a suit. As he stands in front of the three-sided mirror, he says to the tailor, "How do I look?"

With the theater audience totally silent, Marvin yelled out from his seat, "The truth?"

I know. Inappropriate, but funny and honest.

Which brings me to Mitch McConnell and Paul Ryan, who know full well that Donald Trump is a train wreck driving our democracy off the rails. Yet, they do nothing but acquiesce and capitulate to President Crazypants's whims. They need to take a page from Marvin Braverman, who had the cojones to yell out the truth.

S is for Stock Market. One of the things Donald Trump likes to take credit for is the rising stock market. What he doesn't mention is that he inherited a booming stock market from President Obama, a market that kept reaching record highs. He keeps telling his base that the market numbers show how great he's doing. They, of course, believe him. The irony is that the majority of his hard-core base probably doesn't own stocks. They don't play the stock market; they go to the supermarket. Their daily lives are more affected by the numbers at Piggly Wiggly than the numbers at NASDAQ. I hope they figure that out. So, to you Trump diehards out there (all two of you who bought this book), remember that the price of Apple is not going to help you with the price of apples.

S is for Style. Why do all tyrants have bad hair and terrible fashion sense? I don't get it. They're the most powerful people in their countries, yet they can't find one person who knows how to cut hair or put together an outfit?

Hitler was usually to be found wearing a brown Nazi uniform. Admittedly, the red armband added a pop of color, but brown was *soooo* 1922. The Führer's hair and mustache were flat-out awful, too. First of all, it was a bad cut, cropped short near the ears with one long bang hanging down the side. Even worse, it was greasy. On a hot day, you could cook a schnitzel on his head. And the mustache? How did that even start? Was he grooming one morning and suddenly had to stop mid-shave when Eva Braun marched in dangling a whip and some handcuffs? It was such a bad mustache. I've never, ever seen any other human being wearing it, and that includes my aunt Annunziata.

Good thing they don't have much electricity in North Korea. Kim Jong-un looks best in bad light. As a chubbette, he faces certain challenges, but that hairdo is not going to make his face look any less round. The only thing that would elongate Kim's face is a feedbag. His outside is as bad as his inside. As they say in Sicily, *faccia brutta*.

Even Ghaddafi tried to enhance his façade by wrapping what he considered a stunning schmata on his head. And Mussolini, to his credit, knew enough to shave his pate so as to avoid the dreaded male-pattern baldness fringe.

I have no idea if Hitler thought he looked nice, or if Kim Jong-un thinks he is the Fabio of Pyongyang, but Donald Trump clearly thinks of himself as a hottie. Donald must spend copious amounts of time fixing the 'do, spraying on the orange tan, Turtle Waxing the teeth, and making sure his tie is long enough to cover his gut. Maybe that's why he's up at 3:00 in the morning, tweeting: he's under the dryer starting his daily beauty regimen.

If I were The Donald, I'd either (a) start earlier, or (b) start over. If Trump spent less time brushing his hair and more time brushing up on facts, the country might start looking better.

S is for Superlatives. As I've already mentioned, Donald Trump loves hyperbole. But not just any old hyperbole—the greatest, the finest, the best hyperbole. And that's no exaggeration.

S is for Supreme Court. I never thought my civil rights, my daughter's civil rights, and my grandson's civil rights would hinge on the continuing good health of an eighty-four-year-old Jewish woman from Brooklyn, Ruth Bader Ginsburg. (If I had known that old age was the criterion, I'd have asked Bill Clinton to nominate my mother's friend Estelle Weinstein to the Court. Estelle is indefatigable. The woman never sleeps; she plays mah-jongg 24 hours a day, 365 days a year, even on Rosh Hashanah and Yom Kippur, and almost always wins.)

During the campaign, some of my friends said they were

going to sit out the election because they hated Trump and didn't like Hillary. I told them that their vote was important, if for no other reason than that a seat on the Supreme Court was open (and had been kept open by that great constitutionalist Mitch McConnell, who had changed the very document he "so reveres" to suit his agenda). Hillary would have nominated a better candidate than Trump. And now that Trump is in the White House, and Neil Gorsuch is on the Supreme Court, I say to my friends who sat out the election, "Happy now? When Gorsuch overturns *Roe v. Wade* and you get pregnant, don't come crying to me." Of course, most of these women are in their sixties, so if they get pregnant, they shouldn't call me. They should call Ripley's.

Neil Gorsuch believes corporations are people, and he overwhelmingly rules in their favor in his decisions and opinions. If Joseph and Mary had been busted for squatting in the manger, Gorsuch would have ruled in favor of the slumlord who ran that condemned barn, thrown the Three Wise Men in jail for trespassing, and sent Jesus to foster care.

S is for Surrogate. These days, when people hear the word *surrogate*, they probably think of a pretty but strapped-for-cash girl from Oklahoma carrying a baby for some good-looking couple from San Francisco. But when I hear the word *surrogate*, I think of the cadre of Kool-Aid-drinking sycophants who speak on Donald Trump's behalf, primarily his rotating corps of spokespeople. The original mouthpiece who made a deal with the devil was Kellyanne Conway, whom I've already discussed ad nauseam, with an emphasis on the "nauseam." Then there was Stephen Miller, one of Trump's right-wing policy wonks, who was so hateful and offensive he was dragged off the national stage faster than passengers get dragged off United Airlines flights. Then came my favorite explainer-du-jour, Sean Spicer. I was going to say "apologist-du-jour," but as previously noted, Trump never apologizes for anything, so "explainer" will have to do.

I've got to be honest: I got a certain pleasure out of watching Sean Spicer try to stammer his way through a press conference. Every time he was asked to explain one of Trump's lies, he stammered and cajoled and deflected. It reminded me of when I begged my calculus teacher for a D so I could graduate. But as much as I enjoyed the schadenfreude I experienced when Sean got caught in a lie, I also felt sorry for him. Unlike Stephen Miller, who is a true believer, and Kellyanne, who is a paid believer, I get the impression Sean Spicer knew that what he was saying was complete bullshit but that he had to say it anyway. Plus, we all know that Spicer was speaking to an audience of one, and if he didn't answer correctly, he might have ended up in Guantánamo. Couple that with the fact that Spicer, not unlike his boss, is factually challenged, and every press conference turned into Must See TV. And that's what Trump wants in a press secretary: high ratings!

Here are some of the actual things Sean Spicer said in public (or, as I like to call them, "Spicerisms"):

- Magnetometers kept crowds off the Mall at the inauguration (not true).

- A new style of ground covering made it appear as though the crowd was sparse (not true).

- The DC subway rider usage numbers proved that Trump's was the largest inauguration crowd ever (not true).

- Paul Manafort played a very limited role (in the campaign) for a very limited time (not true).

- Even Hitler didn't sink to using chemical weapons (not true).

From what I hear, Sean Spicer was even more of a hot mess offstage. Here are some of the Spicerisms uttered in private:

- Sean Hannity's IQ is higher than Stephen Hawking's.

- Andrea Mitchell's feet are made out of liverwurst.

- There are Islamic terrorists hiding in Abe Lincoln's nose on Mount Rushmore.

- Susan Sarandon is a Cuban spy named Raúl.

- President Duterte of the Philippines is on the short list for canonization.

T is for Tammy Wynette. Country star Tammy Wynette's biggest hit song was "Stand by Your Man," which became an anthem for subservient women stoically staying in bad, sexless marriages. Think of poor Pat Nixon in her cloth coat, a flask in her purse, standing beside Tricky Dick while he sweated his way through press conferences telling people he was not a crook. Pat stood by her man (the way Melania is standing by her man), even when Dick had to resign the presidency before being impeached. I can only pray that Melania shows the same courage Pat displayed, when her Donald is forced to resign before *he's* impeached. FYI: Tammy Wynette may have sung that anthem, but she was no dummy. She was married eight times.

T is for Taxes. To Donald Trump, *taxes* is a dirty word, one of the few dirty words he hates to use. Trump's tax returns are harder to find than a period at the end of one of Kellyanne Conway's sentences. During the campaign, Deceptive Donny said he was being audited by the IRS and wasn't allowed to release his taxes until the audit was done. (According to the IRS, not true. FYI: even Nixon, the Sultan of Sneaky, released his taxes while he was under audit *and* under investigation for Watergate.) Then Trump said that the American people "don't care about his taxes." Again, not true. I'm an American people and I care—and according to current polls, so do 72 percent of the rest of the American people. Then his son Benito . . . I mean, Hans, said that his father's tax return was twelve thousand pages and would take too long to go through. Not true.

There are plenty of great accountants with OCD in this country who would be thrilled to read those pages, and who could use the extra work. Even Trump's favorite "intelligence gathering agency," WikiLeaks, thinks something is fishy.

@wikileaks
Trump's breach of promise over the release of his tax returns is even more gratuitous than Clinton concealing her Goldman Sachs transcripts.
9:15 AM—22 Jan 2017

Actually, WikiLeaks is only Donald Trump's fifth-favorite intelligence gathering agency; it comes after Breitbart News, Alex Jones's Infowars, the *National Enquirer*, and the lady he overheard talking to her friend Selma at the airport.

There are a lot of theories as to why Trump won't release his tax returns. I'm going with that he doesn't want us to find out he's claimed Vladimir Putin as a dependent.

T is for Tea Bag. See: "O is for Orange." Though Donald Trump's face is orange, the areas around and under his eyes are pale white. I'm not sure why. I'm guessing he's either part raccoon or he's been tea-bagged by a mime.

T is for Tea Party. The original tea party was a protest where angry citizens dumped tea in Boston Harbor yelling, "No taxation without representation." The Tea Party that emerged in 2009 was composed of angry citizens who stood in parking lots with tea bags on their heads, holding signs saying things against Obama like LIER IN CHEIF and COMMANDER AND THEIF. I don't want to be picky, but it's *i* before *e* except after *c*, or when sounding like *a* as in *neighbor* and *weigh*. So, it's *chief*, not *cheif*, okay? Got that? Next week, we'll go over the use of dangling participles. I promise it won't hurt.

T **is for Tea-Bagged.** Though Donald Trump's face is orange, the areas around and under his eyes are pale white. I'm not sure why. I'm guessing he's either part raccoon or he's been tea-bagged by a mime.

T **is for Teddy Roosevelt.** The old Rough Rider was the last Republican president not to have maternal issues. Think about it: Ike had Mamie, Reagan called his wife "Mommy," Bush Sr. married his mommy, W. needed his mommy, and Trump thinks his mother was a 5, maybe a 6.

T **is for Ted Nugent.** Redneck rocker Ted Nugent was "invited" by the Secret Service for "interviews" at least twice for making threatening and incendiary remarks toward President Obama. After that, any decent, normal elected official would have steered clear of this aging musical misanthrope, if for no other reason than bad optics. But not Donald Trump. He invited Ted to perform at the inauguration. Presumably, that means that Jesse James (Sandra Bullock's ex, who loves Nazi memorabilia) can't hold a tune. (That said, neither can Ted Nougat.)

T **is for Temperament.** During the 2016 campaign, Hillary and the Democrats kept saying that Trump was "temperamentally unfit for office." In hindsight, they were being way too polite. Hillary should have slipped on her big-boy pantsuit and yelled, "That is one crazy motherfucker!"

T **is for Terrible Twos.** Toddlers go through a phase at about two years old when they cry, they whine, they break things, they have tantrums, they won't eat, and they throw food. Experts believe the cause of this is that children's brains develop faster than their language skills, and when they can't express what they're thinking, they get frustrated and act out. This phase usually ends at about three years old. Usually. There are exceptions. I know of one world leader who is sixty-eight years late and counting.

T **is for Terrorism.** During the 2016 election, Candidate Trump told America he was going to get rid of ISIS in his first thirty days in office. Apparently, the calendar app on his iPhone broke. Months later, ISIS is still ticking, and since I have no plans of vacationing in Iran or buying a time share in Syria, I'm more afraid of Trump and Pence than I am of

Sheik Al-Sheik or his kooky nephew Sheik Sheik Sheik Your Booty.

T is for **Tiffany.** Donald named his daughter for his favorite jewelry store, Tiffany. She's lucky he doesn't shop at Hammacher Schlemmer.

T is for **Tiny Hands.** You know what they say about men with tiny hands? Tiny mittens. A lot has been made of the size of Donald Trump's hands and fingers. Critics say they're minute; Trump, of course, says they're *uuuuuge*. My own estimate is that on the size scale, they fall somewhere between stumps and the hands of a small Filipino child. But other than the women whose pussies he plans on grabbing, who cares about the size of his fingers? I don't. I care about the size of his brain, which, sadly, appears to be smaller than his hands.

T is for **Toadies.** Toadies are sycophants who grovel and fawn, give up all sense of pride or self-respect, are humiliated and shit on by the celebrity they're fawning over, get shit on again, and then come back for more. Alternate definition: Chris Christie.

T is for **Toe Fungus.** People keep stopping me on the street and asking me, "Joy, would you rather have Donald Trump as president, or would you rather have toe fungus?" The answer is: Toe fungus. It's curable.

T is for Trade Agreements. Donald Trump knows *a lot* about making trades. He traded in Ivana for Marla, and traded in Marla for Melania. (I think Melania's got another twenty thousand miles on her until he trades her in for a newer model.) One of the first things Donald Trump did in office was go after the Trans-Pacific Partnership, or as Bernie Sanders kept yelling, "TPP, TPP!" Let's be honest, Bernie was obsessed. I can't get the image out of my head of him screaming, "TPP, TPP, TPP!" At night, when my husband gets a little too frisky, I yell out, "TPP, TPP!" and we stop and calm down and discuss trade tariffs.

Believe it or not, Bernie and Donald Trump were on the same page when it came to getting out of the TPP. Neither one of them liked it. The only difference is Bernie described it in complex economic terms, while Trump simply called it a "horrible deal." I have no idea what's in the TPP—I haven't read it, and I don't plan to read it. I'm still only halfway through *Fifty Shades of Grey* and I'm not going to put it down to read a government document until the spankings begin.

T is for Transgender. Republicans spend more time worrying about other people's junk than Sanford and Son. In April 2016, when Trump was asked about the "transgender bathroom crisis," he said, "People should go to the bathroom where they feel comfortable . . . even in Trump Tower." (Or maybe on a mattress in Moscow?) But in less than a year, in February 2017, he overturned President Obama's law protecting transgender students' right to use the bathroom they feel comfortable in. How is this even an issue? I'd like Trump to name one transgender person who is a national threat.

I only know a few transgender celebrities: Chaz Bono, Caitlyn Jenner, and Laverne Cox. I think Laverne is the only one who has had the full surgery; the others may still be in various stages of transitioning. Chaz (née Chastity) was really brave to be among the first celebrities to publicly come out as gay. Then, a few years later, he came out as transgender. Coming out is a daunting prospect for most young people—I can't imagine how difficult it must be when your mother is Cher. Think about it: Your mother is a big star, an Oscar winner, and a staple in every drag queen's act . . . and you have to come home and tell her you're turning in your ovaries. I was an absolute wreck the day I had to tell my mother I wasn't a virgin. And I was thirty-seven! I give Chaz credit. Good for him.

And I give Caitlyn (née Bruce) Jenner lots of props, too. Again, I'm not sure what stage of the transition Caitlyn is at. She's clearly had hormones and implants. Going from being the best male athlete in the world to being a middle-aged suburban woman takes, pardon the pun, a lot of balls. Caitlyn wasn't just "some guy." When other guys sat down to eat their Wheaties for breakfast, Bruce Jenner was the guy they saw looking out at them from the front of the cereal box. It took a lot of courage for Caitlyn to do what she did. So, my question is: Since the current GOP platform is the most anti-LGBTQ platform *ever*, why is she still a Republican? If Caitlyn had the courage to change genders, I'm sure she has the courage to change parties. Go where you're wanted, Cait! The Democrats would love to have you.

T **is for Trazodone.** My favorite sleeping pill. I'm taking one now. All this Trump talk is giving me agita.

T **is for Tweets and Twits.** Tweeting is a preferred method of communication among middle school and high school students—and between Donald Trump and the American people.

Donald Trump loves tweeting almost as much as he loves himself. Morning, noon, and night, The Donald tweets. The White House is open for tweeting 24/7. It's like a 7-Eleven. Four o'clock in the morning, a time when most seventy-year-old men would be sleeping or counting out Cialis pills, Trump's tiny fingers are flying over those keys like a World War II Luftwaffe pilot. Four in the morning, and Agent Orange is sitting there in his silk pajamas, with the lights on, typing away.

Twitter is perfect for Trump. He can communicate only in 140 characters or less, which breaks down to one character for each of his personalities. Tweeting is also a method of bullying, because you can tweet what you want and have no obligation to read any replies. A nasty tweet is basically a fuck-you, like hanging up on a caller or slamming a door in someone's face. In addition to the sampling of tweets in the *S* section, here are a couple of Trump's especially petty, vindictive, small-minded, childish tweets:

@realDonaldTrump

. . . John McCain has failed miserably to fix the
situation and to make it possible for Veterans to
successfully manage their lives.

11:15 AM—18 Jul 2015

@realDonaldTrump

I hear that sleepy eyes @chucktodd will be fired like
a dog from ratings starved Meet The Press? I can't
imagine what is taking so long!

5:36 PM—12 Jul 2015

@realDonaldTrump

Meryl Streep, one of the most over-rated actresses in
Hollywood, doesn't know me but attacked last night at
the Golden Globes.

3:27 AM—9 Jan 2017

@realDonaldTrump

@Macys was one of the worst performing stocks on the
S&P last year, plunging 46%. Very disloyal company.
Another win for Trump! Boycott.

3:15 AM—7 Jan 2016

@realDonaldTrump
Did Crooked Hillary help disgusting (check out sex tape and past) Alicia M become a U.S. citizen so she could use her in the debate?
2:30 AM—30 Sep 2016

Donald Trump may be a bad president and a terrible human being, but he's an outstanding mean girl.

U is for Ubiquitous. Donald Trump is like Starbucks or the Zika virus—he's everywhere. Radio, press, Internet, TV— no matter where you go, there he is. I was watching a rerun of *Baywatch* last week, and I swear I saw him flouncing up the beach in a red Speedo, being chased by Pamela Anderson and the Hoff.

For all Trump's complaining about the media, they cover him 24/7. If he so much as burps, MSNBC breaks into its coverage of *Lockup* to bring us "Breaking News: Trump Belches in Bethesda." First of all, *not* everything Trump does is "breaking news." His saying or doing something stupid, disruptive, selfish, or damaging isn't even news; it's Trump being Trump. Breaking news should be saved for when he does something right, or smart, or in the best interest of someone other than himself. Since that's never going to happen, maybe Brian Williams can just make it up.

U is for Uganda. Idi Amin Dada was a cruel dictator who forever tarnished the reputation of Uganda. (Yes, "Dada" was his actual real last name, and no, it's not related to the early twentieth-century art movement, and yes, that's what Hans and Fritz call their father when he tucks them in at night. FYI: Amin dropped his last name for professional, show-biz reasons, just like Cher, Adele, and Carrot Top.)

Idi Amin's eight-year presidency, from 1971 to 1979, was marked by corruption, nepotism, political repression, economic chaos, murder, and delusion. (He thought he was the king of Scotland.) Amin had multiple children with multiple wives and liked to mock other world leaders (Henry Kissinger, Queen Elizabeth, Leonid Brezhnev) with crazy telegrams. He was also rumored to be a cannibal. In a 2003 story by Riccardo Orizio of the *New York Times*, Amin was quoted as saying, "I don't like human flesh. It's too salty for me." Which means of course that he's tried it—and I'm sure it wasn't in one of Uganda's myriad five-star restaurants offering tasting menus; he probably just snacked on one of his enemies.

Except for the murder and the cannibalism, does any of this sound frighteningly familiar? Replace telegrams with tweets, and what've we got? That's right, Donald Trump Dada. But if these parallels ring true, then the most upsetting thing in the preceding paragraph isn't the corruption or the nepotism or even the murder; it's the phrase "eight-year presidency." I don't know that I can survive that. And if not, I just hope I taste good with ketchup and a side of fries.

is for **UUUUUGE**. Trump doesn't mispronounce words because he's a student of etymology. He mispronounces them because e's a *uuuuuge orse's ass*.

U **is for Unchristian.** In his first overseas trip since assuming office, Donald Trump made a speech in Saudi Arabia. He mentioned God no fewer than seven times in thirty-three minutes. I don't think he's mentioned God that many times in his seventy years on the planet, and that includes the five and a half times he was having sex. I guess he was trying to show his Arab "friends" that he was the voice of morality in the Western world. (He must've figured they didn't know of his anti-Islam slurs, or that he dissed the Pope in 2016.)

But he's not the voice of morality. I'll bet he breaks at least four of the Ten Commandments every morning before he's even had coffee. So, why does Trump keep mentioning God? Because one of his handlers told him to, that's why. They figure his Republican base will like it. I don't claim to be an expert on Christianity, but from what I gather, Jesus was a role model with Christian values who would never, ever, have made massive financial cuts to services for the poor, women, and children in *His* budget. That's just what Donald did.

U **is for Unpredictable**. You know who likes unpredictability? Poker players, mystery writers, and Ashton Kutcher. That's about it. The rest of the friggin' world is not so thrilled with it; foreign countries don't want to be punk'd. Stock markets, for example, which are the basis for our capitalist economy, hate instability. They like things nice and steady and calm, kind of like my cat Benito Pussolini once his kitty downers kick in.

Foreign governments like predictability; they like to know who are their allies and who are their enemies. Surviving in today's world is not a game of *Survivor*. Donald Trump prides himself on being unpredictable, though. And if he were sitting at a poker table at one of his casinos, that would be fine . . .

Oh, wait, I'm sorry. His casinos all closed or went bankrupt. I mean if he were sitting at a poker table at someone *else's* casinos, that would be fine, but not when he's sitting in the Oval Office or the Situation Room. When the nuclear button is at your disposal, I think "predictable" is way better than "quick-fingered." I feel much safer with my cat Benito than Trump. Maybe Melania can slip some kitty downers into his ice cream.

U is for Utah. When I think of Utah, like most Americans, I think of Donny and Marie, the Mormon Tabernacle Choir, and Mitt Romney's underpants. For the record, I like Donny and Marie, the choir sings great, and I've never seen Mitt's underpants. But what I (and the people of Utah) *should* be thinking about are the great national parks in the state: Zion National Park, Arches National Park, and Bryce Canyon National Park. These three parks, along with the Grand Canyon and Larry King, are some of the country's oldest treasures. The Donald wants to do away with a lot of the protections the parks have, so he can open them up for drilling. The last thing we need in Utah is more gas. If you think I'm kidding, spend half an hour listening to Orrin Hatch. Admittedly, I'm not the outdoorsy type; I don't whittle, or husk, or, God knows, hike—I need a Sherpa simply to get across Amsterdam Avenue on the Upper West Side of Manhattan—but just because I have a close relationship with my sofa doesn't mean we should let the oil companies own our parks. It's bad enough they own our Congress.

U **is for** *Uuuuuuge!* For some odd reason, Donald Trump doesn't pronounce the *h* in *huge*. He treats it like a silent letter and, instead, says, "uge." Everything he's going to do is going to be *uuuuge*. The wall, the economy, and Hillary's prison cell—they're all going to be *uuuuuge* . . .

There are some words in American English that employ a silent *h* at the front, like *herbs*. Other words have a silent *h* in the middle, like *shepherd*, which is just an elision. But Trump doesn't mispronounce words because he's a student of etymology. He mispronounces them because e's a *uuuuuge orse's ass*.

V is for **Vatican**. Even though I was raised Catholic, I don't know a lot about God or religion. I never went to Catholic school; I hated the uniforms. But I do know it's not a great idea to take on the Pope. After Pope Francis said, "A person who thinks only about building walls is not Christian," Trump responded, "For a religious leader to question a person's faith is disgraceful." Calling the Pope "disgraceful" may not send you directly to hell, but you are now on report that you dissed the man who has a direct line to God. Why would anyone risk pissing off a guy with those kinds of connections?

V is for **Vladdy Baby.** I'm very worried that because Trump idolizes Putin so much, next week we'll see The Donald half-naked riding a Shetland pony around Mar-a-Lago.

V is for **Vegas**. I would like to move the White House, Camp David, Trump Tower, and Mar-a-Lago to Las Vegas. Because what happens in Vegas stays in Vegas. And nothing would please me more than to have the Family Trump stay there—and never leave.

V is for **Vegetable**. Michelle Obama built a vegetable garden at the White House. Melania Trump is putting in a panic room.

V **is for Vetting.** "Vetting" is how Melania Trump pronounces *wedding*. She should know; her husband's had three "vettings." Vetting is also the process by which potential government employees are screened to make sure they're cleared for work. It's basically a very deep and thorough background check. Apparently, The Donald either didn't fully vet a lot of his people or he did and just didn't care that they had dicey backgrounds. For example, I don't imagine he spent much time vetting Ivanka—not because she's his daughter or because he has a crush on her, but because she makes money for the family, so therefore, she's A-OK to come on board! He must've vetted Steve Bannon, and it didn't bother him that Bannon ran a website for neo-Nazis. Which makes me wonder: how could he not have known that Michael Flynn, Paul Manafort, and Carter Page were in business with the Russians? After all, Trump himself is in business with Russians. (His son Hans said so.) I think the next "vetting" Melania attends will be between General Flynn and his cellmate, Sergei (or, as he's known on Grindr, "the Siberian Husky").

V **is for Vitriol.** Vitriol is defined as "abusive, corrosive language used to censure, place blame, or create ill-will," or, as I like to think of it, any Donald Trump speech. Saying that there is a problem with illegal immigration is a fair topic for conversation; calling Mexicans "rapists and thugs" is vitriolic speech, the main purpose of which is to place blame and create animosity. If what's being said is true, sometimes the vitriol is well deserved. For example, referring to the 9/11 attackers as "monsters" or calling the guy at next table who's eating egg salad with his mouth open "disgusting" is harsh but nonetheless true. But Trump spits out venomous statements that are either patently false or aimed at people who don't deserve it.

Trump once said that "Arianna Huffington is unattractive, both inside and out. I fully understand why her former husband left her for a man—he made a good decision."

Did Arianna deserve that? Did she, in fact, turn her ex-husband gay? I doubt that, because if that were possible (to actually affect someone's sexual orientation), then all three of Donald Trump's wives, ex and current, would be lesbians. So, what was accomplished with Trump's vitriol? Arianna is still cute, her ex-husband is still gay, and Trump is still an asshole. Yes, I'm being vitriolic, but not only does he deserve it, but it is patently true.

V is for Vladdy Baby. You didn't think I'd forget Putin, did you? Yes, I've mentioned him in other chapters, but given the breadth of his power, the scope of his influence, and his cuckolding of Donald Trump, he could be in every chapter. Even though Putin was "elected" president of Russia, he's a dictator. He "governs" with an iron fist. He's been linked to murder, mayhem, and chaos all over the world. He started the war in Chechnya, he invaded the Ukraine, he annexed Crimea, and he's supporting Assad's reign of terror in Syria. Journalists have vanished, minorities and the media are tormented, and political opponents have mysteriously died. (And that's just a Thursday!)

Trump thinks Putin's a "strong leader." No. My husband's mother—let's call her Pearl—was a strong leader. She ran a mah-jongg game every week in the Bronx and conducted cha-cha lessons in her basement. If you so much as dropped a tile or missed a step, you were banished from the neighborhood for a week, sent home with a piece of kugel until you were eventually welcomed back with open arms and some ruggelah. Pearl was a leader; Putin is a menace.

Another thing that annoys me is that Putin's always photographed riding horses shirtless. In every picture, there's Vlad, sitting high in the saddle on Flicka, nipples ahead. Do I need to see this? Do the horses need to see this? My father loved to go to Belmont or Aqueduct to play the ponies almost every day. And not once, even in the middle of August, did he go topless. Nor did the jockeys, who, by the way, wear silk, a fabric not known for breathing. Maybe Putin thinks horseback riding makes him look macho, like a cowboy. But without the shirt, he looks like he's in an equestrian porn movie. I'm very worried that because Trump idolizes Putin so much, next week we'll see The Donald half-naked riding a Shetland pony around Mar-a-Lago. Haven't we suffered enough?

V is for Voir Dire: I'm an aficionado of TV crime shows. I know more about the court system than the judges do (in the way Trump knows more about ISIS than the generals do).

Which brings me voir dire, the jury selection process in which the opposing lawyers come up with twelve jurors they can agree upon. In theory, this should work, but in practice, it's not so easy. Let's say, hypothetically, that after Donald Trump is impeached, he is charged with various crimes (i.e., obstruction of justice, collusion, treason, ruining the ozone layer with too much hair spray) and goes on trial. In the United States, defendants are supposed to be tried by a jury of their "peers." In Trump's case, coming up with peers will be almost impossible. Where are we going to find twelve narcissistic millionaires with glued-down hair and orange complexions worthy of a Smucker's marmalade jar who only worship tax cuts? They don't exist—oh wait, they do: some of Trump's Cabinet and others in the Republican Party. Except for the hair and complexion, there is no dearth of Trump clones. He *would* get trial by a jury of his peers.

W is for **W.** Up until November 8, 2016, W. held the title of Least-Informed Person Ever to Become President of the United States. Now he's the Least-Informed Person Ever to Become Ex-President of the United States. Hopefully, he'll lose that title to Donald Trump, too.

W is for **Walla Walla.** The Washington State Penitentiary at Walla Walla is a maximum-security prison that would be perfect for Trump: it's got more than fifteen hundred rooms, it's fully staffed, three meals a day, and we, the taxpayers, would pay for his time there. Think of it as the Western White House!

W is for **Walls.** What's up with Republicans and their obsession with walls? They want to either tear them down or put them up. All day long, they're carrying on: "We're going to build this wall; we're going to tear down that wall; we're going to paint this wall; we're going to redo that wall; we're going to make this one out of brick and that one out of wood . . ." There are already plenty of famous walls: the Berlin Wall, the Great Wall of China, Hadrian's Wall, the Walls of Babylon. The world is wall to wall walls. But those walls are not enough for Trump and his supporters.

Trump is obsessed with building a wall between the United States and Mexico to keep illegal immigrants out. The fact that most people fly in from Mexico is an inconvenient fact. If Trump really wants to keep people out, he needs to build a forty-thousand-foot-high wall.

W is for War. George W. Bush started a war in Iraq and a war in Afghanistan; George Bush Sr. waged a war in Kuwait; and Ronald Reagan waged war on the island of Grenada, which is known as "the Island of Spice," famous for nutmeg. In his first hundred days in office, Donald Trump sent missiles into Syria, dropped a mega-bomb on Afghanistan, and threatened North Korea.

This has to stop. The Ancient Greek women had a solution. *Lysistrata* is a Greek play about women who withhold sex from their men until the men stop fighting the Peloponnesian War and negotiate a peace settlement. Works like a charm. The women cut off sex, and faster than you can say, "Not tonight, Pericles, I have a headache," the war is over and both peace and piece are at hand.

While I'm on the subject of war, what's with the "war on Christmas"? How seriously do right-wingers take the phony, nonexistent war on Christmas? In 2013, then-Fox anchor Megyn Kelly stated as a fact, "Everyone knows Santa is white." Kelly's GOP audience gave her full-throated support, ignoring the fact that Santa Claus is a fictitious character and not a real human being. (Don't tell the kids.) They even ignored the fact that he might have been at least half Jewish—Blitzen was actually his third cousin on his mother's side—and had a time-share in Boca Raton.

But the real war is the war on women. When it comes to women, Republicans are living in the past. For comedy's sake, I was going to be specific and say they're living in 1953, but that would imply that Republicans are okay with women having the right to vote (which we didn't get until 1920), and I'm not sure they are. I'll bet the GOP would overturn the Nineteenth Amendment if they could, just like they're trying to overturn *Roe v. Wade* and the Lilly Ledbetter Fair Pay Act, along with the paid maternity provision in the Affordable Care Act. If these conservative men (and some women) had their way, we women would be home, in the kitchen, wearing nothing but Saran Wrap, waiting eagerly for our man to come home so we could serve him a piping hot meal and tell him how wonderful he is. BTW, Saran Wrap causes excessive sweating, so this would work only until the onset of menopause.

W is for Waterboarding. Waterboarding is torture, and Candidate Trump promised he would do far worse than waterboarding. What could be worse than waterboarding? Well . . .

- Giving Mitch McConnell a sponge bath;
- Singing Yiddish karaoke songs with Henry Kissinger;
- Having Ann Coulter speak at a Black Lives Matter meeting;
- Taking Tiny Hands shopping for gloves; or
- Double-dating with Newt and Calista.

W is for Watergate. Watergate was the original "gate" scandal. It preceded Irangate, Contragate, Iraqgate, Monicagate, Bridgegate, Benghazigate, and Parsippanygate. (I'm not sure there was a Parsippanygate, but given that the media have dubbed everything "gate," what are the odds there wasn't a scandal in Parsippany at some point in time?) What I am sure of is that we are in the midst of Trumpgate—unless the media decide to call it Russiagate or Manafortgate or Flynngate.

Watergate and Trumpgate were both created by the same thing: Republican paranoia. Richard "I Am Not a Crook" Nixon was going to win reelection in 1972 by a landslide, yet his minions insisted on burglarizing the Democratic National Committee headquarters in the Watergate complex anyway. This led to the famous question "What did the president know and when did he know it?" As information began leaking, Tricky Dick tried to cover the whole thing up. Eventually, he resigned before being impeached, and Gerald Ford pardoned him so he wouldn't have to go to jail.

W is for **WikiLeaks**. Up until Trump's campaign, I thought WikiLeaks was an adult diaper.

Fast-forward to 2017: Donald Trump's team may have been complicit in Russia hacking into the DNC computers. Once again, the question "What did the president know and when did he know it?" is being asked. What will the Trumpgate investigations turn up? Will Trump be impeached? Will he resign? Will he go to jail?

Will we have to think of his time away in prison as Walla Wallagate?

W is for White People. I'm tired of hearing about the frustrated, angry white people who voted for Donald Trump. Day after day, it's the same thing: "frustrated, angry white voters, blahblahblahblahblah . . ." Look, I'm white and I'm frustrated. And I'm angry. I'm frustrated and angry that Trump conned so many white people into voting for him. But I'm not a complainer; I'm a problem-solver. (Think of me as an Italian Siri.) I have a solution. I think it's time to follow a simple rule: No white people after Labor Day. Basically, they're allowed to come out in the summer and go to the beach to turn brown. And then they're allowed back out.

W is for Why the Fuck Are We Paying for Trips to Mar-a-Lago? Between the White House and Camp David, we, the American people, have paid for two perfectly lovely homes for the president and his family. They are completely furnished, fully staffed, and have free Wi-Fi, ample parking, no noisy neighbors, regular trash pickup, and a full-time doorman. So, if Trump wants to schlep to Mar-a-Lago every weekend, why isn't *he* paying for it? He can't stop telling us how rich he is. Let him open his damned wallet. Not only do we have to pay for the White House and Camp David, but because Melania stayed so long in New York with the kid, we had to pay for that, too. Why should it cost the taxpayers a million bucks a day because she doesn't want to sleep with her husband? She's the one who said, "I do," so when the thirty-million-dollar monthly security bill comes in and she asks, "Who vill pay dis?" the answer is "You vill."

W is for WikiLeaks. Up until Trump's campaign, I thought WikiLeaks was an adult diaper. At rally after rally, Trump kept yelling, "Isn't WikiLeaks great? Don't we love WikiLeaks?" And, at the time, he did, because they were leaking secret information about Hillary Clinton and the DNC. He also had nice things to say about WikiLeaks's founder, Julian Assange, but that doesn't surprise me. Assange is wanted on rape charges back in Sweden. But now that WikiLeaks is leaking info on the Trump campaign's and administration's possible Russia connections, The Donald wants to break up with them. In fact, Jeff Sessions says leakers should be put in prison, and I hear that the Justice Department is preparing charges against Assange. I also hear that Trump was so upset he wet himself. Maybe I should go to the drugstore and buy him some extra-absorbent WikiLeaks.

W is for Willie Nelson. I don't know much about country music, but I love Willie Nelson. Any man willing to wear pigtails outside the house is a man I'd like to know. He's like a country-western Pippi Longstocking. And he's found the perfect way to deal with life in Trump World: Ever been on his tour bus? You can get a contact high just driving near it on the freeway. I think I might try to hitch a ride.

W is for Wiretap. Barack Obama didn't wiretap Trump's apartment any more than Kellyanne Conway's "microwave" spied on Melania vacuuming the hallway. Our intelligence agencies routinely monitor communications between noted Russian and

American officials and leaders. If you don't want to get caught communicating with Russia, don't communicate with Russia. The only wire I care about is the underwire in my bra.

W **is for Wolf Blitzer.** For years, Wolf Blitzer has been the face of CNN. (Sean Hannity and Tucker Carlson are the boobs of Fox.) Wolf Blitzer is a world-famous, well-respected journalist—respected by everyone, that is, except Donald J. Trump.

CNN has become one of Trump's favorite targets as an alleged purveyor of fake news. He probably goes after CNN more than most of the other networks because (a) they're an international news organization with a worldwide audience; (b) unlike Fox, they tell the truth; and (c) unlike Fox, none of their big names is a known sexual predator. I don't care if Trump goes after other news anchors, like Scott Pelley or Lester Holt or that young cute one with the nice hair on ABC, but leave my Wolfie alone! Not that Wolf needs me to come to his aid; he can handle himself. Last April, after it was revealed that Syrian president Assad was gassing his own people, Sean Spicer took his foot out of his mouth long enough to jam his entire leg in there when he said, "Even Hitler didn't use chemical weapons on his own people." And he said this during the week of Passover. Realizing the error of his ways—and by that, I mean Jared Kushner pulled him aside and said, "Dude! What the fuck?"—Sean went on CNN with Wolf to (a) clarify his incredibly ignorant remark; (b) make a broad, tepid apology, and (c) try to walk it back so he wouldn't lose his job. Wolf would have none of it because (a) it was the right thing to do; (b) his parents are Holocaust survivors, and (c) he's Wolf Fucking Blitzer.

X **is for Xenophobia.** Some people probably (a) think this word is spelled with a *z*; (b) have no idea what it means; or (c) think it means having an irrational fear of Xena, Warrior Princess. For the record, the medical definition of *xenophobia* is "fear and hatred of strangers or foreigners or anything that is strange or foreign." Learning this was helpful to me, because I always thought phobias were just about fear, and that hatred was something else. Turns out they go together, like John Boehner and a shot of bourbon. For example, Mike Pence is homophobic—he both fears *and* hates homosexuals. I don't know what he's afraid of—that he'll wake up one morning and have an incredible urge to dump the wife and join the road company of *Hello, Dolly!*? And the argument that religious zealots like Pence use to justify homophobia, "Hate the sin, love the sinner," is a bunch of crap. Would they say the same thing about Jeffrey Dahmer, "Hate the butchery, love the cuisine"?

I don't think Trump is afraid of foreigners. Maybe he just hates them. Fine. Let him hate whomever he wants. The problem is he uses that hatred to instill fear in others. Yet, according to CNN and Homeland Security News Wire, between 2001 and 2014, a total of 3,412 Americans were killed by terrorists (including those killed on 9/11), while 440,095 Americans were killed by handguns. In the year 2014, only 32 Americans were killed by terrorists, while 33,599 were killed by handguns. Technically, Trump should be more afraid of guns than terrorists. And Pence should be more afraid of guns than gays.

XYZ is for XYZ. When I was in elementary school, if one of the boys accidentally had his fly open, all of us kids would yell, "*X-Y-Z*, examine your zipper!" As an adult, I still find myself saying this . . . every time I see Bill O'Reilly or Bill Cosby or Bill Clinton. Which makes me wonder, is there something about the name "Bill" that makes these guys want to free Willy? Does this mean that other men named Bill are going to waltz around flashing their bits? Will I find out that Bill Kristol leans to the right in more than just his politics? You might ask what this has to do with the Great Gasbag. Nothing, really, except that everytime he opens his mouth, I want to say, "Donald, *X-Y-Z*, examine your xenophobia!"

Y is for Sally Yates. Mother Teresa spent years and years washing the feet of the poor, until people took notice and said, "You know something, that Terry woman from Calcutta's a good egg." Sally Yates was acting attorney general for less than a month, but in that amount of time, she managed to become a hero to a lot of Americans. Because, unlike Paul Ryan or Mitch McConnell or most of the members of Congress with "(R)" after their names, she had the cojones to stand up to Donald Trump. Twice.

First came the Mike Flynn situation. Trump had named

him head of national security. As AAG, Yates went to the White House to give The Donald a heads-up about the general's Russian connections and possible vulnerability to blackmail. She went back once more to reinforce her warning. Obviously, she was ignored. And obviously, Trump wasn't happy.

Then The Donald issued his "travel ban," which was in actuality nothing more than a ban on Muslims, which Sally Yates would not enforce because it was unconstitutional. So, Trump did what any self-respecting seven-year-old would do: he fired Yates and then blamed and shamed her. The White House said she had "betrayed the Justice Department," and then Trump tweeted an unsubstantiated accusation that she'd leaked classified information to the press. FYI: since the time of her firing, Trump has rewritten the ban a few different times, and as of this writing, every single court it has come in front of has shot it down. Except the Supreme Court which allowed parts of the travel ban to take effect until they can hear all the arguments.

I don't know what Sally's plans are for the future—I've invited her to join me for my weekly mani-pedis; so far, no answer—but wouldn't it be fun to watch her run against Trump in 2020? And if not, even though she's not Catholic, maybe canonization? If Mother Teresa became a saint for caring for the homeless, surely Sally Yates should get something for standing up to Presidente Stoonad (Sicilian for "dummkopf").

Y is for Yentl. I was channel-surfing the other night, and on one of the networks the movie *Yentl* was playing. There was Barbra Streisand singing, "Papa Can You Hear Me?" and I'm thinking, *No, Barbra, he can't; the man's dead. Why don't you sing something from* Funny Girl? *It's much peppier.* And while watching *Yentl*, I realized that this movie is Republicans' worst nightmare. It's the story of a Jewish girl from a single-parent home who dresses like a Jewish boy so she can get an education and get ahead. Think about it: Jews. Cross-dressing. Empowered women. It'll drive them nuts. Plus, Barbra's a big liberal Democrat. As I write this, I'm planning a movie night. I'm going to invite Steve Bannon, Mike Pence, and Hans and Fritz over to watch *Yentl*. And as a surprise, I'm going to have RuPaul swing by with some kreplach. I can't wait! Barbra, can you hear me?

Y is for Yoko Ono. For years, Yoko Ono was one of the most disliked women in the country because everyone thought she'd broken up the Beatles. After John Lennon was killed, sentiments changed, however, and she became a sympathetic figure. But then she started "singing," and people started hating her again. But that was back in the '80s. Here in the 2000s, Yoko's place atop the Leader Board of Loathing has been taken by Laura Ingraham, who is doing her best to break up the country. The only good thing is that, to the best of my knowledge, Laura Ingraham doesn't sing.

Z is for Zzzzzz. The Lunesta I took three chapters ago is kicking in. I'm getting drowsy now. Wake me in four years when this nightmare is over. Wait a minute. No way Trump is going to last four years. Wake me in a few months; it'll be time to start writing the sequel.

Acknowledgments

There are many people I'd like to acknowledge for all the help they gave me in putting this book together, but I just don't have the time; I'm going shopping.

About the Author

JOY BEHAR is one of the co-hosts of ABC's hit daytime show *The View*. A former schoolteacher, Joy is also a legendary stand-up comedian. She has hosted several of her own TV shows *(The Joy Behar Show; Joy Behar: Say Anything!)*, and has written a number of books, including *Joy Shtick* and *When You Need a Lift*.